CLASSICAL CHINA

CLASSICAL CHINA

Edited by

WILLIAM H. McNEILL

and

JEAN W. SEDLAR

New York
OXFORD UNIVERSITY PRESS
London   1970   Toronto

Preface

Ancient China is more profoundly alien to us than any of the other great classical civilizations of Eurasia. Vast distances separated the cradle of Chinese civilization in the Yellow River valley from centers of high culture in western Asia and Europe; and whatever influences traveled across those distances always remained comparatively slight. Indeed, it is not entirely misleading to think of ancient Near Eastern, Mediterranean, and Indian high culture as variants on a common theme, each tied to the others by continual, however tenuous, contact. By contrast, China stood alone, remote and radically different.

This situation presents the Western historian with special difficulties in undertaking the study of ancient China. We are at the mercy of translators; and translators, in turn, face quite extraordinary problems, since the grammar, vocabulary, and ideographic script of the classical Chinese language differ fundamentally from our own patterns of speech and writing. The meaning of certain passages from ancient Chinese literature is sometimes unclear even to modern Chinese scholars. How much more difficult, then, to find any kind of adequate equivalents for Chinese ideas in English.

A second important problem results from the fact that the China of the Sage Kings, of the Hsia, Shang, and early Chou dynasties, and of Confucius and Mencius, became a model and measure by which the Chinese of subsequent periods attempted

to assess the shortcomings of their own times. Generations of
Chinese scholars pored over the Classics, reading from them (or
into them) whatever they found useful for their own thought.
Few other writings in the history of the world have been so con-
tinuously and carefully scrutinized by so many keen minds;
and few have been interpreted in as many different ways.
When Europeans first became interested in classical Chinese
literature, they naturally fell heir to the Chinese tradition of
scholarship. The result was to emphasize the uniformity of Chinese thought by exaggerating the importance of Confucius and
his school and minimizing the very real variety of Chinese intellectual life throughout history.

In choosing and arranging the selections which follow, the
editors have imitated Alexander the Great's approach to the
Gordian knot. Just as the all-conquering Macedonian cut
through the tangled ropes with one blow of his sword, so have
we chosen to impose upon our Chinese materials an alien (fundamentally Greek) set of classifications. At the same time, we
have taken care to set beside the writings of the Confucian
school samples of other voices from the Chinese past. These selections will, we hope, suggest something of the richness and
variety of viewpoint that flourished in China's early ages, and
which was only slowly wrought into a "Confucian" whole by
later generations of scholars. In this volume, therefore, texts
dealing with similar subjects are grouped together. Compari-
sons and contrasts are thereby made easier; and at the same
time some main themes of Chinese thought and sensibility
ought to become apparent.

A section on "Ethics" comes first, because the dominant
schools of Chinese thought always stressed the importance of
human behavior, and argued that social and political as well as
metaphysical and religious relationships depended upon per-

sonal conduct. "Politics" comes next, being merely ethics writ large, in the view of most Chinese schools—except for the Legalists, who neatly reversed the usual Chinese concept by declaring that the will of the ruler and the good of the state as a whole take precedence over individual welfare. Our third section, "History," was made possible by the fact that historians and chroniclers were an important part of Chinese intellectual life from the earliest times. The Chinese, in common with the Jews and Greeks and unlike all the other peoples of the world, developed a sophisticated historiographical tradition, unique in its chronological precision as far back as the ninth and eighth centuries B.C. Our selections in this section are designed to suggest the variety of subjects treated, the points of view that characterized China's earliest historians, and the impact of ethical and political theories upon their work.

The fourth section, "Religion," deals chiefly with Taoist and Buddhist texts that treat religion as an autonomous subject of study. These are prefaced by examples of Confucian writings that deal with the world of spirits and man's proper relation thereto—though it would be stretching a point to describe such writings as clearly religious in the sense of recognizing religion as a distinct realm of inquiry.

Our final section, "Society," consists of a cluster of poems. These were selected partly on literary grounds—though, inevitably, it was the quality of the translation rather than the original which mattered. But the editors were particularly interested in the sidelights and intimate glimpses of ancient Chinese life that these compositions afford. In contrast to the writings of the first two sections, which are largely theoretical in nature, the poems comment upon the conditions of real life as observed from an individual's viewpoint. Here, surely, a universal human spirit shines through the haze of imprecision imposed by the incommensurabilities that divide classical Chinese antiquity from the contemporary Western world.

Discovery of what unites as well as of what divides mankind is one of the principal goals of a study of world history. It is my hope that a careful perusal of the documents gathered together in this little volume will do something towards this end, de-spite—or perhaps because of—the particular difficulties we face in coming to grips with the civilization of ancient China.

W. H. M.

Chicago, Illinois
February 1970

Contents

* Introductions are listed separately when they pertain to more than one selection in this volume or deal with a general theme rather than a specific text.

IV RELIGION

A. CONFUCIANISM

B. TAOISM

C. BUDDHISM

V SOCIETY

Editorial Note

The present editors are responsible for the introductions and footnotes, which seek to place the various selections in historical context and make them more easily comprehensible to the non-specialist. In many instances, material provided by the translator has been a source of valuable information for the notes; but notes reprinted verbatim (in whole or in part) are followed by "(Tr.)." The texts themselves have been reproduced exactly as they stand in the sources indicated, except for the cuts made necessary by limitations of space and indicated by ellipses.

The editors extend special thanks to Mr. Peter Li of the University of Chicago for his transliteration of names in the *Tso Commentary* into the standard Wade-Giles system, and to Mr. Min-sun Ch'en for assistance with Chinese terms.

Note on Chinese Chronology

Accurate historical records appear in China at an early period. The chronicles of the feudal states, as well as the later dynastic histories of the empire, provide a precise chronology of the reigns of ruling princes. For the period after 814 B.C., all authorities on Chinese chronology are in agreement regarding both absolute and relative dating. For the prior period, however, the Chinese sources themselves disagree; and the materials for an accurate resolution of their differences are largely lacking. The traditional, and most often employed, Chinese chronology is that given by Pan Ku in his *History of the Former Han Dynasty* (first century A.D.). Some authorities, however, favor a rival scheme which appears in the *Bamboo Annals*, the chronicle of the feudal state of Wei. Using the dates for the founding of the three earliest Chinese dynasties, the two systems compare as follows:

DYNASTY	TRADITIONAL DATE	BAMBOO ANNALS DATE
Hsia	2205 B.C.	1994 B.C.
Shang (Yin)	1765 B.C.	1523 B.C.
Chou	1122 B.C.	1027 B.C.

In the absence of scholarly agreement, we have consistently used the traditional dating in the present volume.

Note on Chinese Pronunciation

This book uses the standard Wade-Giles system for the transliteration of Chinese sounds into English. The letters of the alphabet according to this system sound as follows:

Vowels

a	as in *father*
ai	like the *i* in *ice*
ao	like the *ow* in *cow*
e	like the *u* in *up* (except after i or y)
i	like the letter *e* (as in *east*)
ih	like the *ir* in *fir*
o	as in *old*; but sometimes like *o* in *soft*
ou	like the *o* in *occur*
u	like the English *oo*; but very short after *ss* or *tz*

Consonants

Aspirated consonants (i.e., those marked by a sharp expiration of air) are followed by an apostrophe, and generally resemble their English equivalents. Consonants not aspirated roughly resemble the corresponding voiced sounds in English, as follows:

ch'	as in *church*
ch	like *j*
k'	as in *kite*
k	like the *g* in *go*
p'	as in *pear*
p	like *b*
t'	as in *to*
t	like the *d* in *dog*

ts' &	tz'	like *ts* in *hits*
	ts &	
	tz	like *dz*
Also:	hs	similar to the English *sh*
	j	resembles English *r*; *jen* sounds something like *run*
	ss	not distinguished from *s*

Other consonants generally resemble their English equivalents.

As with most systems of transliteration from one language into another, the equivalents are approximate, and only partially correspond to the actual Chinese sounds. Moreover, the same combination of English letters may indicate several distinct sounds in the original Chinese.

Maps

I
Ethics

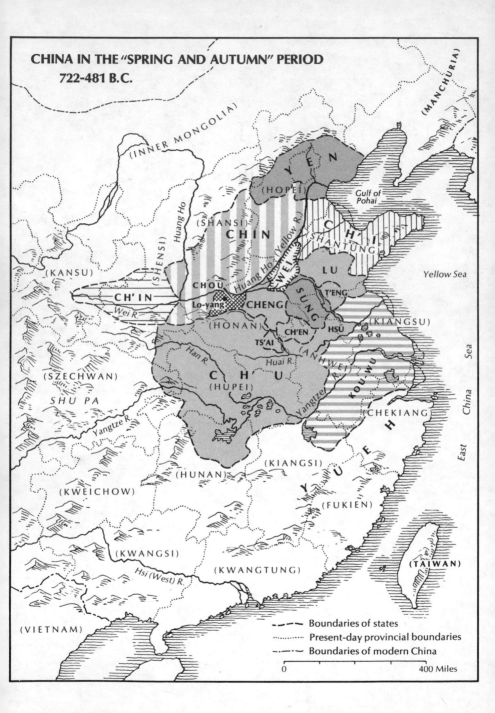

CHINA IN THE "SPRING AND AUTUMN" PERIOD
722–481 B.C.

(MANCHURIA)

(INNER MONGOLIA)

Huang Ho

(SHANSI)

CHIN

Y E N

(HOPEI)

Gulf of
Pohai

C H ' I

SHANTUNG

(KANSU)

(SHENSI)

CHOU

Huang Ho (Yellow R.)

WEI

LU

T'ENG

Yellow Sea

CH'IN

Lo-yang

CHENG

SUNG

HSÜ

(KIANGSU)

Wei R.

(HONAN)

CH'EN

TS'AI

(ANHWEI)

Han R.

Huai R.

Yangtze R.

K O U - W U

(SZECHWAN)

SHU PA

C H U

(HUPEI)

China Sea

Yangtze R.

CHEKIANG

Yangtze R.

(KIANGSI)

Y U E H

(HUNAN)

(FUKIEN)

East

(KWEICHOW)

(KWANGSI)

Hsi (West) R.

(KWANGTUNG)

(TAIWAN)

(VIETNAM)

- - -   Boundaries of states
· · · · ·   Present-day provincial boundaries
- · - · -   Boundaries of modern China

0   400 Miles

Introduction to Confucius

Until very recent times in China, Confucius (K'ung Fu Tzu,* or Master K'ung) was generally regarded as the greatest thinker who ever lived. The complex of ideas attached to his name—human-heartedness, decorum, respect for parents and ancestors—expresses the characteristic attitude of the traditional Chinese. From about the first century B.C. until the twentieth century A.D. Confucianism was recognized, with occasional interruptions, as the official philosophy of the Chinese empire. The Confucian Classics were the basic texts of Chinese education and the subject matter of the civil service examinations, virtually ensuring that the imperial bureaucracy would be imbued with Confucian principles. The all-pervasiveness of Confucian influence in social norms and private morals, the exalted status accorded to Confucius himself, and the general acceptance of his reputed opinions as almost unquestioned truths, gave to Confucianism many of the characteristics which in other civilizations have belonged to religion rather than philosophy.

Confucius himself was born in the small state of Lu on the northeast China plain, in what was then one of the oldest centers of Chinese culture. His traditional dates, 550-479 B.C., are approximately accurate, making him a contemporary of the Buddha, the pre-Socratic philosophers of Greece, and perhaps the Persian Zoroaster. Confucius himself tells us that his background was humble. But he was well educated by the standards of his century—a fact strongly suggesting that he belonged to the lower aristocracy. As a young man he apparently held minor official posts in his native state; his ambition was to gain a position of political influence, but this eluded him. Much of his life evidently was devoted to study and teaching; history does not record how he supported himself. He probably began to evolve his ideas in informal debates with friends, and gradually the force of his intellect and personality attracted others to his

* *Tzu* is a title of respect meaning "Master." It is affixed to the names of many eminent Chinese, e.g., Meng Tzu (Mencius), Mo Tzu, Hsün Tzu, etc.

company. When nearly sixty years old, he began a series of wide-ranging travels to the various courts of China, seeking a prince who would make use of his talents. Preceded by his reputation for learning, he was everywhere received with honor. But no one offered him a position in which he could influence events; and after some ten years of wandering he returned home to Lu.

Confucius' reputation, then, rests upon his ideas rather than his statesmanship. He is said to have been the first independent teacher in China—as opposed to the tutors employed by noble houses—though this is hard to prove. Certainly teaching in his day was not recognized as a profession. The education which Confucius provided included politics, history, and literature, but ignored the aristocrats' traditional training in archery and charioteering. This emphasis on mental rather than physical prowess was undoubtedly an innovation at that time. Confucius' early followers were derided as *ju* ("weaklings"). Within a century of his death, however, the word lost its pejorative significance; and it remains to this day the standard term for "Confucian" (or "literati") in the Chinese language.

Though Confucius described himself as a transmitter rather than a creator of ideas, there can be no doubt that he was both. Certainly he loved the traditional Chinese culture and revered the legendary sage-kings of antiquity, Yao, Shun, and Yü. He liked to speak in archaic formulas and proverbs, and often disparaged the present by comparison with the past. But reverence for antiquity—then as later —was a common trait in China, and Confucius spoke far less about it than most of his followers did. His primary concern was to improve contemporary society; and, without doubt, the conditions of his day left much to be desired. The titular emperor of China exercised a purely nominal authority over all but a small area around his capital; his functions were mainly ceremonial. His supposed vassals, the *de facto* rulers of the various Chinese states, were constantly at war both with one another and with the semi-barbarian states on their borders. The north China plain—the heartland of Chinese culture—had become a vast battleground. Confucius sought to discover the means of ending this chaos.

He said little about the methods he rejected, but it is clear what they were. Obviously, he did not believe that additional warfare could serve any good purpose. At the same time, he refused to look to supernatural beings for assistance. While not denying the existence of gods or spirits—who were supposed to inhabit trees, rocks, rivers, and many other natural phenomena—he preferred not to discuss them. Heaven (*T'ien*), on the other hand, he treated as a remote, impersonal principle which did not intervene in human affairs. The positive basis of Confucius' thought was *Tao*, or the "Way." As used by the Taoist school of philosophy, the term meant something analogous to the course of Nature; Confucius regarded it as the standard of ethics in human affairs.

Conduct in harmony with Tao meant faithfulness and loyalty, reasonableness and moderation, respect for the feelings and rights of others. To the modern mind such precepts are in no way remarkable, but in China of the sixth century B.C. they represented a decided shift of emphasis. In pre-Confucian China, as in other early civilizations, the chief regulator of human behavior was the necessity of pleasing divine beings. The gods and spirits had to be provided with suitable offerings and expressions of devotion according to strictly prescribed formulae. Confucius' insistence upon an internal regulator of conduct—as opposed to the external demands of ritual—was a major innovation in his time. Confucius spoke not of propitiating the spirits, but of cultivating human character. Righteousness, in the broadest possible sense, was his standard for both private and public morals. While respecting the ancient religious ritual, he interpreted it as an aspect of propriety or decorum—a conventional form of social intercourse which directs human behavior into harmonious channels and prevents extremes of emotion.

In later centuries the followers of Confucius were known for their great devotion to book-learning, and similar habits were attributed to the Master as well. But it is unlikely that Confucius himself consulted many books, if only because in his lifetime they were expensive, hard to obtain, and clumsy to use. Legend, nonetheless, has made of him a formidable scholar, and assigned him a role in the composition or editing of the Five Confucian Classics. He is supposed to have selected the 305 poems of the *Book of Songs* from an existing collection of over three thousand, and to have put together the documents which now comprise the *Book of History*. He is similarly reputed to have inspired, if not actually composed, the *Book of Rites*, and to be the author of the *Spring and Autumn Annals* and the appendices to the *Book of Changes*. None of these assertions stands up under critical scrutiny. Most of the material in the Classics postdates Confucius by at least several centuries; and even those portions of the *History* and the *Changes* which preceded him were arranged into the present Classics long after his death. Of the Five Classics, only the *Book of Songs* existed in approximately its present form in the sixth century B.C.; and Confucius probably had nothing to do with selecting its contents.

The one work which is accurately attributed to Confucius is the *Analects* (*Lun Yü,* or "Selected Sayings"). But even this small book —a collection of pithy and disconnected statements on a variety of subjects—did not come from the Master's own hand. It is rather a fourth-century B.C. compilation of his sayings as remembered and passed on by his followers. At one time there were probably several sets of *Analects* in existence, each the product of a different Confucian school. As we have it today, the collection consists of twenty chapters (or "books") of varying dates, of which the third through the ninth contain sayings which probably originated with Confucius himself. Other books are clearly later insertions, and in some cases they contain ideas of which he would scarcely have approved.

The *Analects* remains, nonetheless, the best extant source for the actual opinions of Confucius. Within a few centuries of his death, various notions quite alien to what we know of him became attached to his name. As the Confucian school gained popularity and attracted the patronage of emperors under the Han dynasty (206 B.C.– A.D. 220), an increasing number of ideas that derived from the rival schools of Taoism, Legalism, and Yin-Yang came to be presented under the Confucian label. The Five Classics—supposedly authentic accounts of Confucius' own ideas—are in fact an eclectic mass of divergent and sometimes discordant elements. But in ceasing to be the system of a single and rather obscure individual, Confucianism became a vast intellectual edifice embodying all the major tendencies of Chinese thought. Accepted by ordinary people for its applicability to everyday human concerns and its insistence that government exists for the common welfare, revered by the educated classes for its stress on advancement through merit and its code of gentlemanly behavior, and supported by emperors for its inherent conservatism combined with a reputation for benevolence, Confucianism remained the dominant intellectual system of China until well into the twentieth century.

FROM THE ANALECTS OF CONFUCIUS (LUN YÜ)

Confucius as a Teacher: On Education

II, 15   The Master said, " 'He who learns but does not think,[1] is lost.' He who thinks but does not learn is in great danger."[2]

II, 17   The Master said, "Yu,[3] shall I teach you what knowledge is? When you know a thing, to recognize that you know it, and when you do not know a thing, to recognize that you do not know it. That is knowledge."

VII, 1   The Master said, "I have 'transmitted what was taught to me without making up anything of my own.' I have been faithful to and loved the Ancients. In these respects, I make bold to think, not even our old P'eng[4] can have excelled me."

VII, 2   The Master said, "I have listened in silence and noted what was said. I have never grown tired of learning nor wearied of teaching others what I have learnt. These at least are merits which I can confidently claim."

VII, 4   In his leisure hours the Master's manner was very free and easy, and his expression alert and cheerful.

VII, 8   The Master said, "Only one who bursts with eagerness do I instruct; only one who bubbles with excitement, do I enlighten. If I hold up one corner and a man cannot come back to me with the other three,[5] I do not continue the lesson."

All quotations from the *Analects* are taken from *The Analects of Confucius,* trans. by Arthur Waley, London: George Allen & Unwin, 1958. Reprinted by permission of George Allen & Unwin, Ltd.
  1. The word translated here as "think" (*ssu*) denotes "pay attention" or "observe" rather than "to reason."
  2. The first clause is probably a proverbial saying; the second is Confucius' reply. "Learn" refers to learning the Way of the ancients.
  3. The familiar name of Tzu-lu, one of Confucius' favorite disciples.
  4. A wise old man regarded as the guardian of tradition.
  5. Metaphor from laying out of field-plots? (Tr.)

VII, 18   The "Duke of She"[6] asked Tzu-lu about Master K'ung (Confucius). Tzu-lu did not reply. The Master said, "Why did you not say 'This is the character of the man: so intent upon enlightening the eager that he forgets his hunger, and so happy in doing so, that he forgets the bitterness of his lot and does not realize that old age is at hand. That is what he is.' "[7]

VII, 37   The Master's manner was affable yet firm, commanding but not harsh, polite but easy.

XIII, 9   When the Master was going to Wei,[8] Jan Ch'iu[9] drove him. The Master said, "What a dense population!" Jan Ch'iu said, "When the people have multiplied, what next should be done for them?" The Master said, "Enrich them." Jan Ch'iu said, "When one has enriched them, what next should be done for them?" The Master said, "Instruct them."

XV, 35   The Master said, "When it comes to Goodness one need not avoid competing with one's teacher."

On Goodness

[The word *jen* in Chinese is the generic term for "human being." Here rendered as "Goodness," it is most often translated into English as "humanity" or "human-heartedness." *Jen* is perhaps the most important single concept in the *Analects*, though Confucius nowhere defines it precisely. He speaks of it in a very broad sense as the sum of the qualities which the ideal human being ought to possess, i.e., humanness in the highest degree. Courtesy, loyalty, and unselfishness lie "in its direction," though they are not the whole of it. In Confucius' use of the term, *jen* is in fact a more than human quality. He conceded that the sage-kings of antiquity had possessed it, but refused to apply the word to any living person.]

6. The "Duke of She" was a noble of the state of Ch'u (lived 523-475 B.C.). By reputation a man of principle, he is supposed to have discussed matters of government with Confucius. His title, however, he had invented for himself.
   7. According to the traditional chronology Confucius was sixty-two at the time this was said. (Tr.)
   8. A small state just to the west of Lu.
   9. One of the three disciples mentioned as accompanying Confucius on his travels (the others were Tzu-lu and Yen Hui).

I, 3   The Master said, " 'Clever talk and a pretentious manner'[1] are seldom found in the Good."

I, 6   The Master said, "A young man's duty is to behave well to his parents at home and to his elders abroad, to be cautious in giving promises and punctual in keeping them, to have kindly feelings towards everyone, but seek the intimacy of the Good. If, when all that is done, he has any energy to spare, then let him study the polite arts."[2]

II, 24   The Master said, "Just as to sacrifice to ancestors other than one's own is presumption, so to see what is right and not do it is cowardice."

IV, 2   The Master said, "Without Goodness a man
     Cannot for long endure adversity,
     Cannot for long enjoy prosperity.
The Good Man rests content with Goodness; he that is merely wise pursues Goodness in the belief that it pays to do so."

IV, 3, 4   Of the adage "Only a Good Man knows how to like people, knows how to dislike them," the Master said, "He whose heart is in the smallest degree set upon Goodness will dislike no one."

VII, 15   The Master said, "He who seeks only coarse food to eat, water to drink and bent arm for pillow, will without looking for it find happiness to boot. Any thought of accepting wealth and rank by means that I know to be wrong is as remote from me as the clouds that float above."

XII, 2   Jan Yung[3] asked about Goodness. The Master said, "Behave when away from home[4] as though you were in the presence of an important guest. Deal with the common people

1. A traditional phrase. (Tr.)
2. I.e., learn to recite the *Songs*, practice archery, deportment, and the like. (Tr.)
3. One of the disciples most often mentioned in the *Analects*.
4. I.e., in handling public affairs. (Tr.)

as though you were officiating at an important sacrifice. Do not do to others what you would not like yourself. Then there will be no feelings of opposition to you, whether it is the affairs of a State that you are handling or the affairs of a Family."[5]

XV, 23   Tzu-kung[6] asked saying, "Is there any single saying that one can act upon all day and every day?" The Master said, "Perhaps the saying about consideration: 'Never do to others what you would not like them to do to you.' "[7]

5. A ruling clan. (Tr.)
6. Tzu-kung was one of Confucius' most successful followers: he held important diplomatic positions between 495 and 468 B.C.
7. The same sentiment in different words appears in *Analects* V, 11 and in XII, 2 (above).

On the Gentleman

[*Chün tzu* originally meant "ruler's son" or "aristocrat"—the descendant of a ruling house. Because aristocrats were bound by a special code of manners and morals, the term by extension came to denote superiority of character as well as of birth. Like the English word "gentleman," which at one time signified only a member of the upper classes of society, *chün tzu* in time came to describe anyone, regardless of heredity or social position, who conformed to a certain standard of behavior.

The elaborate code of the gentleman prevailing in traditional China was closely associated with Confucianism. Confucius himself, however, was more concerned with the general moral qualities of the gentleman than with the exact details of his behavior. The *Analects*, for the most part, describe the *chün tzu* in quite unspecific terms as sincere, polite, fair-minded, and so on. But the majority of Confucius' followers attached great importance to the minutiae of proper conduct—the bodily movements, facial expressions, color and material of clothing, and polite phrases suitable for every occasion.]

I, 8   The Master said, "If a gentleman is frivolous,[1] he will lose the respect of his inferiors and lack firm ground[2] upon which to build up his education. First and foremost he must learn to be faithful to his superiors, to keep promises, to refuse

1. I.e., irresponsible and unreliable in his dealings with others. (Tr.)
2. The sentence runs awkwardly and is probably corrupt. (Tr.)

the friendship of all who are not like him. And if he finds he has made a mistake, then he must not be afraid of admitting the fact and amending his ways."

II, 13   Tzu-kung[3] asked about the true gentleman. The Master said, "He does not preach what he practises till he has practised what he preaches."

III, 7   The Master said, "Gentlemen never compete. You will say that in archery they do so. But even then they bow and make way for one another when they are going up to the archery-ground, when they are coming down and at the subsequent drinking bout. Thus even when competing, they still remain gentlemen."

IV, 5   "Wealth and rank are what every man desires; but if they can only be retained to the detriment of the Way he professes, he must relinquish them. Poverty and obscurity are what every man detests; but if they can only be avoided to the detriment of the Way he professes, he must accept them. The gentleman who ever parts company with Goodness does not fulfil that name. Never for a moment[4] does a gentleman quit the way of Goodness. He is never so harried but that he cleaves to this; never so tottering but that he cleaves to this."

IV, 16   The Master said, "A gentleman takes as much trouble to discover what is right as lesser men take to discover what will pay."

VI, 25   The Master said, "A gentleman who is widely versed in letters and at the same time knows how to submit his learning to the restraints of ritual is not likely, I think, to go far wrong."

VIII, 2   . . . The Master said, "When gentlemen deal generously with their own kin, the common people are incited to

3. One of Confucius' most often mentioned disciples; later a diplomat.
4. Literally, "for as long as it takes to eat" one bowl of rice. A common expression, simply meaning a very little while. (Tr.)

Goodness. When old dependents are not discarded, the common people will not be fickle."

IX, 13   The Master wanted to settle among the Nine Wild Tribes of the East. Someone said, "I am afraid you would find it hard to put up with their lack of refinement." The Master said, "Were a true gentleman to settle among them there would soon be no trouble about lack of refinement."

XII, 16   The Master said, "The gentleman calls attention to the good points in others; he does not call attention to their defects. The small man does just the reverse of this."

XIV, 7   The Master said, "It is possible to be a true gentleman and yet lack Goodness. But there has never yet existed a Good man who was not a gentleman."

XIV, 24   The Master said, "The gentleman can influence those who are above him; the small man can only influence those who are below him."

XIV, 27, 28   When the Master said, "He who holds no rank in a State does not discuss its policies," Master Tseng[5] said, " 'A true gentleman, even in his thoughts, never departs from what is suitable to his rank.' "[6]

XV, 1   . . . The Master said, "A gentleman can withstand hardships; it is only the small man who, when submitted to them, is swept off his feet."

XV, 18   The Master said, "A gentleman is distressed by his own lack of capacity; he is never distressed at the failure of others to recognize his merits."

5. Tseng Shen was an influential disciple. The school he established may later have played an important role in compiling the *Analects*.
6. Tseng illustrates Confucius' saying by quoting an old maxim, which also figures, in practically identical form, in the first appendix of the *Book of Changes*. (Tr.)

XV, 20   The Master said, " 'The demands that a gentleman makes are upon himself; those that a small man makes are upon others.' "

XV, 21   The Master said, "A gentleman is proud, but not quarrelsome, allies himself with individuals, but not with parties."

[Chapter X of the *Analects* is a ritual text describing the correct behavior of a gentleman under various circumstances. It demonstrates the extensive interest of many Confucians in the precise details of ritual conduct and the conscious attention they gave to the cultivation of proper attitudes and gestures. Originally this text had nothing to do with Confucius himself. But some of his followers apparently were disturbed that the Master's traditional sayings gave so few clues as to his own behavior. This text was therefore adapted and inserted into the *Analects* as though it were a description of of Confucius himself; the word "gentleman" was changed to "Master K'ung" (Confucius).]

X, 1   At home in his[1] native village his manner is simple and unassuming, as though he did not trust himself to speak. But in the ancestral temple and at Court he speaks readily, though always choosing his words with care.

X, 2   At Court when conversing with the Under Ministers his attitude is friendly and affable; when conversing with the Upper Ministers, it is restrained and formal. When the ruler is present it is wary, but not cramped.

X, 3   When the ruler summons him to receive a guest, a look of confusion comes over his face and his legs seem to give beneath his weight. When saluting his colleagues he passes his right hand to the left, letting his robe hang down in front and behind; and as he advances with quickened step, his attitude is one of majestic dignity.

When the guest has gone, he reports the close of the visit, saying, "The guest is no longer looking back."

1. The gentleman's.

X, 4   On entering the Palace Gate he seems to shrink[2] into himself, as though there were not room. If he halts, it must never be in the middle of the gate, nor in going through does he ever tread on the threshold.[3] As he passes the Stance[4] a look of confusion comes over his face, his legs seem to give way under him and words seem to fail him. While, holding up the hem of his skirt, he ascends the Audience Hall, he seems to double up and keeps in his breath, so that you would think he was not breathing at all. On coming out, after descending the first step his expression relaxes into one of satisfaction and relief. At the bottom of the steps he quickens his pace, advancing with an air of majestic dignity. On regaining his place he resumes his attitude of wariness and hesitation.

X, 5   When carrying the tablet of jade,[5] he seems to double up, as though borne down by its weight. He holds it at the highest as though he were making a bow,[6] at the lowest, as though he were proffering a gift. His expression, too, changes to one of dread and his feet seem to recoil, as though he were avoiding something. When presenting ritual-presents, his expression is placid. At the private audience his attitude is gay and animated.

X, 6   A gentleman[7] does not wear facings of purple or mauve, nor in undress does he use pink or roan.[8] In hot weather he wears an unlined gown of fine thread loosely woven, but puts on an outside garment before going out-of-doors. With a black robe he wears black lambskin; with a robe of undyed silk, fawn. With a yellow robe, fox fur. On his undress robe the fur cuffs are long; but the right is shorter than the left.[9] His bedclothes must

2. In order to demonstrate his insignificance.
3. This prohibition may be derived from a primitive custom of burying the dead underneath thresholds.
4. The place where the ruler takes up his stand when seeing off important guests? (Tr.)
5. Symbol of the ruler's feudal investiture; the *kuei*. (Tr.)
6. On a level with his forehead. (Tr.)
7. Here the compilers have forgotten to alter *chün-tzu* (gentleman) to K'ung Tzu (Confucius). (Tr.)
8. These colours were reserved for times of fasting and mourning. (Tr.)
9. Waley suggests that the shortness of the right sleeve was originally intended to leave the right hand free for using the sword.

be half as long again as a man's height.[10] The thicker kinds of fox and badger are for home wear. Except when in mourning, he wears all his girdle-ornaments.[11] Apart from his Court apron, all his skirts are wider at the bottom than at the waist. Lambskin dyed black and a hat of dark-dyed silk must not be worn when making visits of condolence.[12] At the Announcement[13] of the New Moon he must go to Court in full Court dress.

X, 10   When the men of his village are drinking wine he leaves the feast directly the village-elders have left. When the men of his village hold their Expulsion Rite,[14] he puts on his Court dress and stands on the eastern steps.[15]

X, 11   When sending a messenger to enquire after someone in another country, he prostrates himself twice while speeding the messenger on his way. . . .

X, 14   On entering the Ancestral Temple, he asks about every detail.

X, 15   If a friend dies and there are no relatives to fall back on, he says, "The funeral is my affair." On receiving a present from a friend, even a carriage and horses, he does not prostrate himself. He does so only in the case of sacrificial meat being sent.

X, 16   In bed he avoids lying in the posture of a corpse.[16] When at home he does not use ritual attitudes. When appearing before anyone in mourning, however well he knows him, he must put on an altered expression, and when appearing before anyone in sacrificial garb, or a blind man, even informally, he must be

10. He does not, of course, undress, but simply draws the bedclothes over him. (Tr.)
11. Which are lucky talismans; or (in a more sophisticated vein of explanation) symbolic ornaments indicating his rank. Those of an ordinary gentleman were of jade. (Tr.)
12. I.e., "plain" articles must be worn, approximating to those worn by the mourner. (Tr.)
13. To the Ancestors, who are kept informed of everything that goes on below. (Tr.)
14. The driving away of evil spirits at the close of the year. (Tr.)
15. The place occupied by one who is presiding over a ceremony. (Tr.)
16. I.e., with his face to the North, where lies the land of the Dead. (Tr.)

sure to adopt the appropriate attitude. On meeting anyone in deep mourning he must bow across the bar of his chariot; he also bows to people carrying planks.[17] When confronted with a particularly choice dainty at a banquet, his countenance should change and he should rise to his feet. Upon hearing a sudden clap of thunder or a violent gust of wind, he must change countenance.

X, 17   When mounting a carriage, he must stand facing it squarely and holding the mounting-cord. When riding he confines his gaze,[18] does not speak rapidly or point with his hands.

17. Traditionally explained as meaning "census tablets." (Tr.)
18. Does not look about promiscuously. (Tr.)

On Filial Piety

[The word translated as "filial piety" (*hsiao*) seems originally to have meant the ceremonial forms of expressing reverence toward dead ancestors. Because the ancestors were believed to reside in Heaven, where they watched over the destiny of their descendants down below, filial piety was an essentially religious obligation. By Confucius' time, *hsiao* had acquired the additional meaning of solicitude for living parents. The *Analects* uses the word in both senses.

But filial piety as practiced by most Confucians had little in common with the standpoint of Confucius himself. Certainly Confucius believed that the respect of young people for their elders was essential to both family and social harmony. At the same time, he stressed that acts of devotion must be the outward expression of inward feelings, and he definitely disapproved of elaborate funerals. However, within a century of his death, the Confucian school had come to regard filial piety as a supremely important aspect of ethics. The proper behavior of children toward parents and elder relatives was governed by numerous minute stipulations. Statements in the *Analects* supporting this later notion of filial piety (found especially in Books I and II) almost certainly do not emanate from Confucius himself.]

II, 5   Meng I Tzu[1] asked about the treatment of parents. The Master said, "Never disobey!" When Fan Ch'ih[2] was driving his

1. A young noble of Lu whose father had sent him to study with Confucius.
2. Another of Confucius' disciples.

carriage for him, the Master said, "Meng asked me about the treatment of parents and I said, 'Never disobey!' " Fan Ch'ih said, "In what sense did you mean it?" The Master said, "While they are alive, serve them according to ritual. When they die, bury them according to ritual and sacrifice to them according to ritual."[3]

II, 7   Tzu-yu[4] asked about the treatment of parents. The Master said, " 'Filial sons' nowadays are people who see to it that their parents get enough to eat. But even dogs and horses are cared for to that extent. If there is no feeling of respect, wherein lies the difference?"

IV, 18   The Master said, "In serving his father and mother a man may gently remonstrate with them. But if he sees that he has failed to change their opinion, he should resume an attitude of deference and not thwart them; may feel discouraged, but not resentful."

XIII, 18   The "Duke of She"[5] addressed Master K'ung saying, "In my country there was a man called Upright Kung.[6] His father appropriated a sheep, and Kung bore witness against him." Master K'ung said, "In my country the upright men are of quite another sort. A father will screen his son, and a son his father—which incidentally does involve a sort of uprightness."

3. Here and elsewhere "sacrifice" means offerings in general and not only animal sacrifice. (Tr.)
4. Tzu-yu was evidently one of the more important disciples; certain sayings in the *Analects* are attributed to him rather than to Confucius.
5. A noble of the state of Ch'i with whom Confucius held conversations.
6. A legendary paragon of honesty. (Tr.)

On Ritual and Music

[The word *li* ("ritual") originally signified the sacrifices performed in honor of ancestral spirits by the heads of noble families or clans. Subsequently its meaning expanded to include other ceremonies as well, not necessarily religious in nature—marriage, mourning, feasts, archery contests, political meetings. Finally, *li* came to be equated with proper behavior in general: good manners, dignity, decorum. Confucius regarded *li* as a socially desirable means of expressing emotion, a method of disciplining the feelings and thereby guarding against excess. In theory *li* was supposed to be only the outward manifestation of inner feelings, though it tended to degenerate into stereotyped formulae regarded as valid in themselves.

Yüeh ("music") was a much broader concept than its English equivalent, since it included not only instrumental and vocal music, but also the words of songs and the dancing which accompanied them. Music was closely related to ritual; for both formed part of the rites of sacrifice. In the Classics music occupies an important place. The verses of the *Book of Songs* were all, or almost all, designed to be sung; a *Book of Music* apparently once existed as a separate Classic; and a theoretical chapter on music is included in the *Book of Rites*. Music was thus an essential element in the Chinese concept of the complete life, ranking far higher than a mere diversion or polite accomplishment, as it has often been regarded in the West. Confucian theory noted that music consists of a harmonious and rhythmic set of relationships; this explained its power to produce order and tranquillity in the human spirit. Ritual and music were regarded as complementary, and often mentioned together in a single phrase. Ritual was supposed to guide a man's external conduct, music to regulate his inner being. The ultimate purpose of both was to produce an individual in harmony with himself and with society.]

III, 3   The Master said, "A man who is not Good, what can he have to do with ritual? A man who is not Good, what can he have to do with music?"

III, 4   Lin Fang[1] asked for some main principles in connexion with ritual. The Master said, "A very big question. In ritual at large it is a safe rule always to be too sparing rather than too lavish; and in the particular case of mourning-rites, they should be dictated by grief rather than by fear."

III, 17   Tzu-kung[2] wanted to do away with the presentation[3]

1. Possibly a disciple of Confucius, though this is the only mention of him in the *Analects*.
2. Tzu-kung was one of the more important disciples.
3. By the Duke to his State officers. (Tr.)

of a sacrificial sheep at the Announcement[4] of each New Moon. The Master said, "Ssu! You grudge sheep, but I grudge ritual."

IV, 13   The Master said, "If it is really possible to govern countries by ritual and yielding, there is no more to be said. But if it is not really possible, of what use is ritual?"[5]

VII, 9   If at a meal the Master found himself seated next to someone who was in mourning, he did not eat his fill. When he had wailed at a funeral, during the rest of the day he did not sing.[6]

VII, 17   The occasions upon which the Master used correct pronunciations[7] were when reciting the *Songs* or the *Books* and when practising ritual acts. At all such times he used the correct pronunciation.

VIII, 2   The Master said, "Courtesy not bounded by the prescriptions of ritual becomes tiresome. Caution not bounded by the prescriptions of ritual becomes timidity, daring becomes turbulence, inflexibility becomes harshness."

VIII, 8   The Master said, "Let a man be first incited by the *Songs*, then given a firm footing by the study of ritual, and finally perfected by music."

XII, 1   Yen Hui[8] asked about Goodness. The Master said, " 'He who can himself submit to ritual is Good.' If (a ruler)

---

4. To the Ancestors, who are kept informed of everything that goes on below. (Tr.)

5. The saying can be paraphrased as follows: If I and my followers are right in saying that countries can be governed solely by correct carrying out of ritual and its basic principle of "giving way to others," there is obviously no case to be made out for any other form of government. If on the other hand we are wrong, then ritual is useless. . . . (Tr.)

6. Both of these are common ritual prescriptions. (Tr.)

7. Whereas in daily life he used the Lu dialect. (Tr.)

8. Yen Hui was Confucius' favorite disciple. Confucius remarked of him (*Analects* VI, 5) that, whereas others could not occupy themselves with Goodness for more than a month, Yen Hui could do so for three.

could for one day 'himself submit to ritual,' everyone under Heaven would respond to his Goodness. For Goodness is something that must have its source in the ruler himself; it cannot be got from others." . . .

XVII, 11   The Master said, "Ritual, ritual! Does it mean no more than presents of jade and silk? Music, music! Does it mean no more than bells and drums?"

Introduction to Mo Tzu

Mo Tzu, or Mo Ti (480-390 B.C.), was born the year before Confucius' death, a native either of Confucius' state of Lu or of nearby Sung (both in present-day Shantung province). Tradition records that he was of humble origin, studied with followers of Confucius, and subsequently broke away to found his own school. For several centuries his fame was no less than that of Confucius himself. The book called *Mo Tzu*, in which he criticizes the Confucians on many points, appears to be a reasonably accurate presentation of his doctrines. It was probably written either by Mo Tzu himself or by his immediate disciples, and it is the earliest surviving work of Chinese literature which contains complete essays and dialogues of some length.

Whereas the Confucians in most cases belonged to the landed gentry, Mo Tzu and his followers seem to have been soldiers—professional military retainers of the great territorial lords. Their school is unique in the history of Chinese philosophy for its closely knit organization and the tight control of the leader over its members. The chief of the Mohists was called "Great Master"; he held office for life, and apparently held life-or-death power over his followers. The group took part in military exercises, and on at least one occasion prepared to engage in a war between two of the Chinese states. Nine of the extant chapters of the *Mo Tzu* deal with the means of fighting a defensive war and resisting attacks upon cities.

It is arguable that Mo Tzu's most famous idea—his advocacy of universal love—was merely an extension of the ethics of the military unit. The warriors of feudal China traditionally regarded themselves as members of a brotherhood in which the rule was share and share alike. Mo Tzu argued that this ethic, if faithfully applied, would eliminate all the ills of contemporary China. Universal love to him was not an emotion; it was a strictly utilitarian principle. The stated purpose of his philosophy was to create a well-ordered and wealthy society free from war and strife. In Mo Tzu's opinion, the Confucian stress on filial piety and loyalty to relatives leads merely to invidious distinctions, jealousies, and discord. If the ruler loves everyone equally, he will be loved by all in return; and the result will be social harmony. Moreover, universal love is the Way of Heaven and of the spirits, who will reward the person who practices it.

The Mohist critique of Confucianism fails to draw any distinctions between the actual beliefs of Confucius himself and the practices of his followers, who may well have misunderstood or even consciously misused his doctrines. Mo Tzu (no doubt with some exaggeration) pictures his Confucian contemporaries as pompous and arrogant hypocrites. Still, on many important matters he actually agreed with them. Despite his military background, he regarded war as an unmitigated evil. He valued the Confucian virtues of goodness (*jen*) and righteousness (*li*), while interpreting them in his own fashion: the good and righteous man is one who practices universal love. Like the Confucians, he revered traditional ways, and often supported his arguments by reference to precedent. He agreed that hereditary rulers should govern their states through ministers selected for character and talent rather than for their noble antecedents.

In other respects, his disagreement with Confucianism was fundamental. Confucius believed in adherence to principle regardless of the consequences to oneself; Mo Tzu preached that the view of one's immediate superior must always be accepted—a notion no doubt derived from his military frame of reference. Confucius desired to regulate human emotions through suitable rituals and music; Mo Tzu preferred to ignore the feelings entirely, and dismissed music and ceremonies as a waste of time and resources. Confucius paid no attention to the spirits; Mo Tzu (who probably reflected the popular view) taught that they should be properly served and respected. Indeed, spirits were essential to his system of ethics as the agents for rewarding good, or punishing evil, behavior on the part of mankind.

Followers of Mo Tzu were among the chief participants in the efflorescence of Chinese philosophy which characterized the period of the Warring States (403-221 B.C.). But with the unification of China under a single dynasty, Mohism was at a severe disadvantage. The tendency under the empire was for a single, official doctrine to predominate; and the Han dynasty's support of Confucianism gave that school an undoubted advantage. The class of private military retainers to which Mo Tzu and many of his adherents belonged had long been in decline; it now disappeared entirely, together with most of the independent territorial lords. Moreover, the Mohist ideal of universal love was at best realizable in small and closely knit groups; it was far less suited to the structure of an empire than was the Confucian hierarchy of five relationships.* Except for Taoism, which was a basically private doctrine, the non-Confucian philosophical schools all ceased to exist as separate entities in Han times. Their ideas were either forgotten or were swallowed up in the conglomeration of variant doctrines which now assumed the name of Confucianism.

* Between ruler and subject, father and son, husband and wife, elder brother and younger brother, and friend and friend.

FROM THE MO TZU

On Goodness

[Like Confucius, Mo Tzu also spoke occasionally of *jen*, though in his system the central place of honor is occupied by the idea of universal love. Apparently in his day *jen* had come to be associated with certain Confucian notions of which he disapproved. Attention to ritual and filial piety, at least as practiced by contemporary Confucians, he regarded as useless and hypocritical. To Mo Tzu, the person who has *jen* is one who makes no distinctions between himself and others, family and strangers, countrymen and foreigners, but loves everyone in the world equally.]

Mo Tzu said: It is the business of the benevolent man to try to promote what is beneficial to the world and to eliminate what is harmful. Now at the present time, what brings the greatest harm to the world? Great states attacking small ones, great

All selections from the *Mo Tzu* are taken from *Mo Tzu. Basic Writings*, trans. by Burton Watson, New York and London: Columbia University Press, 1963, pp. 39-40, 83-6, 127-9, 67-9, 76-7. Reprinted by permission of Columbia University Press.

families overthrowing small ones, the strong oppressing the weak, the many harrying the few, the cunning deceiving the stupid, the eminent lording it over the humble—these are harmful to the world. So too are rulers who are not generous, ministers who are not loyal, fathers who are without kindness, and sons who are unfilial, as well as those mean men who, with weapons, knives, poison, fire, and water, seek to injure and undo each other.

When we inquire into the cause of these various harms, what do we find has produced them? Do they come about from loving others and trying to benefit them? Surely not! They come rather from hating others and trying to injure them. And when we set out to classify and describe those men who hate and injure others, shall we say that their actions are motivated by universality or partiality? Surely we must answer, by partiality, and it is this partiality in their dealings with one another that gives rise to all the great harms in the world. Therefore we know that partiality is wrong.

Mo Tzu said: Whoever criticizes others must have some alternative to offer them. To criticize and yet offer no alternative is like trying to stop flood with flood or put out fire with fire. It will surely have no effect. Therefore Mo Tzu said: Partiality should be replaced by universality.

But how can partiality be replaced by universality? If men were to regard the states of others as they regard their own, then who would raise up his state to attack the state of another? It would be like attacking his own. If men were to regard the cities of others as they regard their own, then who would raise up his city to attack the city of another? It would be like attacking his own. If men were to regard the families of others as they regard their own, then who would raise up his family to overthrow that of another? It would be like overthrowing his own. Now when states and cities do not attack and make war on each other and families and individuals do not overthrow or injure one another, is this a harm or a benefit to the world? Surely it is a benefit.

When we inquire into the cause of such benefits, what do we find has produced them? Do they come about from hating others and trying to injure them? Surely not! They come rather from

loving others and trying to benefit them. And when we set out
to classify and describe those men who love and benefit others,
shall we say that their actions are motivated by partiality or by
universality? Surely we must answer, by universality, and it is
this universality in their dealings with one another that gives
rise to all the great benefits in the world. Therefore Mo Tzu has
said that universality is right.

From Sec. 16, "Universal Love"

Mo Tzu said: Now if the gentlemen of today wish to practice
benevolence and righteousness, they must not fail to examine
the origin of righteousness. If they must not fail to examine the
origin of righteousness, then what is the origin of righteousness?

Mo Tzu said: Righteousness does not originate with the stupid
and humble, but with the eminent and wise. How do we know
that righteousness does not originate with the stupid and humble, but with the eminent and wise? Righteousness means doing
what is right. How do we know that righteousness means doing
what is right? Because when there is righteousness in the world,
then the world is well ordered, but when there is no righteousness, then it is in disorder. Therefore we know that righteousness
means doing what is right. Now the stupid and humble cannot
decide what is right for the eminent and wise. There must first
be the eminent and wise, who can then decide what is right for
the stupid and humble. Therefore we know that righteousness
does not originate with the stupid and humble, but with the
eminent and wise.

Then who is eminent and who is wise? Heaven is pure eminence and pure wisdom. Therefore righteousness in fact originates with Heaven.

Now people in the world say: "It is perfectly obvious that
the Son of Heaven is more eminent than the feudal lords and
that the feudal lords are more eminent than the ministers. But
we do not know that Heaven is more eminent and wise than
the Son of Heaven!"

Mo Tzu said: I know that Heaven is more eminent and wise
than the Son of Heaven for this reason: If the Son of Heaven
does something good, Heaven has the power to reward him, and

if he does something bad, Heaven has the power to punish him. If the Son of Heaven is suffering from some illness or misfortune, he must fast and purify himself, prepare clean offerings of wine and millet, and make sacrifices to Heaven and the spirits, and then Heaven will take away the affliction. But I have never heard of Heaven praying for blessings from the Son of Heaven. So I know that Heaven is more eminent and wise than the Son of Heaven. But this is not all. I also know it from one of the books of the former kings[1] which explains the enlightened and unfathomable Way of Heaven in these words:

Enlightened and wise is Heaven,
Looking down upon and governing the world below.[2]

This, then, tells us that Heaven is more eminent and wise than the Son of Heaven. I do not know whether there is something even more eminent and wise than Heaven. But, as I have said, Heaven is pure eminence and wisdom. Therefore righteousness in fact originates with Heaven. So Mo Tzu said: If the gentlemen of the world truly desire to honor the Way, benefit the people, and search out the basis of benevolence and righteousness, then they must not fail to obey the will of Heaven.

If one must not fail to obey the will of Heaven, then what does Heaven desire and what does it hate?

Mo Tzu said: The will of Heaven does not desire that large states attack small ones, that large families overthrow small ones, that the strong oppress the weak, the cunning deceive the stupid, or the eminent lord it over the humble. This is what Heaven does *not* desire. But this is not all. It desires that among men those who have strength will work for others, those who understand the Way will teach others, and those who possess wealth will share it with others. It also desires that those above will diligently attend to matters of government, and those below will diligently carry out their tasks. If those above diligently attend to matters of government, then the state will be well or-

1. The phrase "former kings" or "ancient kings" generally refers to the legendary founders of the first three Chinese dynasties, the Hsia (traditional dates: 2205-1766 B.C.), the Shang (1765-1123 B.C.), and the Chou (1122-403 B.C.).

2. This is apparently a quotation from the *Book of Songs* (No. 207 of the Mao text; No. 143 in Waley).

dered. If those below diligently carry out their tasks, then there will be enough wealth and goods. If the state is well ordered and there are enough wealth and goods, then it will be possible to prepare clean offerings of wine and millet and to sacrifice to Heaven and the spirits within the state, and to provide circlets and other ornaments of jade and pearl by which to carry on diplomatic relations with surrounding states. When the state need not worry about the other feudal lords rising in anger against it or about armed clashes on its borders, when it can devote its efforts to feeding the hungry and giving rest to the weary at home and taking care of its own subjects, then its rulers and superiors will be generous and its subordinates and subjects loyal, its fathers and older brothers loving and its sons and younger brothers filial. Therefore, if one clearly understands how to obey the will of Heaven and put it into practice in the world at large, then the government will be well ordered, the population harmonious, the state rich, and wealth and goods plentiful. The people will all have warm clothes and plenty to eat, and will live in comfort and peace, free from care. Therefore Mo Tzu said: If the gentlemen of today truly desire to honor the Way, benefit the people, and search out the basis of benevolence and righteousness, then they must not fail to obey the will of Heaven. . . .

From Sec. 27, "The Will of Heaven"

On the Gentleman

[It should be noted that Mo Tzu's remarks concerning "gentlemanly" behavior refer to the practices of Confucians in his own day, not to the views of Confucius himself.]

. . . The Confucians corrupt men with their elaborate and showy rites and music and deceive parents with lengthy mournings and hypocritical grief. They propound fatalism,[1] ignore

---

1. When Confucius spoke of conduct in harmony with Tao he certainly did not mean passive acceptance of fate. Mo Tzu's assertion that the Confucians of his day were fatalists may indicate that they did not understand the Master's doctrines.

poverty, and behave with the greatest arrogance. They turn their backs on what is important, abandon their tasks, and find contentment in idleness and pride. They are greedy for food and drink and too lazy to work, but though they find themselves threatened by hunger and cold, they refuse to change their ways. They behave like beggars, stuff away food like hamsters, stare like he-goats, and walk around like castrated pigs. When superior men laugh at them, they reply angrily, "What do you fools know about good Confucians?" In spring and summer they beg for grain, and after the harvests have been gathered in they follow around after big funerals, with all their sons and grandsons tagging along. If they can get enough to eat and drink and get themselves put in complete charge of a few funerals, they are satisfied. What wealth they possess comes from other men's families, and what favors they enjoy are the products of other men's fields. When there is a death in a rich family, they are overwhelmed with joy, saying, "This is our chance for food and clothing!"

The Confucians say: "The superior man must use ancient speech and wear ancient dress before he can be considered benevolent." But we answer: The so-called ancient speech and dress were all modern once, and if at that time the men of antiquity used such speech and wore such dress, then they must not have been superior men. Must we then wear the dress of those who were not superior men and use their speech before we can be considered benevolent?

Again the Confucians say: "The superior man should be a follower and not a maker."[2] But we answer: In ancient times Yi invented the bow, Yü invented armor, Hsi-chung invented carts, and the craftsman Ch'iu invented boats. Do the Confucians mean, then, that the tanners, armorers, cart-makers and carpenters of today are all superior men and Yi, Yü, Hsi-chung, and the craftsman Ch'iu were all inferior men? Moreover, someone must have invented the ways which the Confucians follow, so that in following them they are, by their own definition, following the ways of inferior men.

2. Presumably this is a reference to Confucius' description of himself as a creator and not a transmitter.

The Confucians also say: "When the superior man is victorious in battle, he does not pursue the fleeing enemy. He protects himself with his armor, but does not shoot his arrows, and if his opponents turn and run, he will help them push their heavy carts." But we answer: If the contestants are all benevolent men, then they will have no cause to become enemies. Benevolent men instruct each other in the principles of giving and taking, right and wrong. Those without a cause will follow those who have a cause; those without wisdom will follow those who are wise. When they have no valid arguments of their own, they will submit to the arguments of others; when they see good, they will be won by it. How then could they become enemies? And if both parties in the struggle are evil, then although the victor does not pursue his fleeing opponents, protects himself with his armor but refrains from shooting them, and helps them push their heavy carts if they turn and run—though he does all these things, he will still never be considered a superior man. Let us suppose that a sage, in order to rid the world of harm, raises his troops and sets out to punish an evil and tyrannical state. But, having gained victory, he employs the methods of the Confucians and orders his soldiers, saying: "Do not pursue the fleeing enemy! Protect yourselves with your armor but do not shoot your arrows, and if your opponents turn and run, help them push their heavy carts." Then the evil and disorderly men will get away alive, and the world will not be rid of harm. This is to inflict cruelty upon the parents of the world and do the age a great injury. Nothing could be more unrighteous.

Again the Confucians say: "The superior man is like a bell. Strike it and it will sound; do not strike it and it will remain silent." But we answer: The superior man exerts the utmost loyalty in serving his lord and strives for filial piety in serving his parents. If those whom he serves achieve goodness, he will praise them; and if they have any fault, he will admonish them. This is the way of a subject. Now if one sounds only when struck and remains silent otherwise, then one will be concealing his knowledge and sparing his strength, waiting in dumb silence until he has been questioned. Though he may know of some way to bring benefit to his lord or parents, he will not mention it unless asked.

A great revolt may be about to break out, bandits to rise up, or some trap to spring, and no one knows of it but himself, and yet, though he is actually in the presence of his lord or his parents, he will not mention it unless asked. This is the most perverse kind of treason! As subjects such men are disloyal; as sons they are unfilial. They are disrespectful in serving their elder brothers and unfaithful in their dealings with others. . . .

From Sec. 39, "Against Confucians"

On Filial Piety

. . . There are still many gentlemen in the world today who are in doubt as to whether elaborate funerals and lengthy mourning are actually right or wrong, beneficial or harmful. Therefore Mo Tzu said: Let us try examining the matter. If we follow the rules of those who advocate elaborate funerals and lengthy mourning and apply them in the state, then, we are told, the funeral of a king or high minister will require several inner and outer coffins, a deep grave, numerous grave clothes, a large amount of embroidery for decorating the coffins, and a large grave mound. If the family of the deceased happen to be humble commoners the wealth of the family will be exhausted, and if they are feudal lords their treasuries will be emptied. After the above articles have been supplied, one still needs gold, jewels, and pearls to adorn the corpse, and bundles of silk, carriages, and horses to inter in the grave. In addition there must be draperies and hangings, tripods, baskets, tables, mats, vessels, basins, spears, swords, feather banners, and articles of ivory and hide to bury with the dead before the requirements are fulfilled. And as to those who are chosen to accompany the dead, in the case of a Son of Heaven anywhere from several ten to several hundred persons will be sacrificed, while in the case of generals or high ministers the number will be from several to several tens.

And what are the rules to be observed by the mourner? We are told that he must wail and cry in a sobbing voice at irregular intervals, wearing hemp mourning garments and with tears running down his face. He must live in a mourning hut, sleep on a straw mat, and use a clod of earth for a pillow. In addition he is urged not to eat so as to appear starved, to wear thin clothes so as to appear cold, to acquire a lean and sickly look and a dark complexion. His ears and eyes are to appear dull, his hands and feet lacking in strength, as though he had lost the use of them. And in the case of higher officials we are told that during a period of mourning they should be unable to rise without support or to walk without a cane. And all this is to last for three years.[1]

Now if the rulers and high officials are to adopt these practices, they cannot appear at court early and retire late, attend to the five ministries and six bureaus, encourage farming and forestry, and fill the granaries. If the farmers are to adopt these practices, they cannot leave their homes early and return late, planting their fields and cultivating their crops. If the artisans are to adopt these practices, they cannot construct boats and carts and fashion dishes and utensils, while if women are to adopt these practices they cannot devote themselves day and night to spinning and weaving.

Thus we see that in elaborate funerals much wealth is buried, while lengthy mourning prevents people from going about their activities for long periods of time. If the wealth and goods that have already been produced are to be bundled up and buried in the ground, and the means of future production are to be prohibited for long periods of time, and one still hopes in this way to enrich the state, then it is like prohibiting planting and still hoping for a harvest. One could never acquire wealth that way!

Thus if one hopes to enrich the state, this is obviously not the way to do it. But if one hopes to increase the population, then are elaborate funerals and lengthy mourning perhaps of benefit? Again we find that the answer is no.

Now suppose one follows the rules of those who advocate elaborate funerals and lengthy mourning and applies them in government. We are told that one should mourn three years on the

1. Not three whole years, but into the third year, i.e., twenty-five months. On the whole, Mo Tzu's description of elaborate funerals and mourning practices follows what was prescribed by the Confucians, though the latter stressed that mourning practices were never to be carried to the point where they endangered the health of the mourner. . . . (Tr.)

death of a ruler, three years on the death of a parent, three years for a wife or eldest son, one year for paternal uncles, brothers, and younger sons, five months for other close relatives, and several months for aunts, sisters, and cousins on the maternal side. There are rules requiring one to appear emaciated, to acquire a lean and sickly look, a dark complexion, ears and eyes that are dull, hands and feet that are lacking in strength and useless. And in the case of higher officials we are told that they should be unable to rise without support or to walk without a cane. And all of this in most cases is to last three years. Yet if these practices are adopted and people really are reduced to a starved condition, then the common people will be unable to bear the cold in winter or the heat in summer, and countless numbers of them will sicken and die. Moreover, the relations between men and women will in many cases be disrupted. To hope in this way to increase the population is like ordering a man to fall upon his sword and wishing him long life. . . .

Therefore Mo Tzu prescribes the following rules for funerals and burials: a coffin three inches thick is sufficient to bury rotting bones; three pieces of clothing are sufficient to cover rotting flesh. The hole in the ground should not be deep enough to reach dampness, nor so shallow that the gases escape above ground. A mound sufficiently large to mark the spot is all that is needed. Mourners may weep going to and from the burial, but after that they should devote themselves to making a living. Sacrifices should be carried out at appropriate times in order to fulfill one's filial duty to parents. Thus in this way the rules of Mo Tzu neglect the benefits of neither the living nor the dead.

So Mo Tzu said: If the officials and gentlemen of the world today sincerely desire to practice benevolence and righteousness and become superior men, if they wish to act in accordance with the way of the sage kings and to benefit the people of China, they ought to adopt moderation in funerals as a principle of government. They should not fail to examine the matter.

From Sec. 25, "Moderation in Funerals"

Introduction to Hsün Tzu

Hsün Tzu (ca. 298-238 B.C.) ranks with Confucius and Mencius as one of the three great thinkers of classical Confucianism. He was a native of Chao state (now south Hopei and Shansi)—an area considerably to the west of the main centers of Chinese culture. Hsün Tzu studied in the state of Ch'i (in eastern Shantung), whose ruler was at that time the most lavish patron of learning in China; he held high official posts in the large southern state of Ch'u, and he lived for considerable periods in widely separated regions of China. His experience of the world was thus broader than that of either Confucius or Mencius. He was a famous scholar and teacher in his own time as well as a high government official. Hsün Tzu's ideas are preserved in the book called by his name, some of which he probably wrote himself, though other parts apparently were composed by his disciples. In addition, the *Book of Rites* (*Li Chi*)—one of the Five Confucian Classics—was almost certainly compiled by men of his school.

Hsün's firsthand experience of a variety of cultural milieus led him to observe that not all peoples conform to a single standard of behavior. Quite probably this was the basis for his conclusion that goodness is not an automatic product of human nature, but the result of culture and training. His experience of practical administration (something lacking in the careers of Confucius and Mencius) undoubtedly also gave him a hard-headed view of human character. He believed that human beings in their natural state are barbaric, unjust, and given to extremes of passion; they can be made righteous and wise only through a process of acculturation. Nor did he trust individuals to evolve their own standards of conduct: in his opinion, a fixed body of correct principles had already been handed down from the sage-kings of antiquity. Hsün Tzu laid great stress on the importance of ceremonial forms. While attacking the belief in spirits as superstitious and illogical, he nevertheless wished to maintain traditional rituals as a measure of social control. For this reason he defended the rites in honor of spirits and ancestors and justified them on rational and utilitarian grounds.

The reputation of Hsün Tzu declined substantially after his death, owing at least partly to his unpopular opinion that human nature is basically evil (a point on which he disagreed with Mencius). Nonetheless, his influence upon subsequent Chinese thought can scarcely be overestimated. His works fell into neglect, but his ideas were incorporated to a very large extent into what was perhaps the most influential of the Confucian Classics—the *Book of Rites* (*Li Chi*). Hsün's assertion that all men are born with similar natures and that differences are due to training rather than inborn merit became the standard Chinese view, with all its egalitarian implications for social mobility through education. His insistence upon the importance of ritual remained the typical Chinese attitude down to modern times. And not least of all, his dogmatic outlook on truth tended to prevail over the far greater open-mindedness of Confucius. Later Confucians generally believed that correct doctrines had been established for all time, that the guardians of these doctrines (scholars and teachers) deserved unquestioning respect, and that new ideas could be at best emendations and explanations of the wisdom of the ancient sages.

FROM THE HSÜN TZU

On Filial Piety

. . . In the funeral rites, one adorns the dead as though they were still living, and sends them to the grave with forms symbolic of life. They are treated as though dead, and yet as though still alive, as though gone, and yet as though still present. Beginning and end are thereby unified.

When a person has died, one first of all washes the hair and body, arranges them properly, and places food in the mouth, symbolizing that one treats the dead as though living. (If the hair is not washed, it is combed with a wet comb in three strokes;

All excerpts from the *Hsün Tzu* are taken from *Hsün Tzu: Basic Writings*, trans. by Burton Watson, New York and London: Columbia University Press, 1963, pp. 103-6, 89, 91-2, 94, 96, 112-15. Reprinted by permission of Columbia University Press.

if the body is not bathed, it is wiped with a wet cloth in three strokes). The ears are closed with wads of silk floss, raw rice is placed in the mouth, and the mouth is stopped with a dried cowry shell. These are acts which are the opposite of what one would do for a living person. One dresses the corpse in underwear and three layers of outer garments and inserts the tablet of office in the sash, but adds no sash buckle; one adds a face cover and eye shield and arranges the hair, but does not put on any hat or hat pin. One writes the name of the deceased on a piece of cloth and fixes it to a wooden tablet,[1] so that the coffin will not be lacking a name. As for the articles placed in the coffin, the hats have bands but no strings to tie them to the head; the jars and wine flagons are empty and have nothing in them; there are mats but no couches or armrests. The carving on the wooden articles and the moulding of the pottery are left unfinished, the rush and bamboo articles are such as cannot be used; the reeds and pipes are complete but cannot be sounded; the lutes and zithers are strung but not tuned. A carriage is buried with the coffin but the horses are taken back home, indicating that the carriage will not be used.

Articles that had belonged to the dead when he was living are gathered together and taken to the grave with him, symbolizing that he has changed his dwelling.[2] But only token articles are taken, not all that he used, and though they have their regular shape, they are rendered unusable. A carriage is driven to the grave and buried there, but it has no bells or leather fixtures, no bit or reins attached. All this is done to make clear that these things will not actually be used. The dead man is treated as though he had merely changed his dwelling, and yet it is made clear that he will never use these things. This is all done in order to emphasize the feelings of grief. Thus the articles used by the dead when he was living retain the form but not the function of the common article, and the spirit articles prepared especially

1. This tablet was supposed to provide a resting place for the spirit of the deceased until the permanent tablet (which would be worshipped by the dead person's descendants) was ready for use.

2. Burying a man's personal possessions with his corpse was an ancient practice in China. Hsün interprets it in the light of his principle of treating the dead as though they have merely changed their residence.

for the dead man have the shape of real objects but cannot be used.[3]

It is true of all rites that, when they deal with the living, their purpose is to ornament joy, when they deal with the dead, to ornament grief, when they pertain to sacrifices, to ornament reverence, and when they pertain to military affairs, to ornament majesty. This is true of the rites of all kings, an unchanging principle of antiquity and the present, though I do not know when the custom began.

The grave and grave mound in form imitate a house; the inner and outer coffin in form imitate the sideboards, top, and front and back boards of a carriage; the coffin covers and decorations and the cover of the funeral carriage in form imitate the curtains and hangings of a door or room; the wooden lining and framework of the grave pit in form imitate railings and roof. The funeral rites have no other purpose than this: to make clear the principle of life and death, to send the dead man away with grief and reverence, and to lay him at last in the ground. At the interment one reverently lays his form away; at the sacrifices one reverently serves his spirit; and by means of inscriptions, eulogies, and genealogical records one reverently hands down his name to posterity. In serving the living, one ornaments the beginning; in sending off the dead, one ornaments the end. When beginning and end are fully attended to, then the duties of a filial son are complete and the way of the sage has reached its fulfillment. To deprive the dead for the sake of the living is niggardly; to deprive the living for the sake of the dead is delusion; and to kill the living and force them to accompany the dead is hideous. To bury the dead in the same general manner that one would send off the living, but to make certain that both living and dead, beginning and end are attended to in the most appropriate and fitting fashion—this is the rule of ritual principle and the teaching of the Confucian school.

What is the purpose of the three-year mourning period? I re-

3. Originally it was believed that the dead person's spirit would use the articles placed with the corpse. Hsün Tzu did not believe in spirits; so he prescribed that the buried articles be defective or incomplete, demonstrating that no spirit could use them.

ply: it is a form which has been set up after consideration of
the emotions involved; it is an adornment to the group and a
means of distinguishing the duties owed to near or distant relatives, eminent or humble. It can neither be lengthened nor
shortened. It is a method that can neither be circumvented nor
changed. When a wound is deep, it takes many days to heal;
where there is great pain, the recovery is slow. I have said that
the three-year mourning period is a form set up after consideration of the emotions involved, because at such a time the pain
of grief is most intense. The mourning garments and the cane
of the mourner, the hut where he lives, the gruel he eats, the
twig mat and pillow of earth he sleeps on—these are the adorn-
ments of the intense pain of his grief.

The three-year mourning period comes to an end with the
twenty-fifth month. At that time the grief and pain have not yet
come to an end, and one still thinks of the dead with longing,
but ritual decrees that the mourning shall end at this point. Is
it not because the attendance on the dead must sometime come
to an end, and the moment has arrived to return to one's daily
life? . . .

From Sec. 19, "A Discussion of Rites"

On Ritual and Music

What is the origin of ritual? I reply: man is born with desires.
If his desires are not satisfied for him, he cannot but seek some
means to satisfy them himself. If there are no limits and degrees to his seeking, then he will inevitably fall to wrangling
with other men. From wrangling comes disorder and from disorder comes exhaustion. The ancient kings[1] hated such disorder,
and therefore they established ritual principles in order to curb
it, to train men's desires and to provide for their satisfaction.
They saw to it that desires did not overextend the means for
their satisfaction, and material goods did not fall short of what
was desired. Thus both desires and goods were looked after and
satisfied. This is the origin of rites. . . .

1. The legendary sage-kings such as Yao, Shun, and Yü.

Rites have three bases. Heaven and earth are the basis of life, the ancestors are the basis of the family, and rulers and teachers are the basis of order. If there were no Heaven and earth, how could man be born? If there were no ancestors, how would the family come into being? If there were no rulers and teachers, how would order be brought about? If even one of these were lacking, there would be no safety for man. Therefore rites serve Heaven above and earth below, honor the ancestors, and exalt rulers and teachers. These are the three bases of rites.

The king honors the founder of his family as an equal of Heaven, the feudal lords would not dare to dismantle the mortuary temples of their ancestors, and the high ministers and officials maintain constant family sacrifices. In this way they distinguish and pay honor to the beginners of their family. To honor the beginning is the basis of virtue.

The Son of Heaven alone performs the suburban sacrifice to Heaven; altars of the soil may not be established by anyone lower than a feudal lord; but sacrifices such as the t'an[2] may be carried out by the officials and high ministers as well. In this way rites distinguish and make clear that the exalted should serve the exalted and the humble serve the humble, that great corresponds to great and small to small.

He who rules the world sacrifices to seven generations of ancestors; he who rules a state sacrifices to five generations; he who rules a territory of five chariots[3] sacrifices to three generations; he who rules a territory of three chariots sacrifices to two generations.[4] He who eats by the labor of his hands is not permitted to set up an ancestral temple. In this way the rites distinguish and make clear that the merit accumulated by the ancestors over the generations is great. Where the merit is great, it will dispense widespread blessing; where the merit is meager, the blessing will be limited. . . .

2. A sacrifice to the gods of the land.
3. In early times an area 10 li square was said to have made up a unit called a ch'eng which was responsible for supplying one war chariot. Hence this is a territory 50 li square. (Tr.)
4. These four categories correspond to the four large divisions of the aristocracy: the Son of Heaven, the feudal lords, the high ministers (ta-fu), and the officials or men of breeding (shih). (Tr.)

All rites begin in simplicity, are brought to fulfillment in elegant form, and end in joy. When rites are performed in the highest manner, then both the emotions and the forms embodying them are fully realized; in the next best manner, the emotional content and the forms prevail by turns; in the poorest manner, everything reverts to emotion and finds unity in that alone.

Through rites Heaven and earth join in harmony,[5] the sun and moon shine, the four seasons proceed in order, the stars and constellations march, the rivers flow, and all things flourish; men's likes and dislikes are regulated and their joys and hates made appropriate. Those below are obedient, those above are enlightened; all things change but do not become disordered; only he who turns his back upon rites will be destroyed. Are they not wonderful indeed? . . .

Ritual uses material goods for its performance, follows the distinctions of eminent and humble in creating its forms, varies its quantities in accordance with differences of station, and varies its degree of lavishness in accordance with what is appropriate. When form and meaning are emphasized and emotional content and practical use slighted, rites are in their most florid state. When form and meaning are slighted and emphasis placed upon emotion and practical use, rites are in their leanest state. When form and meaning, and emotion and practical use, are treated as the inside and outside or the front and back of a single reality and are both looked after, then rites have reached the middle state. Therefore the gentleman understands how to make rites florid and how to make them lean, but he chooses to abide in the middle state, and no matter whether he walks or runs, hurries or hastens, he never abandons it. It is his constant world and dwelling. He who abides in it is a gentleman and a man of breeding; he who abandons it is a commoner. He who dwells in it, who wanders widely and masters all its corners and gradations, is a sage. His bounty is the accumulation of ritual; his greatness is the breadth of ritual; his loftiness is the flourishing

5. In this passage *li* is described in terms more usually applied to *Tao*—the mysterious essence of everything in the universe.

of ritual; his enlightenment is the mastery of ritual. This is what the *Odes* means when it says:

Their rites and ceremonies are entirely according to rule,
Their laughter and talk are entirely appropriate.[6] . . .

From Sec. 19, "A Discussion of Rites"

Music is joy,[7] an emotion which man cannot help but feel at times. Since man cannot help feeling joy, his joy must find an outlet in voice and an expression in movement. The outcries and movements, and the inner emotional changes which occasion them, must be given full expression in accordance with the way of man. Man must have his joy, and joy must have its expression, but if that expression is not guided by the principles of the Way, then it will inevitably become disordered. The former kings hated such disorder, and therefore they created the musical forms of the odes and hymns in order to guide it. In this way they made certain that the voice would fully express the feelings of joy without becoming wild and abandoned, that the form would be well ordered but not unduly restrictive, that the directness, complexity, intensity, and tempo of the musical performance would be of the proper degree to arouse the best in man's nature, and that evil and improper sentiments would find no opening to enter by. It was on this basis that the former kings created their music. And yet Mo Tzu criticizes it. Why?[8]

When music is performed in the ancestral temple of the ruler, and the ruler and his ministers, superiors and inferiors, listen to it together, there are none who are not filled with a spirit of harmonious reverence. When it is performed within the household, and father and sons, elder and younger brothers listen to it together, there are none who are not filled with a spirit of har-

6. From the *Book of Songs*, Mao text no. 209, Waley no. 199 (third stanza).
7. Hsün Tzu's argument here and throughout the section is based upon the fact that the words *yüeh* (music) and *lo* (joy) are written with the same character, a coincidence often exploited by early writers on music. By music, Hsün Tzu means the entire musical performance, including singing, dancing, and musical accompaniment. . . . (Tr.)
8. Mo Tzu considered music a waste of time and money. One of the chapters of the *Mo Tzu* (chapter 32) is entitled "Against Music."

monious kinship. And when it is performed in the community, and old people and young together listen to it, there are none who are not filled with a spirit of harmonious obedience. Hence music brings about complete unity and induces harmony. It arranges its accouterments to comprise an adornment to moderation; it blends its performance to achieve the completion of form. It is sufficient to lead men in the single Way or to bring order to ten thousand changes. This is the manner in which the former kings created their music. And yet Mo Tzu criticizes it. Why?

When one listens to the singing of the odes and hymns, his mind and will are broadened; when he takes up the shield and battle-ax and learns the postures of the war dance, his bearing acquires vigor and majesty; when he learns to observe the proper positions and boundaries of the dance stage and to match his movements with the accompaniment, he can move correctly in rank and his advancings and retirings achieve order. Music teaches men how to march abroad to punish offenders and how to behave at home with courtesy and humility. Punishing offenders and behaving with courtesy and humility are based upon the same principle. If one marches abroad to punish offenders in accordance with the way learned through music, then there will be no one who will not obey and submit; if one behaves at home with courtesy and humility, then there will be no one who will not obey and be submissive. Hence music is the great arbiter of the world, the key to central harmony, and a necessary requirement of human emotion. This is the manner in which the former kings created their music. And yet Mo Tzu criticizes it. Why?

Moreover, music was used by the former kings to give expression to their delight, and armies and weapons were used to give expression to their anger. The former kings were careful to show delight or anger only upon the correct occasions. Therefore, when they showed delight, the world joined with them in harmony, and when they showed anger, the violent and unruly shook with fear. The way of the former kings was to encourage and perfect rites and music, and yet Mo Tzu criticizes such music. Therefore, I say that Mo Tzu's attempts to teach the Way may be compared to a blind man trying to distinguish black from white, a deaf man trying to tell a clear tone from a muddy one, or a traveler trying to get to the state of Ch'u[9] by journeying northward.

Music enters deeply into men and transforms them rapidly. Therefore, the former kings were careful to give it the proper form. When music is moderate and tranquil, the people become harmonious and shun excess. When music is stern and majestic, the people become well behaved and shun disorder. When the people are harmonious and well behaved, then the troops will be keen in striking power and the cities well guarded, and enemy states will not dare to launch an attack. In such a case, the common people will dwell in safety, take delight in their communities, and look up to their superiors with complete satisfaction. Then the fame of the state will become known abroad, its glory will shine forth greatly, and all people within the four seas will long to become its subjects. Then at last a true king may be said to have arisen.

But if music is seductive and depraved, then the people will become abandoned and mean-mannered. Those who are abandoned will fall into disorder; those who are mean-mannered will fall to quarreling; and where there is disorder and quarreling, the troops will be weak, the cities will revolt, and the state will be menaced by foreign enemies. In such a case, the common people will find no safety in their dwellings and no delight in their communities, and they will feel only dissatisfaction toward their superiors. Hence, to turn away from the proper rites and music and to allow evil music to spread is the source of danger and disgrace. For this reason the former kings honored the proper rites and music and despised evil music. As I have said before, it is the duty of the chief director of music to enforce the ordinances and commands, to examine songs and writings, and to abolish licentious music, attending to all matters at the appropriate time, so that strange and barbaric music is not allowed to confuse the elegant classical modes. . . .

From Sec. 20, "A Discussion of Music"

9. Ch'u (in the Yangtze Valley) was the southernmost of the major Chinese states.

Introduction to the Five Classics

The Five Classics are those books which the Confucians—the majority of educated Chinese—have traditionally regarded as the highest authorities on the most important questions of life. Two of the Classics are historical works: the *Book of History (Shu Ching)**—a collection of speeches and pronouncements allegedly made by rulers or important officials of the three earliest Chinese dynasties; and the *Spring and Autumn Annals (Ch'un Ch'iu)*†—a bare chronological record of events in Confucius' native state of Lu between 722 and 481 B.C. The *Book of Songs (Shih Ching)*‡ and the *Book of Rites (Li Chi)*§ were both regarded in China as moral treatises—the *Songs* because its apparently simple verses were supposed to contain profounder meanings than appeared on the surface; the *Rites,* more obviously, because of its discussions of ritual, propriety, family relations, and political morality. The *Book of Changes (I Ching),* finally, is an ancient manual of divination which provides formulae for ascertaining the auspicious moment to engage in various activities. A *Book of Music,* sometimes listed as a sixth Classic, has since disappeared as a separate work (although a treatise on music—perhaps a remnant of the former Classic—survives as a chapter of the *Book of Rites*). All these books acquired their status as Classics under the Former Han dynasty (206 B.C.–A.D. 8); but the *Book of Rites* which was then considered the fifth Classic (perhaps the *I Li*) is not identical with the present one (the *Li Chi*).

Modern scholarship has demonstrated that most portions of the Classics are by no means so old as they are supposed to be. Except for the *Songs,* some portions of the *History,* and the original text of the *Changes* (without appendices), all of them were composed in

* Also known as the *Book* (or *Classic*) *of Documents.*
† "Spring and Autumn" actually stands for the four seasons—the book is a year-by-year account of the events in each year which the chroniclers considered significant.
‡ Also known as the *Book* (or *Classic*) *of Poetry* or the *Book of Odes.* Since its verses were set to music, *Songs* is perhaps the most precise designation.
§ Or *Records on Ceremonial; Record of Rituals.*

the period between the death of Confucius and the first century B.C. But the claim of the Classics to high antiquity and the alleged connection with Confucius—whom his followers regarded as the wisest man in history—added enormously to their value in Chinese eyes. Though apparently Confucius himself never defended an idea solely on account of its age, many of his successors carried their reverence for antiquity to great lengths. They felt that correct opinions must necessarily find support in ancient literature. Accordingly, various appropriate documents of allegedly ancient origin were "discovered,"* some of which were accepted into the Classics despite their clearly non-Confucian tendencies. Interestingly enough, neither the internal consistency of the Five Classics, nor their authenticity as true records of Confucius' time and before, was seriously questioned in China until the seventeenth century; and even then the skepticism of critical scholars failed to win wide acceptance. Chinese thinkers still felt impelled to justify their ideas by reference to these traditional books, which remained—together with the *Analects* and the *Mencius*—the principal texts of Chinese education until the twentieth century.

* Certainly the writers of the Classics did not consider themselves as forgers in the usual sense. No doubt they believed they were reconstructing ancient history as it must have been in reality. In post-Confucian China it was common for writers of all sorts of works to attribute them to famous persons of the past. To present a book under one's own name would have been thought presumptuous.

Introduction to the Book of Rites (Li Chi)

The *Book of Rites* (*Li Chi*)—one of the Five Classics—is a compilation of miscellaneous essays dealing with questions of ceremony and general propriety. Its forty-nine chapters are of greatly varying quality and content, and certainly not all by the same hand. Included are discussions of the origin and significance of traditional rites together with directions for ceremonial procedure and dress and proper relations within the family. The rituals it describes are supposed to be of great antiquity; and many of them undoubtedly go back to at least the fourth century B.C. However, even the oldest of them are overlaid with much theoretical analysis and Confucian moralizing. The work as a whole was compiled in the second or first century B.C., probably by followers of the famous Confucian thinker Hsün Tzu (lived *ca.* 298-238 B.C.). In fact, substantial passages seem to have been copied almost verbatim from the writings of Hsün Tzu, though his authorship is not acknowledged.

The *Book of Rites* is a work of great importance in Chinese intellectual history. It bears witness to the development of Confucianism from the relatively simple precepts of the *Analects* to a complicated, eclectic system of thought including many elements of totally non-Confucian origin. The scholars of the Han dynasty who compiled the Classic were eager to surround the emperor with complex ceremonies of allegedly ancient date which emphasized the continuity of the dynasty with the legendary sage-kings of antiquity. In effect, the elaborate intellectual justification given to these rites tended also to perpetuate them. For more than two millennia the educated classes of China venerated the *Book of Rites* as a true account of ancient practices and referred to it as authoritative upon all matters of ritual procedure.

Introduction to
"The Great Learning" and "The Doctrine of the Mean"

"The Great Learning" (*Ta Hsüeh*) and "The Doctrine of the Mean" (*Chung Yung*) are the two most famous chapters of the *Book of Rites*. According to tradition they were written by Confucius' grandson Tzu-ssu; but probably they are composite works dating from about 200 B.C. They represent a type of thought common under the Han dynasty: a combination of Confucian moral precepts with a mysticism akin to Taoism.

The ideal propounded by "The Great Learning" is of an all-pervasive harmony in which every member of society has his assigned place. To achieve this, each person must first perfect himself: only then can he take his proper place within the family. For the ruler, correct family relationships were particularly important: according to a prevalent Chinese belief, the emperor's ability to regulate his own family also determined his success or failure in governing the country. Government was supposed to be merely the family writ large, with the relationship of ruler to subject corresponding to that between farther and son.

"The Doctrine of the Mean" advocates conduct in harmony with the course of nature, which it interprets to mean the exercise of such virtues as justice, tolerance, and equality. The "mean" (*chung*) and "normality" (*yung*) denote a middle course between extremes and a state of mind in which reason and feeling work together.

FROM THE GREAT LEARNING (TA HSÜEH)

On Education

1   . . . Things have their root and their branches; affairs have their end and their beginning. To know what is first and what is last will lead near to what is taught (in the Great Learning).

2   The ancients who wished to illustrate illustrious virtue throughout the kingdom, first ordered well their states. Wishing to order well their states, they first regulated their families. Wishing to regulate their families, they first cultivated their persons. Wishing to cultivate their persons, they first rectified their hearts. Wishing to rectify their hearts, they first sought to be sincere in their thoughts. Wishing to be sincere in their thoughts, they first extended to the utmost their knowledge.

3   The extension of knowledge is by the investigation of things.

4   Things being investigated, their knowledge became complete. Their knowledge being complete, their thoughts were sincere. Their thoughts being sincere, their hearts were then rectified. Their hearts being rectified, their persons were cultivated. Their persons being cultivated, their families were regulated. Their families being regulated, their states were rightly governed. Their states being rightly governed, the whole kingdom was made tranquil and happy.

From *Li Ki: Book of Rites*, trans. by James Legge (Vols. 27 and 28 of *The Sacred Books of the East*), Oxford: At the Clarendon Press, 1885, II, 411-13, 416-21, 423.

From the son of Heaven down to the multitudes of the people, all considered the cultivation of the person to be the root
(of everything besides). It cannot be, when the root is neglected, that what should spring from it will be well ordered. It
never has been the case that what was of great importance has
been slightly cared for, and at the same time what was of slight
importance has been greatly cared for.

This is called "knowing the root," this is called "the perfection of knowledge."

5   What is called "making the thoughts sincere" is the allowing no self-deception;—as when we hate a bad smell and
love what is beautiful, naturally and without constraint. Therefore the superior man must be watchful over himself when he
is alone. There is no evil to which the small man, dwelling retired, will not proceed; but when he sees a superior man, he
tries to disguise himself, concealing his evil, and displaying
what is good. The other beholds him as if he saw his heart and
reins;—of what use (is his disguise)? This is an instance of the
saying, "What truly is within will be manifested without."
Therefore the superior man must be watchful over himself
when he is alone.

15   What is meant by "The cultivation of the person depends on the rectifying of the mind" (may be thus illustrated):
—If a man be under the influence of anger, his conduct will not
be correct. The same will be the case, if he be under the influence of terror, or of fond regard, or of sorrow and distress.
When the mind is not present, we look and do not see; we hear
and do not understand; we eat and do not know the taste of
what we eat. This is what is meant by saying that "the cultivation of the person depends on the rectifying of the mind."

16   What is meant by "The regulation of the family depends on the cultivation of the person" is this:—Men are partial where they feel affection and love; partial where they despise and dislike; partial where they stand in awe and with a
feeling of respect; partial where they feel sorrow and compassion; partial where they are arrogant and rude. Thus it is that
there are few men in the world who love and at the same time
know the bad qualities (of the object of their love), or who hate

and yet know the good qualities (of the object of their hatred). Hence it is said, in the common adage, "A man does not know the badness of his son; he does not know the richness of his growing corn." This is what is meant by saying, that "if his person be not cultivated, a man cannot regulate his family."

17   What is meant by "In order to govern well his state, it is necessary first to regulate his family" is this:—It is not possible for one to teach others while he cannot teach his own family. Therefore the superior man (who governs a state), without going beyond his family, completes the lessons for his state. There is filial piety;—it has its application in the service of the ruler. There is brotherly obedience;—it has its application in the service of elders. There is kindly gentleness;—it has its application in the employment of the multitudes. . . .

18   From the loving (example) of one family, a whole state may become loving, and from its courtesies, courteous, while from the ambition and perverseness of the One man,[1] the whole state may be thrown into rebellious disorder;—such is the nature of the influence. This is in accordance with the saying, "Affairs may be ruined by a single sentence; a state may be settled by its One man."

19   Yao and Shun[2] presided over the kingdom with benevolence, and the people followed them. Chieh and Chou[3] did so with violence, and the people followed them. When the orders of a ruler are contrary to what he himself loves to practise the people do not follow him.

20   Therefore the ruler must have in himself the (good) qualities, and then he may require them in others; if they are not in himself, he cannot require them in others. Never has there been a man who, not having reference to his own character and wishes in dealing with others, was able effectually to instruct them. Thus we see how "the government of the state depends on the regulation of the family."

22   What is meant by "The making the whole kingdom

1. The ruler of the state.
2. Legendary ancient kings proverbial for their virtuous rule.
3. The final kings of the Hsia and Shang dynasties, respectively, known for their extreme wickedness.

peaceful and happy depends on the government of its states" is
this:—When the superiors behave to their aged as the aged
should be behaved to, the people become filial; when they behave to their elders as elders should be behaved to, the people
learn brotherly submission; when they treat compassionately
the young and helpless, the people do the same. Thus the superior man has a principle with which, as with a measuring
square, to regulate his course.

23   What a man dislikes in his superiors, let him not display
in his treatment of his inferiors; and what he dislikes in his inferiors, let him not display in his service of his superiors: what
he dislikes in those who are before him, let him not therewith
precede those who are behind him; and what he dislikes in
those who are behind him, let him not therewith follow those
who are before him: what he dislikes to receive on the right, let
him not bestow on the left; and what he dislikes to receive on
the left, let him not bestow on the right:—this is what is called
"The Principle with which, as with a measuring square, to regulate one's course."

26   In the Book of Poetry it is said,

> "Ere Shang had lost the nation's heart,[4]
> Its monarchs all with God had part
> In sacrifice. From them we see
> 'Tis hard to keep High Heaven's decree."[5]

This shows that by gaining the people, the state is gained; and
by losing the people, the state is lost.

Therefore the ruler should first be careful about his (own)
virtue. Possessing virtue will give him the people. Possessing
the people will give him the territory. Possessing the territory
will give him its wealth. Possessing the wealth, he will have resources for expenditure.

Virtue is the root; wealth is the branches. If he make the root
his secondary object, and the branches his primary object, he

4. Waley (in the *Book of Songs*) translates this as "Before (Shang) lost
its army . . ."

5. III, I, 1, v. 6 of Legge's verse translation of the *Book of Poetry* (*Songs*);
No. 241 of Waley's version.

will only quarrel with the people, and teach them rapine. Hence the accumulation of wealth is the way to scatter the people, and the distribution of his wealth is the way to collect the people. Hence (also), when his words go forth contrary to right, they will come back to him in the same way, and wealth got by improper ways will take its departure by the same.

37   Never has there been a case of the superior loving benevolence, and his inferiors not loving righteousness. Never has there been a case where (his inferiors) loved righteousness, and the business (of the superior) has not reached a happy issue. Never has there been a case where the wealth accumulated in the treasuries and arsenals (of such a ruler and people) did not continue to be his.

FROM THE DOCTRINE OF THE MEAN
(CHUNG YUNG)
On The Gentleman

SECTION I

5   When there are no stirrings of pleasure, anger, sorrow, or joy, we call it the State of Equilibrium. When those feelings have been stirred, and all in their due measure and degree, we call it the State of Harmony. This Equilibrium is the great root (from which grow all the human actings) in the world; and this Harmony is the universal path (in which they should all proceed).

6   Let the State of Equilibrium and Harmony exist in perfection, and heaven[1] and earth would have their (right) places, (and do their proper work), and all things would be nourished (and flourish).

7   Kung-ni (Confucius) said, "The superior man[2] (exhibits) the state of equilibrium and harmony[3]; the small man presents

From *Li Ki: Book of Rites,* trans. by James Legge (Vols. 27 and 28 of *The Sacred Books of the East*), Oxford: At the Clarendon Press, 1885, II, 300-304, 306-7.

1. The material heavens (sky, stars, etc.) rather than the supreme Power called Heaven (*T'ien*).

2. "Superior man" is Legge's translation of *chün tzu*; Waley (in the *Analects*) renders it as "gentleman."

3. Or: embodies the course of the Mean.

the opposite of those states. The superior man exhibits them, because he is the superior man, and maintains himself in them; the small man presents the opposite of them, because he is the small man, and exercises no apprehensive caution."

8   The Master[4] said, "Perfect is the state of equilibrium and harmony! Rare have they long been among the people who could attain to it!"

11   The Master said, "Was not Shun[5] grandly wise? Shun loved to question others, and to study their words though they might be shallow. He concealed what was bad (in them), and displayed what was good. He laid hold of their two extremes, determined the mean between them, and used it in (his government of) the people. It was this that made him Shun!"

12   The Master said, "Men all say, 'We are wise'; but being driven forward and taken in a net, a trap, or a pitfall, not one of them knows how to escape. Men all say, 'We are wise'; but when they have chosen the state of equilibrium and harmony, they are not able to keep in it for a round month."

13   The Master said, "This was the character of Hui[6]:— Having chosen the state of equilibrium and harmony, when he found any one thing that was good, he grasped it firmly, wore it on his breast, and did not let it go."

14   The Master said, "The kingdom, its states, and clans may be perfectly ruled; dignities and emoluments may be declined; but the state of equilibrium and harmony cannot be attained to."

19   (The Master said), "The superior man cultivates a (friendly) harmony, and is not weak;—how firm is he in his fortitude! He stands erect in the middle, and does not incline to either side;—how firm is he in his fortitude! If right ways prevail in (the government of his state), he does not change from what he was in retirement;—how firm is he in his fortitude! If

---

4. "The Master" presumably means Confucius, though whether he actually made the statements here attributed to him is doubtful. It was common practice for Chinese authors to present their own ideas as quotations from some ancient worthy.

5. The legendary emperor of antiquity who supposedly lived ca. 2250 B.C.

6. Yen Hui was Confucius' favorite disciple.

bad ways prevail, he will die sooner than change;—how firm is he in his fortitude!"

22   (The Master said), "The superior man, acting in accordance with the state of equilibrium and harmony, may be all unknown and unregarded by the world, but he feels no regret:—it is only the sage who is able for this."

36   "The superior man does what is proper to the position in which he is; he does not wish to go beyond it. In a position of wealth and honour, he does what is proper to a position of wealth and honour. In a position of poverty and meanness, he does what is proper to a position of poverty and meanness. Situated among barbarous tribes, he does what is proper in such a situation. In a position of sorrow and difficulty, he does what is proper in such a position. The superior man can find himself in no position in which he is not himself.

37   "In a high situation, he does not insult or oppress those who are below him; in a low situation, he does not cling to or depend on those who are above him.

38   "He rectifies himself, and seeks for nothing from others; and thus none feel dissatisfied with him. Above, he does not murmur against Heaven; below, he does not find fault with men.

39   "Therefore the superior man lives quietly and calmly, waiting for the appointments (of Heaven); while the mean man does what is full of risk, looking out for the turns of luck."

40   The Master said, "In archery we have something like (the way of) the superior man. When the archer misses the centre of the target, he turns round and seeks for the cause of his failure in himself."

II
Politics

THE "WARRING STATES" IN 350 B.C.

HSIUNG-NU NOMADS

TUNG-HU NOMADS
(to Yen, 290 B.C.)

(MANCHURIA)

Built ca. 300 B.C.

(to Chao, 300 B.C.)

HU NOMADS

Built ca. 300 B.C.

Huang Ho

(KANSU)

JUNG NOMADS

Built ca. 300 B.C.

Built 353 B.C.

Built ca. 330 B.C.

CHAO

(SHANSI)

(to Han)

(to Wei)

YEN

Gulf of Pohai

CH'I

(SHANTUNG)

ca. 450 B.C.

Yellow Sea

Huang Ho (Yellow R.)

WEI

CHOU

Lo-yang

HAN

LU

TSOU

SUNG

T'ENG

Built 353 B.C.

CH'IN

(SHENSI)

Wei R.

(to Wei)

(HONAN)

(KIANGSU)

Han R.

Huai R.

(to Ch'u, 333 B.C.)

(SZECHWAN)

SHU PA
(to Ch'in, 316 B.C.)

CH'U

(HUPEI)

ANHWEI

YÜEH

(CHEKIANG)

Yangtze R.

Yellow Sea

East China Sea

(KWEICHOW)

(HUNAN)

(KIANGSI)

(FUKIEN)

(KWANGSI)

Hsi (West) R.

(KWANGTUNG)

(TAIWAN)

(VIETNAM)

- – – Boundaries of states
· · · · · Present-day provincial boundaries
– · – · – Boundaries of modern China

0   400 Miles

FROM THE ANALECTS OF CONFUCIUS
(LUN YÜ)*

On Government by Moral Force

[A basic assumption of the Confucian school was that the quality of government depends primarily upon the ruler's moral character. If he was upright, benevolent, and observed the proper rituals, they believed, he would automatically act for the general welfare, and the people would be satisfied with his government. A fixed body of laws was therefore unnecessary. The possibility of well-meaning stupidity, of disasters produced through the best of intentions, was scarcely considered. Between a righteous sovereign and the rest of society, conflicts of interest were inconceivable.]

I, 5   The Master said, "A country of a thousand war-chariots cannot be administered unless the ruler attends strictly to business, punctually observes his promises, is economical in expenditure, shows affection towards his subjects in general, and uses the labour of the peasantry only at the proper times of year."[1]

II, 3   The Master said, "Govern the people by regulations, keep order among them by chastisements, and they will flee from you, and lose all self-respect. Govern them by moral force, keep order among them by ritual[2] and they will keep their self-respect and come to you of their own accord."

* For the Introduction to Confucius, see above, pp. 3-6.
From *The Analects of Confucius*, trans. by Arthur Waley, London: George Allen & Unwin, 1958. Reprinted by permission of George Allen & Unwin, Ltd.
  1. I.e., when their crops do not require attention.
  2. There is some question as to whether Confucius refers merely to government by example—i.e., that if the upper classes follow the proper ritual the masses will follow suit—or whether he thought that ritual as practiced by the ruler had a magical efficacy.

III, 19   Duke Ting[3] asked for a precept concerning a ruler's use of his ministers and a minister's service to his ruler. Master K'ung[4] replied saying, "A ruler in employing his ministers should be guided solely by the prescriptions of ritual. Ministers in serving their ruler, solely by devotion to his cause."

XII, 11   Duke Ching of Ch'i[5] asked Master K'ung about government. Master K'ung replied saying, "Let the prince be a prince, the minister a minister, the father a father and the son a son." The Duke said, "How true! For indeed when the prince is not a prince, the minister not a minister, the father not a father, the son not a son, one may have a dish of millet in front of one and yet not know if one will live to eat it."

XII, 19   Chi K'ang-tzu[6] asked Master K'ung about government, saying, "Suppose I were to slay those who have not the Way in order to help on those who have the Way, what would you think of it?" Master K'ung replied saying, "You are there to rule, not to slay. If you desire what is good, the people will at once be good. The essence of the gentleman is that of wind; the essence of small people is that of grass. And when a wind passes over the grass, it cannot choose but bend."

XIII, 2   Jan Yung, having become steward of the Chi Family, asked about government. The Master said, "Get as much as possible done first by your subordinates. Pardon small offences. Promote men of superior capacity." Jan Yung said, "How does one know a man of superior capacity, in order to promote him?" The Master said, "Promote those you know, and those whom you do not know other people will certainly not neglect."[7]

3. Duke of Lu, died 495 B.C.
4. Confucius.
5. Ch'i was a moderate-sized state just north of Lu in present-day Shantung province. The last years of Duke Ching's reign (d. 490 B.C.) were marred by the intrigues of ministers and by quarrels among his own sons. According to legend, the duke was haunted by the fear of death.
6. Chi K'ang-tzu (d. 469 B.C.) was the noble who exercised the actual ducal power in the state of Lu.
7. I.e., will not fail to call to your attention.

XIII, 6   The Master said, "If the ruler himself is upright, all will go well even though he does not give orders. But if he himself is not upright, even though he gives orders, they will not be obeyed."

XIII, 10   The Master said, "If only someone were to make use of me, even for a single year, I could do a great deal; and in three years I could finish off the whole work."

XIII, 11   The Master said, " 'Only if the right sort of people had charge of a country for a hundred years would it become really possible to stop cruelty and do away with slaughter.' How true the saying is!"

XIII, 13   The Master said, "Once a man has contrived to put himself aright, he will find no difficulty at all in filling any government post. But if he cannot put himself aright, how can he hope to succeed in putting others right?"[8]

XV, 14   The Master said, "To demand much from oneself and little from others is the way (for a ruler) to banish discontent."

8. The play on *cheng* "to straighten, put right" and *cheng* "to govern" makes this passage impossible to translate satisfactorily. (Tr.)

On Public Opinion

II, 19   Duke Ai[1] asked, "What can I do in order to get the support of the common people?" Master K'ung[2] replied, "If you 'raise up the straight and set them on top of the crooked,' the commoners will support you. But if you raise the crooked and set them on top of the straight, the commoners will not support you."

II, 20   Chi K'ang-tzu[3] asked whether there were any form of encouragement by which he could induce the common people

1. Duke of Lu from 494 to 468 B.C. (Tr.)
2. Confucius.
3. Head of the three families who were *de facto* rulers of Lu. Died 469 B.C. (Tr.)

to be respectful and loyal. The Master said, "Approach them
with dignity, and they will respect you. Show piety towards
your parents and kindness toward your children, and they will
be loyal to you. Promote those who are worthy, train those who
are incompetent; that is the best form of encouragement."

XII, 7   Tzu-kung[4] asked about government. The Master
said, "Sufficient food, sufficient weapons, and the confidence of
the common people." Tzu-kung said, "Suppose you had no
choice but to dispense with one of these three, which would you
forgo?" The Master said, "Weapons." Tzu-kung said, "Suppose
you were forced to dispense with one of the two that were left,
which would you forgo?" The Master said, "Food. For from of
old death has been the lot of all men; but a people that no
longer trusts its rulers is lost indeed."

4. Tzu-kung is one of the most frequently mentioned disciples in the *Analects*; he became a prominent diplomat.

Introduction to Mencius

Mencius (or Meng Tzu: "Master Meng"), who lived between 372
and 289 B.C., was the earliest of the major intellectual heirs of Confucius. He was native to a small state in northeast China, and is
supposed to have studied with pupils of Confucius' grandson, Tzu-
ssu. Much of his life he spent traveling from one state to another
expounding his ideas at the various ducal courts; but like Confucius
before him, he failed to win any important office. However, by the
fourth century B.C. itinerant philosophers were no longer the rarity
they had been two centuries before. The rulers of many Chinese
states—ambitious to increase their territories—were eager to hear
the views of eminent thinkers on political subjects. Mencius seems
to have been not only well received, but also lavishly supported by
a series of noble patrons. His book, also called *Mencius*, is a record
of some of his conversations both with rulers of states and with philosophical opponents. Probably compiled by his disciples rather than

by Mencius himself, it appears to be a reasonably accurate account of his ideas. It is also, after the *Analects,* our most reliable source of information about the actual career and opinions of Confucius.

By the fourth century B.C. the traditions of Confucianism were under attack from many sides. One of Mencius' chief purposes was to defend these traditions against opponents, especially the followers of Mo Tzu and the Taoist Yang Chu. Like Confucius, he described himself as a transmitter of ideas rather than an original thinker; but his true role was to expand, or to make explicit, ideas which Confucius had merely suggested. The *Mencius* was from the beginning one of the central scriptures of Confucianism; and it has a strong claim to be regarded also as one of the classics of world literature.

FROM THE MENCIUS

On Government by Moral Force

1 Mencius went to see king Huei of Liang.[1]

2 The king said, "Venerable sir, since you have not counted it far to come here, a distance of a thousand *li,*[2] may I presume that you are provided with counsels to profit my kingdom?"

3 Mencius replied, "Why must your Majesty use that word 'profit?' What I am provided with, are counsels to benevolence and righteousness, and these are my only topics.

4 "If your Majesty say, 'What is to be done to profit my kingdom?' the great officers will say, 'What is to be done to profit our families?' and the inferior officers and the common

All selections from the *Mencius* are reprinted from *The Works of Mencius,* trans. by James Legge (Vol. II of *The Chinese Classics*), Oxford: At the Clarendon Press, 1895.

1. The state of Wei (also called Liang from the name of its capital) was one of the so-called Six States into which China was divided in the fourth century B.C. Wei occupied the southeastern portion of the formerly powerful state of Chin in the northwest. "Huei," meaning "the kindly," was the posthumous title of this king, whom Mencius is thought to have visited in 336 B.C.

2. The *li* was the standard Chinese measure of distance. The exact length of the ancient *li* is uncertain; it was probably equivalent to roughly one-third of a mile. In complimentary style, the king exaggerates the distance that Mencius has traveled.

people will say, 'What is to be done to profit our persons?' Superiors and inferiors will try to snatch this profit the one from the other, and the kingdom will be endangered. In the kingdom of ten thousand chariots, the murderer of his sovereign shall be the chief of a family of a thousand chariots.[3] In a kingdom of a thousand chariots, the murderer of his prince shall be the chief of a family of a hundred chariots. To have a thousand in ten thousand, and a hundred in a thousand, cannot be said not to be a large allotment, but if righteousness be put last, and profit be put first, they will not be satisfied without snatching all.

5   "There never has been a benevolent man who neglected his parents. There never has been a righteous man who made his sovereign an after consideration.

6   "Let your Majesty also say, 'Benevolence and righteousness, and let these be your only themes.' Why must you use that word—'profit?' "

Bk. I, Pt. I, Ch. 1

[King Hsüan of Ch'i asked Mencius how to institute benovolent government.]

20   Mencius replied, "They are only men of education who, without a certain livelihood, are able to maintain a fixed heart. As to the people, if they have not a certain livelihood, it follows that they will not have a fixed heart. And if they have not a fixed heart, there is nothing which they will not do, in the way of self-abandonment, of moral deflection, of depravity, and of wild license. When they thus have been involved in crime, to follow them up and punish them;—this is to entrap the people. How can such a thing as entrapping the people be done under the rule of a benevolent man?

21   "Therefore an intelligent ruler will regulate the livelihood of the people, so as to make sure that, for those above them, they shall have sufficient wherewith to serve their par-

3. A domain of one thousand *li* square was supposed to produce ten thousand war chariots—enough to maintain a king. An area producing only one thousand chariots was that of an inferior lord, or marquis.

ents, and, for those below them, sufficient wherewith to support
their wives and children; that in good years they shall always
be abundantly satisfied, and that in bad years they shall escape
the danger of perishing. After this he may urge them, and
they will proceed to what is good,[1] for in this case the people
will follow after it with ease.

22   "Now[adays], the livelihood of the people is so regulated, that, above, they have not sufficient wherewith to serve
their parents, and, below, they have not sufficient wherewith to
support their wives and children. Notwithstanding good years,
their lives are continually embittered, and, in bad years, they
do not escape perishing. In such circumstances they only try to
save themselves from death, and are afraid they will not succeed. What leisure have they to cultivate propriety and
righteousness?"

Bk. I, Pt. I, Ch. 7

1   Mencius said, "Let it be seen to that (the people's) fields
of grain and hemp are well cultivated, and make the taxes on
them light;—so the people may be made rich.

2   "Let it be seen to that the people use their resources of
food seasonably, and expend their wealth only on the prescribed ceremonies:—so their wealth will be more than can be
consumed.

3   "The people cannot live without water and fire, yet if you
knock at a man's door in the dusk of the evening, and ask for
water and fire, there is no man who will not give them, such is
the abundance of these things. A sage governs the kingdom so
as to cause peas and grain to be as abundant as water and fire.
When peas and grain are as abundant as water and fire, how
shall the people be other than virtuous?"

Bk. VII, Pt. I, Ch. 23

On Public Opinion

[Although China never evolved democratic institutions in the
Western sense of the word—elections, parliaments, an independent

---

1. I.e., behavior in acordance with propriety and righteousness.

judiciary, and so forth—Chinese government was by no means an unmitigated autocracy. The prevailing Confucian philosophy constantly emphasized that government exists for the people's welfare. Confucian tutors instilled this idea into the minds of successive heirs to the throne, who could scarcely have remained uninfluenced by it. Moreover, the good of the people was guaranteed by the Mandate of Heaven. This remarkable theory—an article of faith to all good Confucians—assumed a kind of divine right of rulership contingent upon popular satisfaction with the sovereign's conduct. The notion of the Mandate appears very early in Chinese literature—for example in the oldest parts of the *Book of History*. It was constantly cited by the Confucians and must have had a profound effect upon everyone concerned with government.]

1   King Huei of Liang said, "There was not in the nation a stronger State than Chin,[1] as you, venerable Sir, know. But since it descended to me,[2] on the east we have been defeated by Ch'i,[3] and then my eldest son perished;[4] on the west we have lost seven hundred *li* of territory to Ch'in;[5] and on the south we have sustained disgrace at the hands of Ch'u.[6] I have brought shame on my departed predecessors, and wish on their account to wipe it away, once for all. What course is to be pursued to accomplish this?"

2   Mencius replied, "With a territory which is only a hundred *li* square, it is possible to attain to the royal dignity.[7]

1. Chin, one of the larger Chinese states in Confucius' time, divided in 453 B.C. into three independent parts—Chao, Han, and Wei (also called Liang). They were three of the so-called Six States—the most important ones in China at that time.
2. The king speaks as though the entire former state of Chin belonged to him, rather than merely a third of it.
3. Ch'i (in modern Shantung) was one of the Six States—the "Big Six" of Chinese politics in the fourth century B.C.
4. In 340 B.C. the king's eldest son was taken captive and died soon afterward.
5. The state of Ch'in lay in the Wei River valley to the west of the main area of Chinese civilization; it was regarded as semi-barbarous country, not one of the Six States. In 361 B.C. Ch'in captured the capital of Wei, which was forced to buy peace through various surrenders of territory.
6. This defeat by Ch'u—southernmost of the Six States—was also marked by loss of territory.
7. I.e., become sovereign of all China, like the legendary ancient kings.

3   "If your Majesty will indeed dispense a benevolent government to the people, being sparing in the use of punishments and fines, and making the taxes and levies light,[8] so causing that the fields shall be ploughed deep, and the weeding of them be carefully attended to, and that the strong-bodied,[9] during their days of leisure, shall cultivate their filial piety, fraternal respectfulness, sincerity, and truthfulness, serving thereby, at home, their fathers and elder brothers, and, abroad, their elders and superiors,—you will then have a people who can be employed, with sticks which they have prepared, to oppose the strong mail and sharp weapons of the troops of Ch'in and Ch'u.

4   "The rulers of those states[10] rob their people of their time, so that they cannot plough and weed their fields, in order to support their parents. Their parents suffer from cold and hunger. Brothers, wives, and children are separated and scattered abroad.

5   "Those rulers, as it were, drive their people into pit-falls, or drown them. Your Majesty will go to punish them. In such a case, who will oppose your Majesty?

6   "In accordance with this is the saying,—'The benevolent has no enemy.' I beg your Majesty not to doubt what I say."

Bk. I, Pt. I, Ch. 5

1   Mencius said, "Chieh's and Chou's[11] losing the throne, arose from their losing the people, and to lose the people means to lose their hearts. There is a way to get the kingdom:—get the people, and the kingdom is got. There is a way to get the people:—get their hearts, and the people are got. There is a way to get their hearts:—it is simply to collect for them what they like, and not to lay on them what they dislike.[12]

2   "The people turn to a benevolent rule as water flows downwards, and as wild beasts fly to the wilderness.

8. Small punishments and low taxes were regarded as the chief aspects of benevolent government and the basis for all the other benefits specified.

9. I.e., those able to take the field against an enemy.

10. I.e., Ch'in and Ch'u.

11. The wicked kings whose reigns marked the end of the Hsia and Shang dynasties, respectively.

12. I.e., to protect their lives and property and not lay on heavy taxes and punishments.

3   "Accordingly, as the otter aids the deep waters, driving the fish into them, and the hawk aids the thickets, driving the little birds to them, so Chieh and Chou aided T'ang and Wu,[13] driving the people to them.

4   "If among the present rulers of the kingdom, there were one who loved benevolence, all the other princes would aid him, by driving the people to him. Although he wished not to become sovereign, he could not avoid becoming so."

Bk. IV, Pt. I, Ch. 9

Mencius said, "There are instances of individuals without benevolence, who have got possession of a single state, but there has been no instance of the throne's[14] being got by one without benevolence."

Bk. VII, Pt. II, Ch. 13

1   Mencius said, "The people are the most important element in a nation; the spirits of the land and grain are the next[15]; the sovereign is the lightest.

2   "Therefore to gain the peasantry is the way to become sovereign; to gain the sovereign is the way to become a prince of a state; to gain the prince of a state is the way to become a great officer.

Bk. VII, Pt. II, Ch. 14

[According to the traditional account in the *Book of History*, the ancient sage-king Yao passed over his own sons in order to select as his heir the ablest and most virtuous man in the kingdom—his minister Shun.]

1   Wan Chang said, "Was it the case that Yao gave the

13. T'ang (the traditional founder of the Shang dynasty) replaced Chieh (the last of the Hsia); Wu (founder of the Chou dynasty) succeeded Chou (the last Shang king).
14. I.e., the throne of all China. Mencius' argument from history is based on the legends of such ancient sovereigns as Yao and Shun, Wen and Wu. In his time there had been no effective government of all China for centuries.
15. The prosperity of the country and the happiness of the people were believed to depend on the spirits.

throne to Shun?" Mencius said, "No. The sovereign cannot give the throne to another."

2   "Yes;—but Shun had the throne. Who gave it to him?" "Heaven[1] gave it to him," was the answer.

3   " 'Heaven gave it to him:'—did Heaven confer its appointment on him with specific injunctions?"

4   Mencius replied, "No. Heaven does not speak. It simply showed its will by his personal conduct and his conduct of affairs."

5   " 'It showed its will by his personal conduct and his conduct of affairs:'—how was this?" Mencius's answer was, "The sovereign can present a man to Heaven, but he cannot make Heaven give that man the throne. A prince can present a man to the sovereign, but he cannot cause the sovereign to make that man a prince. A great officer can present a man to his prince, but he cannot cause the prince to make that man a great officer. Yao presented Shun to Heaven, and Heaven accepted him. He presented him to the people, and the people accepted him. Therefore I say, 'Heaven does not speak. It simply indicated its will by his personal conduct and his conduct of affairs.' "

6   Chang said, "I presume to ask how it was that Yao presented Shun to Heaven, and Heaven accepted him; and that he exhibited him to the people, and the people accepted him." Mencius replied, "He caused him to preside over the sacrifices, and all the spirits were well pleased with them;—thus Heaven accepted him. He caused him to preside over the conduct of affairs, and affairs were well administered, so that the people reposed under him;—thus the people accepted him. Heaven gave the throne to him. The people gave it to him. Therefore I said, 'The sovereign cannot give the throne to another.'

7   "Shun assisted Yao in the government for twenty and eight years;—this was more than man could have done,[2] and was from Heaven. After the death of Yao, when the three years' mourning was completed, Shun withdrew from the son of Yao

---

1. *T'ien*—sometimes thought of as the spirits of Heaven collectively.
2. I.e., this was a long time for a man to be second in command (without either displeasing his sovereign or trying to usurp the supreme power for himself).

to the south of South river.[3] The princes of the kingdom, however, repairing to court, went not to the son of Yao, but they went to Shun. Litigants went not to the son of Yao, but they went to Shun. Singers sang not the son of Yao, but they sang Shun. Therefore I said, 'Heaven gave him the throne.' It was after these things that he went to the Middle Kingdom, and occupied the seat of the Son of Heaven. If he had, before these things, taken up his residence in the palace of Yao, and had applied pressure to the son of Yao, it would have been an act of usurpation, and not the gift of Heaven.

8   "This sentiment is expressed in the words of The Great Declaration,[4]—'Heaven sees according as my people see; Heaven hears according as my people hear.' "

Bk. V, Pt. I, Ch. 5

3. The Huang Ho (Yellow) River.
4. A chapter of the *Book of History*.

FROM THE HSÜN TZU *

On Government by Moral Force

. . . If there are laws, but in actual practice they do not prove to be of general applicability, then points not specifically covered by the laws are bound to be left undecided. If men are appointed to posts but they have no over-all understanding of their duties, then matters which do not specifically fall within their jurisdiction are bound to be neglected. Therefore there must be laws that prove applicable in practice and men in office who have an over-all understanding of their duties. There must be no hidden counsels or overlooked ability on the lower levels and all matters must proceed without error. Only a gentleman is capable of such government.

Fair-mindedness is the balance in which to weigh proposals; upright harmoniousness is the line by which to measure them. Where laws exist, to carry them out; where they do not exist,

* For the Introduction to Hsün Tzu, see above, pp. 32-3.
From *Hsün Tzu: Basic Writings*, trans. by Burton Watson, New York and London: Columbia University Press, 1963, pp. 35-7, 56-8, 67-71, 76-7. Reprinted by permission of Columbia University Press.

to act in the spirit of precedent and analogy—this is the best way to hear proposals. To show favoritism and partisan feeling and be without any constant principles—this is the worst you can do. It is possible to have good laws and still have disorder in the state. But to have a gentleman acting as ruler and disorder in the state—from ancient times to the present I have never heard of such a thing. This is what the old text means when it says, "Order is born from the gentleman, disorder from the petty man."

Where ranks are all equal, there will not be enough goods to go around; where power is equally distributed, there will be a lack of unity; where there is equality among the masses, it will be impossible to employ them. The very existence of Heaven and Earth exemplifies the principle of higher and lower, but only when an enlightened king appears on the throne can the nation be governed according to regulation. Two men of equal eminence cannot govern each other; two men of equally humble station cannot employ each other. This is the rule of Heaven. If men are of equal power and station and have the same likes and dislikes, then there will not be enough goods to supply their wants and they will inevitably quarrel. Quarreling must lead to disorder, and disorder to exhaustion. The former kings abhorred such disorder and therefore they regulated the principles of ritual in order to set up ranks. They established the distinctions between rich and poor, eminent and humble, making it possible for those above to join together and watch over those below. This is the basis upon which the people of the world are nourished. This is what the *Documents* means when it says, "Equality is based upon inequality."[1]

If the horses are frightened of the carriage, then the gentleman cannot ride in safety; if the common people are frightened of the government, then the gentleman cannot occupy his post in safety. If the horses are frightened of the carriage, the best thing to do is to quiet them; if the common people are fright-

---

1. Hsün Tzu is quoting out of context. The original sentence, from a chapter of the *Book of History* called "Marquis of Lü on Punishments," appears to mean that justice is uniform even though punishments vary according to circumstances.

ened of the government, the best thing to do is to treat them with kindness. Select men who are worthy and good for government office, promote those who are kind and respectful, encourage filial piety and brotherly affection, look after orphans and widows and assist the poor, and then the common people will feel safe and at ease with their government. And once the common people feel safe, then the gentleman may occupy his post in safety. This is what the old text means when it says, "The ruler is the boat and the common people are the water. It is the water that bears the boat up, and the water that capsizes it." Therefore, if the gentleman desires safety, the best thing for him to do is to govern fairly and to love the people. If he desires glory, the best thing is to honor ritual and treat men of breeding with respect. If he desires to win fame and merit, the best thing is to promote the worthy and employ men of ability. These are the three great obligations of the ruler. If he meets these three, then all other obligations will likewise be met; if he does not meet these three, then, although he manages to meet his other obligations, it will scarcely be of any benefit to him. Confucius has said, "If he meets both his major and minor obligations correctly, he is a superior ruler. If he meets his major obligations but is inconsistent in meeting his minor ones, he is a mediocre ruler. If he fails to meet his major obligations, though he may meet his minor ones correctly enough, I do not care to see any more of him." . . .

From. Sec. 9, "The Regulations of a King"

On Warfare

[War has had its place in Chinese history; but in no other major civilization has the military art been less esteemed. In ordinary times in China civilians dominated the government; soldiers were considered the scum of society. Order in the empire was enforced for the most part not through soldiers and police, but through general acceptance of the Confucian ethic, the authority of the family over its individual members, and the importance attached to public opinion ("face").

Chinese literature contains remarkably little which tends either to glorify military prowess or present war as such in heroic guise.* The Confucian school stressed moral authority and deplored any resort to force: wars, if fought at all, must be for a compelling moral reason. Even the literature dealing with military tactics and strategy maintains the superiority of intelligence over physical force and stresses the difficulties in conquering a well-governed country.]

The lord of Lin-wu and Hsün Tzu were debating military affairs in the presence of King Hsiao-ch'eng of Chao.[1] "May I ask what are the most essential points to be observed in taking up arms?" inquired the king.

The lord of Lin-wu replied, "Above, utilize the most seasonable times of heaven; below, take advantage of the most profitable aspects of the earth. Observe the movements of your enemy, set out after he does, but get there before him. This is the essential point in the art of using arms!"

"Not so!" objected Hsün Tzu. "From what I have heard of the way of the ancients, the basis of all aggressive warfare and military undertaking lies in the unification of the people. If the bow and arrow are not properly adjusted, even the famous archer Yi could not hit the mark. If the six horses of the team are not properly trained, even the famous carriage driver Tsao-fu could not go far. If the officers and people are not devoted to their leaders, even the sages T'ang or Wu could not win victory. The one who is good at winning the support of his people is the one who will be good at using arms. Therefore what is really essential in military undertakings is to be good at winning the support of the people."

"I disagree," said the lord of Lin-wu. "In using arms, one should place the highest value upon advantageous circumstances, and should move by stealth and deception. He who is good at using arms moves suddenly and secretly, and no one knows from whence he comes. Sun Wu and Wu Ch'i[2] employed

---

* Exceptions are the well-known novels of the fourteenth and fifteenth centuries A.D., *The Romance of Three Kingdoms* and *All Men Are Brothers*— but the novel itself was considered an inferior form of literature.

1. The Lord of Lin-wu is identified by commentators as a general of the state of Ch'u. . . . King Hsiao-ch'eng of Chao reigned 265-245 B.C. (Tr.)

2. Two famous generals and military experts of the 4th and 3d centuries respectively. Both are reputed authors of early works on military science, known today as the *Sun Tzu* and *Wu Tzu*. (Tr.)

this method and there was no one in the world who could stand up against them. Why is it necessary to win the support of the people?"

"You do not understand," said Hsün Tzu. "What I am speaking about are the soldiers of a benevolent man, the intentions of a true king. You speak of the value of plots and advantageous circumstances, of moving by sudden attack and stealth—but these are matters appropriate only to one of the feudal lords. Against the soldiers of a benevolent man, deceptions are of no use; they are effective only against a ruler who is rash and arrogant, whose people are worn out; they are effective only against a state in which the ruler and his subjects, superiors and inferiors, are torn apart and at odds. Therefore a tyrant like Chieh may practice deception upon another Chieh, and, depending upon how cleverly he proceeds, may happily achieve a certain success. But for a Chieh to try to practice deception against a sage like Yao would be like trying to break a rock by throwing eggs at it, or trying to stir boiling water with your bare finger. He will be like a man consumed by fire or drowned in water.

"As for the relations between superior and inferior under the rule of a benevolent man, the various generals will be of one mind, and the three armies of the state will work together. Subjects will serve their lord and inferiors will serve their superiors like sons serving a father or younger brothers serving an elder brother. They will be like hands held up to guard the face and eyes, arms clasped to protect the breast and belly. Try to attack such a ruler by deception and you will see the hands fly up in warning and then dart forward in attack.

"Moreover, if the benevolent man rules a state which is ten *li* square, the people for a hundred *li* around will act as listeners for him; if he rules a state of a hundred *li*, a thousand *li* will listen for him; and if he rules a state of a thousand *li*, the whole region within the four seas will listen for him. He will receive clear intelligence and warning, and the whole region will draw about him in unity. Thus the soldiers of a benevolent man, when gathered together, will form themselves into companies; when spread out, they will form in ranks. In striking power they are like the long blade of the famous sword Mu-yeh; what comes beneath it will be cut off. In keenness they are like the sharp point of Mu-yeh; what falls upon it will be pierced through. Drawn up in square encampment and surrounded by sentries, they will be like a solid rock; what butts against it will be smashed, crushed, broken, defeated, and forced to fall back."

. . . .

[The lord of Lin-wu said], "And now may I ask about the regulations of the king's army?"

Hsün Tzu replied, "The general dies with his drums; the carriage driver dies with the reins; the officials die at their posts; the leaders of the fighting men die in their ranks. When the army hears the sound of the drums, it advances; when it hears the sound of the bells, it retreats. Obedience to orders is counted first; achievements are counted second. To advance when there has been no order to advance is no different from retreating when there has been no order to retreat; the penalty is the same. The king's army does not kill the enemy's old men and boys; it does not destroy crops. It does not seize those who retire without a fight, but it does not forgive those who resist. It does not make prisoners of those who surrender and seek asylum. In carrying out punitive expeditions, it does not punish the common people; it punishes those who lead the common people astray. But if any of the common people fight with the enemy, they become enemies as well. Thus those who flee from the enemy forces and come in surrender shall be left to go free. . . .

"A true king carries out punitive expeditions, but he does not make war. When a city is firmly guarded, he does not lay siege to it; when the soldiers resist strongly, he does not attack. When the rulers and their people of other states are happy with each other, he considers it a blessing. He does not massacre the defenders of a city; he does not move his army in secret; he does not keep his forces long in the field; he does not allow a campaign to last longer than one season. Therefore the people of badly ruled states delight in the report of his government; they feel uneasy under their own rulers and long for his coming."

"Excellent," said the lord of Lin-wu.

Ch'en Hsiao[3] said to Hsün Tzu, "When you talk about the use of arms, you always speak of benevolence and righteousness as being the basis of military action. A benevolent man loves others, and a righteous man acts in accordance with what is right. Why, then, would they have any recourse to arms in the first place? Those who take up arms do so only in order to contend with others and seize some spoil!"

Hsün Tzu replied, "This is not something that you would understand. The benevolent man does indeed love others, and because he loves others, he hates to see men do them harm. The righteous man acts in accordance with what is right, and for that reason he hates to see men do wrong. He takes up arms in order to put an end to violence and to do away with harm, not in order to contend with others for spoil. Therefore, where the soldiers of the benevolent man encamp they command a god-like respect; and where they pass, they transform the people. They are like the seasonable rain in whose falling all men rejoice. . . ."

Li Ssu[4] said to Hsün Tzu, "For four generations now Ch'in has won victory. Its armies are the strongest in the world and its authority sways the other feudal lords. It did not attain this by means of benevolence and righteousness, but by taking advantage of its opportunities, that is all."

Hsün Tzu replied, "This is not something that you would understand. When you talk about opportunities, you are speaking of opportunities that are in fact inopportune. When I speak of benevolence and righteousness, I mean opportunities that are in fact great opportunities. This benevolence and righteousness which I speak of are the means whereby government is ordered properly, and when government is properly ordered, then the people will draw close to their superiors, delight in their rulers, and think it a light matter to die for them. Therefore I have said that matters pertaining to the army and the leadership of the generals are of minor importance. Ch'in has been victorious

3. A disciple of Hsün Tzu, otherwise unknown. (Tr.)
4. Li Ssu, who studied for a time under Hsün Tzu, later became prime minister of the state of Ch'in and (in 221 B.C.) of united China.

for four generations, yet it has lived in constant terror and apprehension lest the rest of the world should someday unite and trample it down. These are the soldiers of a degenerate age, not of a nation which has grasped the true principle of leadership. Thus T'ang did not have to wait until he had cornered Chieh on the field of Ming-t'iao before he could accomplish his overthrow; King Wu did not have to wait until his victory on the day *chia-tzu* before he could punish Chou for his evil deeds.[5] They had already assured victory for themselves by all their earlier deeds and actions. This is what it means to employ the soldiers of benevolence and righteousness. Now you do not try to get at the root of the matter, but look for a model in superficial appearances. This is the way to bring disorder to the world!"

.   .   .   .

There are three methods by which you may annex a neighboring state and bring its people under your rule: you may win them over by virtue, by force, or by wealth.

If the people of a neighboring state respect your reputation, admire your virtuous actions, and desire to become your subjects, they will throw open their gates, clear the roads, and welcome you to their cities. If you allow them to follow their old customs and remain in their old homes, the common people will all rest easy and will willingly obey your laws and commands. In this way you will acquire new territory and your power will increase; you will have added to your population and your armies will be stronger than ever. This is what it means to win over a neighbor by virtue.

If the people of a neighboring state do not respect your reputation or admire your virtuous actions, but are awed by your authority and intimidated by force, then, although they will feel no loyalty to you in their hearts, they will not dare to resist annexation. In such cases, however, you will have to enlarge

5. The field of Ming-t'iao was the scene of T'ang's final victory over Chieh, the last ruler of the Hsia; *chia-tzu* was the day of the Chinese sixty-day cycle upon which King Wu won final victory over Chou, the last ruler of the Yin [Shang]. (Tr.) T'ang and Wu were frequently cited by the Confucians as paragons of virtuous rule.

your garrisons and increase your military supplies, and your
government expenditures will increase likewise. In this way
you will acquire new territory but your power will decrease;
you will have added to your population but your armies will be
weaker than before. This is what it means to win over a neighbor by force.

If the people of a neighboring state do not respect your reputation or admire your virtuous actions, but are poor and are
looking for some way to get rich, are starving and in search of
plenty, then they will come to you with empty bellies and gaping mouths, attracted by your food alone. In such a case, you
will have to issue supplies of grain from your storehouses in
order to feed them, hand out goods and wealth to enrich them,
and appoint conscientious officials to look out for them, and
only after three years have passed can you put faith in their
loyalty. In this way you will acquire new territory but your
power will decrease; you will have added to your population
but the state will be poorer than before. This is what it means
to win over a neighbor by wealth. Therefore I say, he who annexes a state by virtue is a true king; he who annexes it by
force will be weakened; and he who annexes it by wealth will
be impoverished. From ancient times to the present it has always been the same.

It is easy enough to annex territory; the difficult thing is to
stabilize and maintain control over it. . . . He who is able to
annex territory but not to hold on to it will invariably be
stripped of his acquisitions; he who can neither annex territory
nor hold on to what he has will surely be destroyed. He who
can hold on to territory will invariably be able to acquire more.
When one can both acquire and hold on to territory, there is no
limit to the amount he can annex. In ancient times T'ang began with the region of Po and King Wu began with Hao, both
of them areas of only a hundred *li* square. The reason they were
able to unite the world under their rule and win the allegiance
of all the other feudal lords was simply this: they knew how to
secure their hold upon their territory. . . .

From Sec. 15, "Debating Military Affairs"

Introduction to Legalism

Legalism in China was the philosophy which emphasized the importance of fixed standards as opposed to personal ethics in government. The term in English is somewhat misleading; for Chinese Legalists were concerned not with the letter of the law, but with increasing the power of state governments both at home and in inter-state relations. In contrast to Confucianism, which dealt mainly with ethical norms, Legalism was an analysis of the realities of political power. As a system of thought, it was unique in China in that it had no recognized founder and no school in the usual sense of a teacher and his students. Certain classical books are commonly called Legalist, although experts do not always agree about just which ones should be included; and a number of statesmen famous in Chinese history are reputed to have governed on Legalist principles.

Legalism was a product of Chinese politics of the fourth and third centuries B.C. The tendency of those times was toward the consolidation of power—the absorption of small states by their larger neighbors; elimination of the nobles' authority over their peasants; direct administration of justice by officials of the central government; centralized collection of taxes. The dream of a united China—which supposedly had existed in antiquity—no longer seemed impossible of achievement; and Legalism pointed to the means. This philosophy, with its willingness to ignore inconvenient traditions and crush vested interests, had particular appeal to men in positions of power. In fact, most of the writers classed as Legalists were either practical administrators or men closely associated with ruling circles. The state of Ch'in—by which China was finally unified in 221 B.C.—was especially noteworthy for its Legalist policies.

The principal dispute between Confucians and Legalists concerned the permissible scope of official judgment as against fixed and impersonal laws. The Confucians pointed out that even the best of laws must be enforced by men; they therefore concluded that if the ruler of a state and his officials were upright, a permanent body of law was unnecessary. Even Hsün Tzu, who admitted the usefulness of laws, assigned them a position of secondary importance. On the other hand, the Legalists asserted that a uniform set of standards ought to apply to the entire population of a country. They conceived of law as virtually automatic in its operation. In their ideal state, the ruler publishes his decrees so that no one can remain ignorant of them. A fixed penalty is imposed for each offense, with no exceptions allowed for rank or extenuating circumstances. Law, in the Legalist view, ought not to be subject to the discretion of magistrates.

Unquestionably Legalism—with its emphasis on state power rather than popular welfare—represented a regression from Confucius' high standard of political morality. But Confucianism also presupposed a social system that was rapidly becoming obsolete. The Confucian virtues of righteousness and propriety belonged to the unwritten code of the nobility, adequate in the political sphere only as long as governments were managed by aristocrats related by ties of blood and marriage. Custom, good sense, and general ethical principles were sufficient to guide the conduct of a feudal lord in judging the affairs of peasants whom he knew personally. But by the fourth and third centuries B.C., communications had improved in China, knowledge had expanded, and prosperity had been enhanced through the increasing use of iron implements in agriculture. The old social structure, based upon rigid class distinctions, was slowly breaking down; and men of humble background could sometimes obtain positions of power. Bureaucrats representing the central government gradually replaced hereditary lords as tax-collectors and judges over the peasantry. Obviously, they required a set of fixed standards to judge by: and the ruler's interest in unifying his territories demanded that these should be more or less uniform. In many respects, Legalism was a philosophy for a new and more complex age.

Nonetheless, Legalism quickly acquired an evil reputation in China. The idea of the supremacy of law was tainted by association with the harsh government of the state of Ch'in, and later with the Ch'in dynasty's rule of united China (221-206 B.C.). Perhaps more importantly, the Chinese concept of law never became linked to any higher principle, e.g. natural law, the order of the universe, or the will of Heaven. The idea of law as guarantor of the civil rights of the citizen did not exist at all. Law to the Chinese mind was merely the set of fines and penalties imposed for transgressing a more or less arbitrary list of regulations. It was decidedly inferior to *li*—the code of manners and morals observed by gentlemen in their mutual relations. *Li* was unwritten law; it had nothing to do with government; and the penalties for its non-observance were, at most, the disapproval or ostracism of one's peers.

Legalism was plainly not a philosophy capable of winning popular allegiance; and the rulers of China never openly espoused it. From Han times onward Confucianism—which emphasized ethical government and popular welfare—was the official doctrine of the empire. But Legalism in fact had considerable influence upon the policies of Chinese governments. The mere attempt to control large areas effectively from a single center made necessary such Legalist measures as a uniform currency, weights, and measures; abolition of independent political authorities; and the use of fixed bureaucratic procedures. Despite their sometimes elaborate professions of Confucianism, no Chinese governments could afford to ignore the realities of political power. In practice this meant that Legalist ideas were frequently camouflaged as Confucian, or even interpolated into the Confucian Classics. The distinctions between the two philosophies thus became obscured; and Legalism emerged as an important element in the eclectic Confucianism which prevailed under the Han dynasty.

Introduction to the Book of Lord Shang

Kung-sun Yang, the later Lord Shang (died 338 B.C.) was among the most famous statesmen of ancient China. Born a member of the ruling house of Wei, he failed to gain high office in his native state. In 361 B.C. he joined the entourage of Duke* Hsiao of Ch'in, and subsequently became his prime minister. Shang Yang's policy was Legalist in orientation. Tradition credits him with laying the foundation for the future power of Ch'in, by which all China was unified in the following century. Though he was probably not personally responsible for all the measures attributed to him, there is

---

* The rulers of the individual Chinese states were generally called Dukes in the fourth century B.C.; by the third century, however, some of them felt bold enough to entitle themselves Kings.

no question but that Shang Yang was a remarkable statesman and
a prime mover in Ch'in's centralizing policy.

The immediate object of this policy was to enhance the power of
the Duke's government vis-a-vis every other source of power within
the state. Thus Shang Yang acted to abolish the almost unlimited
authority of lords over the peasants on their domains, restrict the
discretion enjoyed by towns in the management of their own affairs,
and break up the extended family groups in which the eldest male
controlled the activities of his relatives. To be sure, this trend
toward centralization had been evident long before his time. Already in the seventh century B.C., we hear of districts in Ch'in—
usually on the frontiers—directly administered by officials of the
central government. But Shang Yang made this system apply to the
entire state. About 350 B.C. he organized the territory of Ch'in into
thirty-one districts (*hsien*), each governed by a prefect (*ling*) appointed by the Duke. Henceforth the prefects, rather than the territorial lords, were charged with collecting taxes and administering
justice among the peasants. In place of the old noble titles derived
from landholding, Shang Yang created a scale of eighteen ranks
bearing purely honorary significance. He deprived the towns and
villages of their semi-independent status and decreed double taxa-
tion for every household in which more than one adult male resided.

A cardinal principle of Legalism was that fixed laws and penalties
are more important to a state than virtuous ministers. Shang Yang
believed that the laws should be so strict, and the penalties so harsh,
that no one would dare to commit any crime. He instituted a system
of mutual responsibility, dividing the population into groups of five
or ten persons in which each individual was charged with reporting
any illegal behavior on the part of the others. All members of the
group were considered equally guilty of a crime committed by any
one of them; and entire families could be held liable for the trans-
gression of a single member. This severe system appears to have
achieved the desired results; for various writings of the period report that the population of Ch'in was exceptionally orderly and
law-abiding.

The most important act attributed to Shang Yang is his reform
of land tenure. While theoretically the landlords were subject to
the state ruler, in practice they enjoyed great freedom in administering their domains. Shang Yang is supposed to have abolished the
legal attachment of the peasants of Ch'in to the land they tilled,
granting them outright ownership and the right to sell their plots

or buy others. In fact, this liberation of the peasantry had been going on for decades; Shang Yang probably did no more than legalize an existing situation and make it universal throughout Ch'in. Certainly he also took steps to increase agricultural production. He is supposed to have eliminated the paths between individual plots of land, thus increasing the space available for cultivation. Apparently he also granted ownership rights to persons willing to colonize and cultivate the hitherto unsettled lands on Ch'in's western frontiers.

Legalist theory regarded certain occupations as basic to life, i.e. agriculture, weaving, some tool production; while considering others as merely secondary and therefore dispensable, i.e. trade and artisanry. In accordance with this idea, Shang Yang directed all citizens of Ch'in to work either at agriculture or weaving; those who refused were to become slaves. His regulations hampered trade by the imposition of heavy tolls, and fixed high prices upon luxuries like wine and meat. Trade in grain—the dietary staple of north China—he forbade entirely. Shang Yang considered full granaries to be the best guarantee of prosperity and security for the state. His decrees served not only to conserve resources but also to weaken the position of the nobility—the chief patrons (and sometimes financiers) of merchants and artisans.

The ultimate purpose of Shang Yang's measures was to maximize the influence of Ch'in beyond its own borders. By increasing the revenue available to the central Ch'in government and extending its authority over its citizens, his centralizing policy enhanced the capacity of Ch'in to make war. At the same time, he openly encouraged the military virtues. He decreed that office and rank in Ch'in would henceforth be granted only for military accomplishments and could not be derived from landed estates. Finally, he took stern measures against brigandage and the private wars of the nobility. Indeed, his personal position of influence in Ch'in unquestionably owed something to his success as a general. In 352 and again in 340 B.C.—through treachery rather than strategy—he led the Ch'in armies to decisive victories over the state of Wei (his native country), and won significant accretions of territory for his employer.

In reward for his services, Shang Yang received as his personal fief fifteen towns in a district called Shang and the title "Lord of Shang."* But he did not have long to enjoy this new eminence. His

* In contravention of his own decree banning titles derived from landholding.

harsh laws and severe penalties had won him many enemies; and
when Duke Hsiao died in 338 B.C. his base of power was gone. The
new Duke, whom Shang Yang had once humiliated,* listened
willingly to rumors that he was plotting rebellion. The former
prime minister was sentenced to be torn to pieces by chariots; and
his entire family was exterminated.

The *Book of Lord Shang* sets forth the ideas by which this famous
statesman is supposed to have governed. Allegedly written by Shang
Yang himself, the book is clearly a later production. It contains
various anachronisms; and its twenty-four paragraphs (chapters)
are not all by a single author. The older portions—especially Paragraphs Two and Three—seem to represent the remains of a work
written during or shortly after Shang Yang's lifetime. The later
parts date from the third century B.C., and show an unmistakable
resemblance to the style of the *Han Fei Tzu*. Quite possibly these
two Legalist classics were both composed within the same circles.

From the Legalist standpoint, Shang Yang's policies were an
unqualified success. His centralized political system proved to be the
most efficient in China, giving Ch'in an undoubted advantage over
the other Chinese states, where conservative tradition was stronger
and the landed nobility far more powerful. By the middle of the
third century B.C., Ch'in had become the dominant power on the
Chinese scene; and in 221 B.C. the king of Ch'in became the First
Emperor of united China. Much of the credit for this momentous
achievement belongs to Shang Yang, who laid the foundation for
Ch'in's military strength and evolved the system of government
which in large measure was later applied throughout the whole
Chinese empire.

* By causing him to be punished for an offense as though he were an ordinary citizen.

FROM THE BOOK OF LORD SHANG

Agriculture and War (Paragraph 3)

The means, whereby a ruler of men encourages the people, are
office and rank; the means, whereby a country is made pros-

From *The Book of Lord Shang*, trans. by J. J. L. Duyvendak, London: Arthur Probsthain; Chicago: University of Chicago Press, 1928, pp. 185-6,
189-96. Reprinted by permission of Arthur Probsthain and the University of
Chicago Press.

perous, are agriculture and war. Now those, who seek office and
rank, never do so by means of agriculture and war, but by art-
ful words and empty doctrines. That is called "wearying the
people." The country of those, who weary their people, will
certainly have no strength, and the country of those, who have
no strength, will certainly be dismembered. . . .

But now the people within the territory all say that by avoiding agriculture and war, office and rank may be acquired, with
the result that eminent men all change their occupations, to
apply themselves to the study of the *Odes* and *History*[1] and to
follow improper standards; on the one hand, they obtain prominence, and on the other, they acquire office and rank. Insignifi-
cant individuals will occupy themselves with trade and will
practise arts and crafts, all in order to avoid agriculture and
war, thus preparing a dangerous condition for the state. Where
the people are given to such teachings, it is certain that such a
country will be dismembered. . . .

However, nowadays, the ruler, in his appointments, takes
into consideration talent and ability and cleverness and intelligence, and thus clever and intelligent men watch for the likes
and dislikes of the ruler, so that officials are caused to transact
their business in a way which is adapted to the ruler's mind. As
a result there is no consistency of conduct in the officials, the
state is in disorder and there is no concentration. Sophists (are
honoured) and there is no law. Under such circumstances, how
can the people's affairs be otherwise than many and how can
the land be otherwise than fallow?

If, in a country, there are the following ten things: odes and
history, rites and music, virtue and the cultivation thereof, benevolence and integrity, sophistry and intelligence, then the
ruler has no one whom he can employ for defence and warfare.
If a country is governed by means of these ten things, it will be
dismembered, as soon as an enemy approaches, and, even if no
enemy approaches, it will be poor. But if a country banishes
these ten things, enemies will not dare to approach, and even if
they should, they would be driven back. When it mobilizes its

1. Two of the Confucian Classics: the *Book of Songs* (also known as the
Book of Odes) and the *Book of History*.

army and attacks, it will gain victories; when it holds the army in reserve, and does not attack, it will be rich. A country that loves strength makes assaults with what is difficult and thus it will be successful. A country that loves sophistry makes assaults with what is easy and thus it will be in danger.

Therefore sages and intelligent princes are what they are, not because they are able to go to the bottom of all things, but because they understand what is essential in all things. Therefore the secret of their administration of the country lies in nothing else than in their examination of what is essential. But now, those who run a state, for the most part, overlook what is essential, and the discussions at court, on government, are confused and efforts are made to displace each other in them: thus the prince is dazed by talk, officials confused by words, and the people become lazy and will not farm. The result is that all the people within the territory change and become fond of sophistry, take pleasure in study, pursue trade, practise arts and crafts, and shun agriculture and war and so in this manner (the ruin of the country) will not be far off. When the country has trouble, then, because studious people hate law, merchants are clever in bartering and artisans are useless, the state will be easily destroyed.

Indeed, if farmers are few, and those who live idly on others are many, then the state will be poor and in a dangerous condition. Now, for example, if various kinds of caterpillars, which are born in spring and die in autumn, appear only once, the result is that the people have no food for many years. Now, if one man tills and a hundred live on him, it means that they are like a great visitation of caterpillars. Though there may be a bundle of the *Odes* and *History* in every hamlet and a copy in every family, yet it is useless for good government, and it is not a method whereby this condition of things may be reversed. Therefore the ancient kings made people turn back to agriculture and war. For this reason is it said: "Where a hundred men farm and one is idle, the state will attain supremacy; where ten men farm and one is idle, the state will be strong; where half farms and half is idle, the state will be in peril." That is why those, who govern the country well, wish the people to take to agriculture. If the country does not take to agriculture, then, in its quarrels over authority with the various feudal lords, it will not be able to maintain itself, because the strength of the multitude will not be sufficient. Therefore the feudal lords vex its weakness and make use of its state of decadence; and if the territory is invaded and dismembered, without the country being stirred to action, it will be past saving.

A sage knows what is essential in administrating a country, and so he induces the people to devote their attention to agriculture. If their attention is devoted to agriculture, then they will be simple, and being simple, they may be made correct. Being perplexed it will be easy to direct them, being trustworthy, they may be used for defence and warfare. Being single-minded, opportunities of deceit will be few and they will attach importance to their homes. Being single-minded, their careers may be made dependent on rewards and penalties; being single-minded, they may be used abroad.

Indeed, the people will love their ruler and obey his commandments even to death, if they are engaged in farming, morning and evening; but they will be of no use, if they see that glib-tongued, itinerant scholars succeed in being honoured in serving the prince, that merchants succeed in enriching their families and that artisans have plenty to live upon. If the people see both the comfort and advantage of these three walks of life, then they will indubitably shun agriculture; shunning agriculture, they will care little for their homes; caring little for their homes, they will certainly not fight and defend these for the ruler's sake. . . .

When a country is in peril and the ruler in anxiety, it is of no avail to the settling of this danger, for professional talkers to form battalions.[2] The reason why a country is in danger and its ruler in anxiety lies in some strong enemy or in another big state. Now if a prince is unable to vanquish that strong enemy or to destroy that big state, he improves his defences, makes the best use of the topographical conditions, consolidates the strength of the people and thus meets the foreign attack. After

2. Lit., "bands of five men," squads. (Tr.)

this the danger may be averted and supremacy yet attained. That is why an intelligent prince, in improving the administration, strives for uniformity, removes those who are of no use, restrains volatile scholars and those of frivolous pursuits and makes them all uniformly into farmers. Thereafter the reigning dynasty may become rich and the people's strength may be consolidated.

Nowadays, the rulers of the world are all anxious over the perilous condition of their countries and the weakness of their armies, and they listen at all costs to the professional talkers; but though these may form battalions, talk profusely and employ beautiful expressions, it is of no practical use. When a ruler loves their sophistry and does not seek for their practical value, then the professional talkers have it all their own way, expound their crooked sophistries in the streets, their various groups become great crowds, and the people, seeing that they succeed in captivating kings, dukes and great men, all imitate them. Now, if men form parties, the arguments and discussions in the country will be of confusing diversity; the lower classes will be amused and the great men will enjoy it, with the result that amongst such a people farmers will be few and those, who, in idleness, live on others will be many. These latter being numerous, farmers will be in a perilous position, and this being so, land will be left lying fallow. If study becomes popular, people will abandon agriculture and occupy themselves with debates, high-sounding words and discussions on false premises; abandoning agriculture, they will live on others in idleness and seek to surpass one another with words. Thus the people will become estranged from the ruler and there will be crowds of disloyal subjects. This is a doctrine, which leads to the impoverishment of the state and to the weakening of the army. Indeed, if a country employs people for their talking then the people will not be nurtured in agriculture; so it is only an intelligent prince, who understands that by fondness of words one cannot strengthen the army nor open up the land. Only when a sage rules the country will he strive for singleness of purpose and for the consolidation of the people in agriculture and for that alone.

Introduction to Han Fei Tzu

Han Fei Tzu (died 233 B.C.) was the leading theoretician of Legalism. By birth he was a prince of the state of Han; and his close association with a governing class undoubtedly colored his political outlook. He studied, however, with Hsün Tzu, the leading Confucian thinker of his time. Han Fei Tzu himself seems never to have held any major office. His plans for strengthening the state of Han were ignored by its leading ministers; and he contented himself with writing essays. In 233 B.C. he represented his native state on a mission to Ch'in. When it appeared that the king of Ch'in wished to appoint him to office, one of the king's officials* arranged to have Han Fei Tzu thrown into prison, where he was persuaded to commit suicide.

The book called *Han Fei Tzu* is the fullest and maturest surviving exposition of the Legalist philosophy. It preserves a number of essays by Han Fei himself, apparently almost as he wrote them, intermixed with other Legalist treatises and some material which is not Legalist at all. In part, Han Fei Tzu opposed Confucianism; in part, he reinterpreted it to accord with his own way of thought. His views were authoritarian, like those of Hsün Tzu; and he too regarded human nature as fundamentally evil. But he failed to share his teacher's faith in the redeeming power of education and culture. While Confucians insisted that government ministers should be chosen for their upright characters, Han Fei thought that all officials were potentially dishonest; each should be encouraged to act as a check upon the others. Government should direct itself to the broad masses, who in Han Fei's opinion were ignorant and incapable of seeing beyond their own immediate interests. Given these presuppositions, he concluded that a strict set of laws and penalties, impartially enforced, was indispensable to public order.

Han Fei Tzu's standpoint was that of the ruler rather than of the people at large. Like other Legalists, he tended to ignore the fact—so well understood by Mencius, for example—that at least the tacit

---

* This was Li Ssu, later the first prime minister of united China. Both men had studied under Hsün Tzu; Li Ssu is said to have feared Han Fei Tzu's brilliance.

consent of the populace is required if any government is to function. On the other hand, his criticism of the abuses of personal government as practiced in his day was probably well founded. He saw that an impersonal set of standards was necessary and inevitable, at least to some extent, if a single government wished to control large territories. Han Fei Tzu's analyses of government aims and practices are coolly rational. The ethical deficiencies of his position are undeniable; but at the same time he avoided the rather naïve idealism of some Confucians. Though he came to share the general obloquy which later fell upon Legalism, many of his ideas, while publicly abhorred, were nonetheless practiced by Chinese governments. Han Fei Tzu was one of China's greatest minds; and his book ranks among the major works of Chinese literature.

FROM THE HAN FEI TZU

On Pretensions and Heresies/Chapter 19

. . . In ancient times, the early kings[1] exerted their forces to renovate the people and doubled their efforts to clarify the law. As the law was made clear, loyal subjects were encouraged. As punishment was made definite, wicked subjects were suppressed. It was Ch'in whose loyal subjects were encouraged and wicked ones were suppressed and whose territory was expanded and sovereign was glorified.[2] It was the states to the east of Mount Hua whose officials formed factions, associated for selfish purposes and thereby obscured the right way of government and committed crookedness in secret, and whose territories were dismembered and sovereigns humiliated. That disorderly and weak states go to ruin, is known to everybody. That orderly and strong states attain supremacy has been the beaten track since antiquity.

Kou-chien, King of Yüeh, believed in the Ta-p'eng Tortoise[3]

From *The Complete Works of Han Fei Tzu*, trans. by W. K. Liao, Vol. I, London: Arthur Probsthain, 1939, pp. 158-68.

1. The legendary sage-kings whom the Confucians especially revered.
2. In Han Fei Tzu's lifetime (he died in 233 B.C.), Ch'in had already won major victories over many of the other Chinese states. Ch'in's final conquest of China occurred in 221 B.C.
3. Divination by means of cracks produced in tortoise shells was an ancient practice.

and waged a war with Wu,[4] but did not win, till finally he had to surrender himself as vassal and went personally to serve the King of Wu.[5] Upon his return, he threw away the tortoise, clarified the law, and renovated the people, with a view to giving Wu his revenge. In the end Fu-ch'a, King of Wu, was taken captive.[6] Therefore, whoever believes in devils and deities, neglects the law.

Similarly, whoever relies on other feudal lords, endangers his native soil. . . .

[Examples from Chinese history are cited.]

To-day, Han, being a small state, is relying upon big powers. Her sovereign, paying little attention to the law, takes every word from Ch'in.[7] The above-mentioned small states [of Ts'ao, Hsing, Hsü, and Cheng], having relied upon Wei, Ch'i, Ching, and Wu for support, went to ruin one after another. Thus reliance on others is not sufficient to extend the native soil. Yet Han never looks at these instances. . . . All these states, indeed, never clarified laws and prohibitions in order to govern their peoples, but relied on foreign powers entirely, and thereby drove their Altars of the Spirits of Land and Grain to extinction.[8]

Thy servant, therefore, says: If measures for political order are clarified, the state, though small in size, will become rich. If reward and punishment are dignified and of faith, the people, though small in number, will become strong. If reward and punishment follow no regulations, the state, however large in size, will have weak soldiers. For the soil is no longer its territory, the people no longer its subjects.[9] Without territory and

4. Both Yüeh and Wu were states of southeastern China.
5. In 494 B.C. (Tr.)
6. In 473 B.C. (Tr.)
7. The state of Han lay directly east of Ch'in.
8. These were the altars on which sacrifices were made to the spirits. Destruction of the altars was the worst possible disaster for a state, for the spirits would cease to protect the land and grain if they failed to receive appropriate offerings.
9. Han Fei Tzu defined a state as the combination of three factors: territory, people, and sovereignty.

people, even Yao and Shun never could reign supreme nor could the three dynasties ever become strong.[10]

Moreover, when the sovereign gives indiscriminately, ministers take inconsiderately. Those who discard legal rules, praise the early kings, and thereby illustrate the achievements of the ancients, are entrusted by the ruler with the state affairs. Thy servant, therefore, says: Such an act is to hope for ancient achievements and reward modern men with ancient rewards. In consequence, the sovereign gives wrongly, ministers take idly. If the sovereign gives wrongly, then ministers will expect undue rewards; if ministers take idly, meritorious services will not be held in high esteem. If men of no merit receive rewards, the state exchequer will run low and the people will resent it; if the state exchequer runs low and the people resent it, then nobody will apply his strength to his duties. Therefore, who over-uses reward loses the people; who over-uses penalty cannot hold the people in awe. If reward is not sufficient to encourage, and penalty is not sufficient to prohibit the people, then the state, however large in size, will fall into danger.

Hence the saying: "Who knows few things, should not be allowed to scheme for enterprises; who practises loyalty in small ways, should not be allowed to take charge of judicial administration."

. . . "Small loyalty is the betrayer of big loyalty." Thus, if the ruler puts men loyal in small ways in charge of judicial administration, they will pardon criminal offences. To pardon culprits and thereby love them, is to enjoy temporary peace with the inferiors, whereas it stands in the way of governing the people.

At the time when Wei was clarifying and establishing laws and upholding mandates without fail, men of merit were infallibly rewarded; men guilty of crimes were infallibly censured; her strength was sufficient to rectify All-under-Heaven[11] and her authority prevailed among the neighbours on the four sides. As soon as laws came to be neglected and rewards became arbi-

10. Yao and Shun were ancient sage-kings often cited for their supposedly exemplary rule; the "three dynasties" are those traditionally considered the earliest in Chinese history: the Hsia, Shang (Yin), and Chou.
11. I.e., China—all of the world which mattered.

trary, the state was dismembered day after day. Similarly, at the time when Chao was enacting state laws and training a big army, she had a large population and a strong army and extended her territory into Ch'i and Yen. As soon as the state laws came to be neglected and the personnel in charge of the state affairs became weak, the state was dismembered day after day. Again, at the time when Yen was upholding the law and scrutinizing official decisions in detail, to the east she seized counties from the Ch'i State and to the south occupied the whole territory of Central Hills. When the upholders of the law died, the official decisions became useless, the attendants disputed with each other, and public opinion had to follow the lead of the inferiors; then the army became weak, the soil was dismembered, and the state fell under the spell of the surrounding enemies. Hence the saying: "Who clarifies the law, is strong; who neglects the law, is weak." The causes of strength and weakness are so vivid. Yet sovereigns of this age never attempt to foster the cause of strength. No wonder their states are doomed to ruin.

There is an ancient proverb saying: "The family that has a definite occupation, does not have to starve in time of famine; the state that has definite laws, does not go to ruin in case of emergency." Indeed, if the ruler discards definite laws and follows private opinions, then ministers will pretend to wisdom and ability; if ministers pretend to wisdom and ability, then laws and prohibitions will not hold good. In other words, when arbitrary opinions prevail, the way of governing the state dwindles. Therefore, the right way to govern the state is to remove the injurers of the law. In that case, there will be neither bewilderment by pretensions to wisdom and ability nor deception by pretensions to name and fame.

Of yore, Shun ordered officials to drain the Great Deluge. One official set himself to work before the order came, and accomplished merit. However, Shun executed him. Once Yü received the feudal lords in audience in the vicinity of Kuei-chi. As the Ruler of Fang-feng arrived late, Yü beheaded him.[12] From this viewpoint it is clear that if those who went ahead of orders were

12. Yü was a legendary king of antiquity. These incidents are recorded in the *Book of History*.

executed and those who lagged behind orders were beheaded, the ancients must have held conformity to orders in high esteem.

For illustration, if the mirror keeps clean and has no obstacle, then the beautiful and the ugly can be compared; if the balance keeps right and has no obstacle, then the light and the heavy can be weighed. Indeed, when you shake the mirror, the mirror cannot keep clear; when you shake the balance, the balance cannot keep even. The same is true of the law. Therefore, the early kings took Tao[13] as the constant standard, and the law as the basis of government. . . . Indeed, the true path [Tao] and the law are absolutely reliable, wisdom and ability are liable to errors. Similarly, to hang up the balance and know the plane, and to turn round the compasses and know the circle, is an absolutely reliable way.

The intelligent sovereign makes the people conform to the law and thereby knows the true path; wherefore with ease he harvests meritorious results. To discard the compasses and trust to skilfulness, and to discard the law and trust to wisdom, leads to bewilderment and confusion. The violent sovereign lets the people pretend to wisdom but does not know the true path; wherefore in spite of his toil he gets no credit. If the sovereign discards laws and prohibitions and imprudently grants requests and audiences, then ministers will obtain posts from the sovereign for sale and accept pay from their inferiors. For this reason, profits go to private families and authority rests with ministers. In consequence, the people have no mind to exert their strength to serve the sovereign but merely strive to develop friendships with their superiors. If the people are fond of developing friendships with their superiors, then goods and cash will flow upwards and proficient speakers will be taken into service. Should that be the case, men of merit would decrease, wicked ministers would advance, and talented ministers would withdraw, till the sovereign falls into bewilderment and does not know what to do, and the masses flock together but do not know whom to obey. This is the fault of discarding laws and prohibitions, leaving merits and services behind, exalting names and reputations, and granting requests and audiences. . . .

13. Or the Way, meaning the natural order of the universe.

It is the duty of the sovereign to make clear the distinction between public and private interests, enact laws and statutes openly, and forbid private favours. Indeed, to enforce whatever is ordered and stop whatever is prohibited, is the public justice of the lord of men. To practise personal faith to friends, and not to be encouraged by any reward nor to be discouraged by any punishment, is the private righteousness of ministers. Wherever private righteousness prevails, there is disorder; wherever public justice obtains, there is order. Hence the necessity of distinction between public and private interests. . . .

Therefore, the early kings, in order to encourage ministers, made rewards clear, and, in order to overawe them, made penalties severe. For, when rewards and penalties were clarified, the people would risk their lives in the cause of their native soil; when the people were resolved to risk their lives, the army would become strong and the sovereign would be honoured. When reward and penalty were not clearly enacted, men of no merit would expect undue rewards; when men found guilty were pardoned by grace, the army would become weak and the sovereign would become ignoble. Therefore, the early kings and their worthy counsellors applied their strength and exerted their wisdom to make laws clear and penalties severe. Hence the saying: "That public and private interests must be clearly distinguished and laws and prohibitions must be carefully enacted, the early kings already understood."

Introduction to the Art of War by Sun Tzu

The Art of War (or Thirteen Chapters) is probably the oldest extant military treatise from anywhere in the world which discusses war from a strictly rationalistic viewpoint. The author of this remarkable book is said to have been one Sun Wu, a general reputedly employed by the state of Wu in the late sixth century B.C. But scholars now agree that the traditional identification is improbable: the book's connection with Sun Wu is presumably an instance of

the ancient Chinese practice of ascribing new compositions to famous men of the past. The consistent style and thematic development of *The Art of War* do tend to affirm, however, that it is the
work of a single author. Whatever his actual identity, he was certainly a man of extensive military experience—perhaps Sun Pin
(also called Sun Tzu), a well-known general of the middle of the
fourth century B.C. Philological evidence is consistent with this
dating; and the work can scarcely be any later, for it never mentions cavalry, a prominent element in the wars of the third century
B.C.

Certainly the whole tone of *The Art of War* identifies it as a
product of the age of Warring States (403-221 B.C.). It presupposes
the existence of a multi-state system, while at the same time regarding the unification of all China as a practicable goal. It takes for
granted large state-supported armies rather than feudal levies, professional generals who are not necessarily of noble rank, and the
extensive use of maneuver and tactics—all of which were unknown
in an earlier period. The author of the book, whoever he was, held
a view of war devoid of the knightly values and reliance upon supernatural assistance which characterized the conflicts of feudal
times. His standpoint is thoroughly professional, emphasizing training and discipline, the organization of supply, and the morale of
both soldiers and civilians. War he treats not as a personal contest
between leaders, but as the rational means for unifying China. But
whereas thinkers like Mencius believed that a ruler's benevolence
would in itself be sufficient for this purpose, Sun Tzu asserted the
importance of military methods.

The ideal of *The Art of War* is victory with a minimum resort to
force. For this reason it places primary emphasis upon well-planned
maneuvers, deceptive tactics, and espionage—all designed to outwit
the enemy rather than overpower him. The book's concept of limited war and of victory by indirect means, of cleverness as superior
to brute force, has remained a prominent theme in the Chinese military tradition ever since. A number of famous generals are known
to have followed its precepts, including in the twentieth century
Mao Tse-tung—an avid student of ancient military literature. *The
Art of War* went through many editions; few literary works can
boast of so long and distinguished a list of commentators. With its
rational approach and balanced analysis of the elements of success,
it remains relevant even today as a statement of the general principles of warfare.

FROM THE ART OF WAR

Waging War/Chapter 2

1   Sun Tzu said: In the operations of war, where there are in the field a thousand swift chariots, as many heavy chariots,[1] and a hundred thousand mail-clad soldiers,[2] with provisions enough to carry them a thousand *li*,[3] the expenditure at home and at the front, including entertainment of guests, small items such as glue and paint, and sums spent on chariots and armour, will reach the total of a thousand ounces of silver per day. Such is the cost of raising an army of 100,000 men.

2   When you engage in actual fighting, if victory is long in coming, the men's weapons will grow dull and their ardour will be damped. If you lay siege to a town, you will exhaust your strength.

3   Again, if the campaign is protracted, the resources of the State will not be equal to the strain.

4   Now, when your weapons are dulled, your ardour damped, your strength exhausted and your treasure spent, other chieftains will spring up to take advantage of your extremity. Then no man, however wise, will be able to avert the consequences that must ensue.

5   Thus, though we have heard of stupid haste in war, cleverness has never been seen associated with long delays.

6   There is no instance of a country having benefited from prolonged warfare.

7   It is only one who is thoroughly acquainted with the evils

From *Sun Tzu on the Art of War*, trans. by Lionel Giles, London: Luzac & Co., 1910, pp. 9-25, 33-41, 55-63, 160-70. Reprinted by permission of Luzac & Co.

1. The swift chariots were used for attack, the heavier ones for defense.

2. The swift chariot, carrying a driver, a spearman, and an archer, formed the nucleus around which 72 foot-soldiers were grouped. Each heavy chariot was accompanied by 25 foot-soldiers. The army was thus divided into battalions of 100 men each.

3. *Ca.* 350 miles. In modern China 2.78 *li* make a mile, though the measure may have varied somewhat in ancient times.

of war that can thoroughly understand the profitable way of carrying it on.

8   The skilful soldier does not raise a second levy, neither are his supply-waggons loaded more than twice.[4]

9   Bring war material with you from home, but forage on the enemy. Thus the army will have food enough for its needs.

10   Poverty of the State exchequer causes an army to be maintained by contributions from a distance. Contributing to maintain an army at a distance causes the people to be impoverished.

11   On the other hand, the proximity of an army causes prices to go up; and high prices cause the people's substance to be drained away.

12   When their substance is drained away, the peasantry will be afflicted by heavy exactions.

13, 14   With this loss of substance and exhaustion of strength, the homes of the people will be stripped bare, and three-tenths of their incomes will be dissipated; while Government expenses for broken chariots, worn-out horses, breast-plates and helmets, bows and arrows, spears and shields, protective mantlets,[5] draught-oxen and heavy waggons, will amount to four-tenths of its total revenue.

15   Hence a wise general makes a point of foraging on the enemy. One cartload of the enemy's provisions is equivalent to twenty of one's own,[6] and likewise a single picul of his provender is equivalent to twenty from one's own store.

16   Now in order to kill the enemy, our men must be roused to anger; that there may be advantage from defeating the enemy, they must have their rewards.

17   Therefore in chariot fighting, when ten or more chariots have been taken, those should be rewarded who took the first.

---

4. I.e., once before crossing the frontier and again on his homeward march. The idea is that speed is more important than superiority of numbers or supplies; thus the clever general will not waste time in waiting for reinforcements.

5. It is not entirely clear what is meant by "mantlets"—apparently some sort of movable roof or screen used to protect besiegers from the enemy.

6. Because twenty cartloads will be consumed in the process of transporting one cartload to the front. . . . (Tr.)

Our own flags should be substituted for those of the enemy, and the chariots mingled and used in conjunction with ours. The captured soldiers should be kindly treated and kept.

18   This is called, using the conquered foe to augment one's own strength.

19   In war, then, let your great object be victory, not lengthy campaigns.

20   Thus it may be known that the leader of armies is the arbiter of the people's fate, the man on whom it depends whether the nation shall be in peace or in peril.

Attack by Stratagem/Chapter 3

1   Sun Tzu said: In the practical art of war, the best thing of all is to take the enemy's country whole and intact; to shatter and destroy it is not so good. So, too, it is better to capture an army entire than to destroy it, to capture a regiment, a detachment or a company entire than to destroy them.

2   Hence to fight and conquer in all your battles is not supreme excellence; supreme excellence consists in breaking the enemy's resistance without fighting.

3   Thus the highest form of generalship is to baulk the enemy's plans; the next best is to prevent the junction of the enemy's forces;[7] the next in order is to attack the enemy's army in the field; and the worst policy of all is to besiege walled cities.

4   The rule is, not to besiege walled cities if it can possibly be avoided.

The preparation of mantlets, movable shelters,[8] and various implements of war, will take up three whole months; and the piling up of mounds over against the walls will take three months more.

5   The general, unable to control his irritation, will launch his men to the assault like swarming ants, with the result that

7. I.e., to isolate an enemy from his allies. In Sun Tzu's time armies were commonly composed of forces from more than one state.

8. They were wooden missile-proof structures on four wheels, propelled from within, covered over with raw hides, and used in sieges to convey parties of men to and from the walls, for the purpose of filling up the encircling moat with earth. . . . (Tr.)

one-third of his men are slain, while the town still remains un-
taken. Such are the disastrous effects of a siege.

6   Therefore the skilful leader subdues the enemy's troops
without any fighting; he captures their cities without laying
siege to them; he overthrows their kingdom without lengthy
operations in the field.

7   With his forces intact he will dispute the mastery of the
Empire, and thus, without losing a man, his triumph will be
complete.

This is the method of attacking by stratagem.

8   It is the rule in war, if our forces are ten to the enemy's
one, to surround him; if five to one, to attack him; if twice as
numerous, to divide our army into two.

9   If equally matched, we can offer battle; if slightly inferior
in numbers, we can avoid the enemy; if quite unequal in every
way, we can flee from him.

10   Hence, though an obstinate fight may be made by a
small force, in the end it must be captured by the larger force.

11   Now the general is the bulwark of the State: if the bulwark is complete at all points, the State will be strong; if the
bulwark is defective, the State will be weak.

12   There are three ways in which a ruler can bring misfortune upon his army:—

13   (1) By commanding the army to advance or to retreat,
being ignorant of the fact that it cannot obey. This is called
hobbling the army.

14   (2) By attempting to govern an army in the same way
as he administers a kingdom, being ignorant of the conditions
which obtain in an army. This causes restlessness in the soldier's minds.

15   (3) By employing the officers of his army without dis-
crimination,[9] through ignorance of the military principle of
adaptation to circumstances. This shakes the confidence of the
soldiers.

16   But when the army is restless and distrustful, trouble is
sure to come from the other feudal princes. This is simply
bringing anarchy into the army, and flinging victory away.

9. I.e., not using the right man in the right place.

17   Thus we may know that there are five essentials for victory: (1) He will win who knows when to fight and when not to fight. (2) He will win who knows how to handle both superior and inferior forces.[10] (3) He will win whose army is animated by the same spirit throughout all its ranks. (4) He will win who, prepared himself, waits to take the enemy unprepared. (5) He will win who has military capacity and is not interfered with by the sovereign. Victory lies in the knowledge of these five points.

18   Hence the saying: If you know the enemy and know yourself, you need not fear the result of a hundred battles. If you know yourself but not the enemy, for every victory gained you will also suffer a defeat. If you know neither the enemy nor yourself, you will succumb in every battle.

Energy/Chapter 5

1   Sun Tzu said: The control of a large force is the same in principle as the control of a few men: it is merely a question of dividing up their numbers.[11]

2   Fighting with a large army under your command is nowise different from fighting with a small one: it is merely a question of instituting signs[12] and signals.[13]

3   To ensure that your whole host may withstand the brunt of the enemy's attack and remain unshaken—this is effected by manœuvres direct and indirect.

4   That the impact of your army may be like a grindstone dashed against an egg—this is effected by the science of weak points and strong.

5   In all fighting, the direct method may be used for joining battle, but indirect methods will be needed in order to secure victory.

10. I.e., with a smaller force to defeat a larger one, and vice versa.
11. That is, cutting up the army into regiments, companies, etc., with subordinate officers in command of each. . . . (Tr.)
12. "Signs" are explained by one Chinese commentator as the flags and banners which enable a soldier to recognize his own company or regiment, and thus prevent confusion.
13. [D]rums and gongs, which from the earliest times were used to sound the advance and the retreat respectively. . . . (Tr.)

6   Indirect tactics, efficiently applied, are inexhaustible as Heaven and Earth, unending as the flow of rivers and streams: like the sun and moon, they end but to begin anew; like the four seasons, they pass away but to return once more.

7   There are not more than five musical notes, yet the combinations of these five give rise to more melodies than can ever be heard.

8   There are not more than five primary colours, yet in combination they produce more hues than can ever be seen.

9   There are not more than five cardinal tastes, yet combinations of them yield more flavours than can ever be tasted.

10   In battle, there are not more than two methods of attack —the direct and the indirect; yet these two in combination give rise to an endless series of manœuvres.

11   The direct and the indirect lead on to each other in turn. It is like moving in a circle—you never come to an end. Who can exhaust the possibilities of their combination?

12   The onset of troops is like the rush of a torrent which will even roll stones along in its course.

13   The quality of decision is like the well-timed swoop of a falcon which enables it to strike and destroy its victim.

14   Therefore the good fighter will be terrible in his onset, and prompt in his decision.

15   Energy may be likened to the bending of a crossbow; decision, to the releasing of the trigger.

16   Amid the turmoil and tumult of battle, there may be seeming disorder and yet no real disorder at all; amid confusion and chaos, your array may be without head or tail, yet it will be proof against defeat.

17   Simulated disorder postulates perfect discipline; simulated fear postulates courage; simulated weakness postulates strength.[14]

18   Hiding order beneath the cloak of disorder is simply a question of subdivision; concealing courage under a show of timidity presupposes a fund of latent energy; masking strength with weakness is to be effected by tactical dispositions.

14. The original of this passage is cryptic; but the meaning evidently is: To lead the enemy on by feigned disorder in your ranks, you must first have perfect discipline, etc.

19   Thus one who is skilful at keeping the enemy on the move maintains deceitful appearances, according to which the enemy will act. He sacrifices something, that the enemy may snatch at it.

20   By holding out baits, he keeps him on the march; then with a body of picked men he lies in wait for him.

21   The clever combatant looks to the effect of combined energy, and does not require too much from individuals. Hence his ability to pick out the right men and to utilise combined energy.

22   When he utilises combined energy, his fighting men become as it were like unto rolling logs or stones. For it is the nature of a log or stone to remain motionless on level ground, and to move when on a slope; if four-cornered, to come to a standstill, but if round-shaped, to go rolling down.

23   Thus the energy developed by good fighting men is as the momentum of a round stone rolled down a mountain thousands of feet in height. So much on the subject of energy.

Manœuvring/Chapter 7

1   Sun Tzu said: In war, the general receives his commands from the sovereign.

2   Having collected an army and concentrated his forces, he must blend and harmonise the different elements thereof before pitching his camp.

3   After that, comes tactical manœuvring, than which there is nothing more difficult. The difficulty of tactical manœuvring consists in turning the devious into the direct, and misfortune into gain.

4   Thus, to take a long and circuitous route, after enticing the enemy out of the way, and though starting after him, to contrive to reach the goal before him, shows knowledge of the artifice of deviation.

5   Manœuvring with an army is advantageous; with an undisciplined multitude, most dangerous.

6   If you set a fully equipped army in march in order to snatch an advantage, the chances are that you will be too late. On the other hand, to detach a flying column for the purpose involves the sacrifice of its baggage and stores.

7   Thus, if you order your men to roll up their buff-coats, and make forced marches without halting day or night, covering double the usual distance at a stretch, doing a hundred *li* in order to wrest an advantage, the leaders of all your three divisions will fall into the hands of the enemy.[15]

8   The stronger men will be in front, the jaded ones will fall behind, and on this plan only one-tenth of your army will reach its destination.

9   If you march fifty *li* in order to outmanœuvre the enemy, you will lose the leader of your first division, and only half your force will reach the goal.

10   If you march thirty *li* with the same object, two-thirds of your army will arrive.

11   We may take it then that an army without its baggage-train is lost; without provisions it is lost; without bases of supply it is lost.

12   We cannot enter into alliances until we are acquainted with the designs of our neighbours.

13   We are not fit to lead an army on the march unless we are familiar with the face of the country—its mountains and forests, its pitfalls and precipices, its marshes and swamps.

14   We shall be unable to turn natural advantages to account unless we make use of local guides.

15   In war, practise dissimulation, and you will succeed. Move only if there is a real advantage to be gained.

16   Whether to concentrate or to divide your troops, must be decided by circumstances.

17   Let your rapidity be that of the wind, your compactness that of the forest.

18   In raiding and plundering be like fire, in immovability like a mountain.[16]

19   Let your plans be dark and impenetrable as night, and when you move, fall like a thunderbolt.

20   When you plunder a countryside, let the spoil be divided

---

15. I.e., maneuvers of this type should be confined to short distances.
16. That is, when holding a position from which the enemy is trying to dislodge you, or perhaps . . . when he is trying to entice you into a trap. (Tr.)

amongst your men; when you capture new territory, cut it up
into allotments for the benefit of the soldiery.[17]

21   Ponder and deliberate before you make a move.

22   He will conquer who has learnt the artifice of deviation.
Such is the art of manœuvring.

The Use of Spies/Chapter 13

1   Sun Tzu said: Raising a host of a hundred thousand men
and marching them great distances entails heavy loss on the
people and a drain on the resources of the State. The daily expenditure will amount to a thousand ounces of silver. There will
be commotion at home and abroad, and men will drop down exhausted on the highways. As many as seven hundred thousand
families will be impeded in their labour.[18]

2   Hostile armies may face each other for years, striving for
the victory which is decided in a single day. This being so, to
remain in ignorance of the enemy's condition simply because
one grudges the outlay of a hundred ounces of silver in honours
and emoluments,[19] is the height of inhumanity.[20]

3   One who acts thus is no leader of men, no present help to
his sovereign, no master of victory.

4   Thus, what enables the wise sovereign and the good general to strike and conquer, and achieve things beyond the reach
of ordinary men, is foreknowledge.

5   Now this foreknowledge cannot be elicited from spirits;
it cannot be obtained inductively from experience, nor by any
deductive calculation.

17. I.e., hold the invaded territory by letting the soldiers sow and harvest
the land.
18. The allusion is to an ancient system of land-tenure known as the *ching*
(or well-field) system, whereby sections of land were divided into nine
equal portions (resembling the Chinese character for "well"). The central
field was reserved for tax purposes; individual families held the other eight
fields. In time of war, one of the eight families was required to furnish a
soldier for the army, while the other seven contributed to his support. Thus
the levy of 100,000 men would affect the livelihood of 700,000 families.
19. I.e., for spies.
20. I.e., through accurate intelligence of the enemy's condition, one is able
to terminate a war quickly. It is folly to begrudge a comparatively small
outlay for spies when a long drawn-out war is far more costly.

6   Knowledge of the enemy's dispositions can only be obtained from other men.

7   Hence the use of spies, of whom there are five classes: (1) Local spies; (2) inward spies; (3) converted spies; (4) doomed spies; (5) surviving spies.

8   When these five kinds of spy are all at work, none can discover the secret system. This is called "divine manipulation of the threads." It is the sovereign's most precious faculty.

9   Having local spies means employing the services of the inhabitants of a district.

10   Having inward spies, making use of officials of the enemy.

11   Having converted spies, getting hold of the enemy's spies and using them for our own purposes.

12   Having doomed spies, doing certain things openly for purposes of deception, and allowing our own spies to know of them and report them to the enemy.

13   Surviving spies, finally, are those who bring back news from the enemy's camp.

14   Hence it is that with none in the whole army are more intimate relations to be maintained than with spies. None should be more liberally rewarded. In no other business should greater secrecy be preserved.

15   Spies cannot be usefully employed without a certain intuitive sagacity.

16   They cannot be properly managed without benevolence and straightforwardness.

17   Without subtle ingenuity of mind, one cannot make certain of the truth of their reports.

18   Be subtle! be subtle! and use your spies for every kind of business.

.   .   .   .

III

History

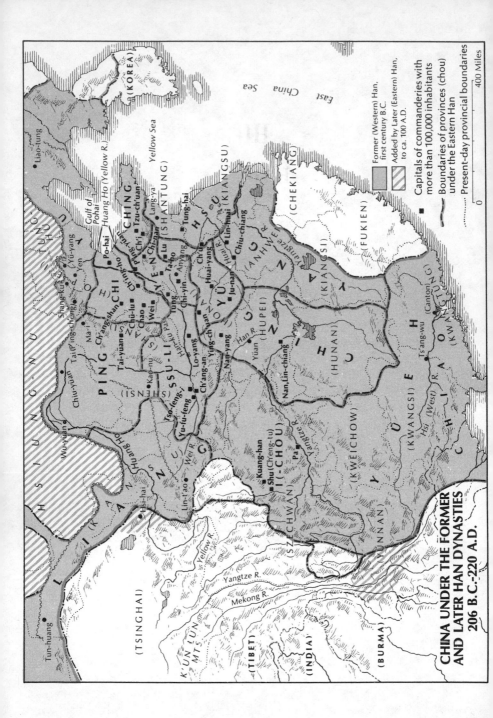

CHINA UNDER THE FORMER
AND LATER HAN DYNASTIES
206 B.C.-220 A.D.

Former (Western) Han,
first century B.C.

Added by Later (Eastern) Han,
to ca. 100 A.D.

■ Capitals of commanderies with
   more than 100,000 inhabitants

Boundaries of provinces (chou)
   under the Eastern Han

(SZECHWAN) Present-day provincial boundaries

0   400 Miles

Introduction to the Book of History

From the earliest recorded times, the Chinese people have shown enormous concern and respect for their own historical past. The *Book of History* (*Shu Ching*)—traditionally the oldest of the Five Classics—was thus a work of high importance. Containing documents allegedly dating from the three earliest Chinese dynasties, it deals with themes common to historical chronicles the world over: the deeds of kings and nobles, sacrifices to the gods, military expeditions, and the organization of government. But it is by no means a comprehensive account of early Chinese history. It describes chiefly the founders of dynasties—who are invariably presented as paragons of righteousness—and the last of their descendants to hold power— who are always models of wickedness. Each document (or "book") of the *History* is a unit in itself; and though the same persons may be mentioned in several documents, there is no connecting narrative.

The *Book of History* is in fact more a treatise on ethics than a work of history in the usual sense. Its account of actual events is employed largely to set the stage for appropriate moral discourse. Historical circumstances are treated not as significant in themselves, but as illustrations of general principles or occasions for edifying speeches. Many of the documents bear such titles as "instructions," "announcement," or "counsels" and consist primarily of direct speech. They are in fact didactic pronouncements on the subject of proper government, presented as the actual utterances of historical personages.

Confucius himself was reputed to be the editor of the *Book of History*. According to tradition, he selected its present fifty-four documents from an original group of 3,240 and composed prefaces for them. But modern scholarship has demonstrated that three-quarters of the material in this Classic could not have existed in Confucius' lifetime; and his connection even with the remainder is dubious. Only about fifteen of the documents in the *History* are probably genuine in the sense of having been written shortly after the events they purport to relate; and none of these go back any farther than the first decades of the Chou dynasty (began 1122 B.C.). Another thirteen documents were written in the several centuries after Confucius; and the remainder are regarded by most authoritis as forgeries dating from the third century A.D.

Introduction to the Canon of Yao

Chinese tradition asserts that the sage-kings of antiquity surpassed all of their successors in wisdom and benevolent government. Semi-historical figures like Yao and Shun, Yü, Wen, and Wu were the accepted models of kingly virtue; few extended political discussions in China managed to escape the use of their names. Beginning in the century after Confucius, the references to them in Chinese literature are legion. Thinkers of such diverse viewpoints as Mo Tzu and Mencius agreed that the rulers of their own times would profit enormously by imitating the deeds of these former sovereigns.

Among the most frequently cited examples of royal uprightness were the ancient emperors Yao and Shun. According to the traditional chronology, they reigned for a total of one hundred fifty years at the beginning of Chinese history,* just prior to the foundation of the first Chinese dynasty, the Hsia (2205-1766 B.C.). To them are attributed various deeds associated with the founding of civilization, e.g. regulation of the flood waters and establishment of the proper times for agriculture. The opening document of the *Book of History*, known as the "Canon of Yao" (*Yao Tien*),** claims to record their accomplishments. While admittedly not as ancient as the events it purports to recount (it begins with the phrase: "Examining into antiquity, we find . . ."), its authenticity as a historical source was generally accepted in China until quite recent times.

* Tradition is vague about the origins of the Chinese people. The usual account begins with a Creator, P'an-ku, followed by twelve Celestial Sovereigns, eleven Terrestrial Sovereigns, and nine Human Sovereigns, representing the triad of heaven, earth, and man. They were followed by the Five Ti, among whom were the Yellow Emperor, Yao, and Shun.
** Sometimes it appears as two documents, known respectively as the "Canon of Yao" (*Yao Tien*) and the "Canon of Shun" (*Shun Tien*).

Only in the twentieth century did scholars discover that Yao and Shun are purely mythological personages who appeared in Chinese legend only shortly before the time of Confucius. Their names are not mentioned on any of the genuinely ancient archaeological objects of the Shang or early Chou period,* or in the *Book of Songs*, which is likewise pre-Confucian. Confucius himself in the *Analects* refers to them only obliquely as virtuous rulers of antiquity; he nowhere suggests that their conduct should set the standard for contemporary governments. But within a century of his death, the legend of Yao and Shun had grown mightily. Its most significant aspect—the assertion that Yao and Shun had passed over their own sons in order to bequeath the throne to the ablest and most righteous man in the kingdom—is clearly a post-Confucian invention. The *Analects* never mentions it (except in Book XX, a late interpolation), though Confucius could scarcely have ignored a tradition so much in accord with his own convictions, if he had known of it. He himself never challenged the hereditary principle of rulership, though this would have been a logical extension of his belief that government office should be the reward of merit. Presumably it was sufficiently daring for him to suggest even that important officials should be chosen without regard for family connections. All available evidence indicates that in Confucius' lifetime, as before, high offices were handed down in noble families as a matter of course.

But when educated Chinese came to accept the idea that office should be the reward of merit, they needed supporting evidence from history. Pointing to ancient precedent was the most compelling kind of argument, and the need soon produced the supply. As a by-product of the intellectual efflorescence of the "Warring States" period (403-221 B.C.), numerous allegedly ancient documents came to light. The "Canon of Yao" is a composition of this sort. Written in the late fifth or the fourth century B.C., it is in some respects based upon genuine tradition. But the idea that Yao and Shun selected their heirs on the basis of merit has no known foundation in historical fact. Quite possibly it is a projection of a similar, and more ancient, story told about the founders of the Chou dynasty.** Though accepted in China for more than two millennia as an account of real events, the "Canon of Yao" actually expresses the political ideal which its authors wished to see established in the future.

---

* Traditional dates for the Shang period: 1765-1123 B.C.; for the Chou: 1122-403 B.C.
** See below, "The Numerous Regions," pp. 114-19.

FROM THE CANON OF YAO (YAO TIEN)

Part I[1]

1   Examining into antiquity, (we find that) the Ti Yao[2] was
styled Fang-hsün.[3] He was reverential, intelligent, accomplished,
and thoughtful,—naturally and without effort. He was sincerely courteous, and capable of (all) complaisance. The bright
(influence of these qualities) was felt through the four quarters
(of the land), and reached to (heaven) above and (earth)
beneath.

He made the able and virtuous distinguished, and thence proceeded to the love of (all in) the nine classes of his kindred, who
(thus) became harmonious. He (also) regulated and polished
the people (of his domain), who all became brightly intelligent.
(Finally), he united and harmonized the myriad states; and so
the black-haired people were transformed. The result was (universal) concord.

2   He commanded the Hsis and Hos,[4] in reverent accordance
with (their observation of) the wide heavens, to calculate and
delineate (the movements and appearances of) the sun, the
moon, the stars, and the zodiacal spaces, and so to deliver respectfully the seasons to be observed by the people.

He separately commanded the second brother Hsi to reside
at Yü-i,[5] in what was called the Bright Valley, and (there) respectfully to receive as a guest the rising sun, and to adjust and
arrange the labours of the spring. "The day," (said he), "is of

From *The Sacred Books of China*, Part I, *The Shu King* (also known as *The
Sacred Books of the East*, Vol. III), trans. by James Legge, Oxford: At the
Clarendon Press, 1899, pp. 32-6, 38-41. (All parentheses inserted by trans-
lator.)

1. Part I corresponds to what in some versions is the complete "Canon of
Yao"; Part II is the "Canon of Shun."
2. "Ti" means "the Divine One" and is used as a synonym for "Emperor."
The name "Yao" may originally have meant "high," "lofty," "grand."
3. This may have been the emperor's proper name, though some Chinese
scholars have asserted that it means "The Highly Meritorious."
4. The Hsis and Hos were apparently two families of brothers who were
commanded to regulate the calendar in order to determine the proper times
for planting and harvesting.
5. Somewhere in eastern China: probably the Shantung peninsula.

the medium length, and the star[6] is in Niao[7];—you may thus exactly determine mid-spring. The people are dispersed (in the fields), and birds and beasts breed and copulate."

He further commanded the third brother Hsi to reside at Nan-chiao[8], (in what was called the Brilliant Capital), to adjust and arrange the transformations of the summer, and respectfully to observe the exact limit (of the shadow). "The day," (said he), "is at its longest, and the star is in Huo[9];—you may thus exactly determine mid-summer. The people are more dispersed; and birds and beasts have their feathers and hair thin, and change their coats."

He separately commanded the second brother Ho to reside at the west, in what was called the Dark Valley, and (there) respectfully to convoy the setting sun, and to adjust and arrange the completing labours of the autumn. "The night," (said he), "is of the medium length, and the star is in Hsü[10];—you may thus exactly determine mid-autumn. The people feel at ease, and birds and beasts have their coats in good condition."

He further commanded the third brother Ho to reside in the northern region, in what was called the Sombre Capital, and (there) to adjust and examine the changes of the winter. "The day," (said he), "is at its shortest, and the star is in Mao[11];—you may thus exactly determine mid-winter. The people keep in their houses, and the coats of birds and beasts are downy and thick."

The Ti said, "Ah! you, Hsis and Hos, a round year consists of three hundred, sixty, and six days. Do you, by means of the intercalary month, fix the four seasons, and complete (the period of) the year. (Thereafter), the various officers being regulated in accordance with this, all the works (of the year) will be fully performed."

6. The star which reaches its highest altitude at dusk (at a specified season and point of observation).

7. "Niao" is the general name for the seven constellations belonging to the southern quarter (one-fourth) of the moon's revolution around the earth.

8. In the extreme south of what was then China.

9. The central constellation of the eastern quarter.

10. The central constellation of the northern quarter.

11. The central constellation of the southern quarter.

3   The Ti said, "Who will search out (for me) a man according to the times, whom I can raise and employ?" Fang-ch'i said,
"(Your) heir-son Chu is highly intelligent." The Ti said, "Alas!
he is insincere and quarrelsome:—can he do?"

The Ti said, "Who will search out (for me) a man equal to
the exigency of my affairs?" Huan-tao said, "Oh! the merits of
the Minister of Works[12] have just been displayed on a wide
scale." The Ti said, "Alas! when all is quiet, he talks; but when
employed, his actions turn out differently. He is respectful
(only) in appearance. See! the floods assail the heavens!"

The Ti said, "Ho! (President of) the Four Mountains,[13] destructive in their overflow are the waters of the inundation. In
their vast extent they embrace the hills and overtop the great
heights, threatening the heavens with their floods, so that the
lower people groan and murmur! Is there a capable man to
whom I can assign the correction (of this calamity)?" All (in
the court) said, "Ah! is there not Kun[14]?" The Ti said, "Alas!
how perverse is he! He is disobedient to orders, and tries to injure his peers." (The President of) the Mountains said, "Well
but—. Try if he can (accomplish the work)." (Kun) was employed accordingly. The Ti said (to him), "Go; and be reverent!" For nine years he laboured, but the work was unac-
complished.

The Ti said, "Ho! (President of) the Four Mountains, I have
been on the throne seventy years. You can carry out my commands;—I will resign my place to you." The Chief said, "I have
not the virtue;—I should disgrace your place." (The Ti) said,
"Show me some one among the illustrious, or set forth one
from among the poor and mean." All (then) said to the Ti,
"There is an unmarried man among the lower people, called
Shun of Yü[15]." The Ti said, "Yes, I have heard of him. What

12. The Emperor Shun will later banish as criminals both Huan-tao and
the minister he recommends.
13. "President of the Four Mountains" appears to be the title of the prime
minister. The four mountains marked the eastern, western, northern, and
southern limits of the country—enclosing the territory within the sphere
of the prime minister's authority.
14. This Kun is supposed to have been the father of the future emperor Yü,
who later successfully regulated the floods.
15. The name "Shun" may mean "Benevolent Sage." Yü was the place
from which he came.

have you to say about him?" The Chief said, "He is the son of a blind man. His father was obstinately unprincipled; his (step-)mother was insincere; his (half-)brother Hsiang was arrogant. He has been able, (however), by his filial piety to live in harmony with them, and to lead them gradually to self-government, so that they (no longer) proceed to great wickedness." The Ti said, "I will try him; I will wive him, and thereby see his behaviour with my two daughters." (Accordingly) he arranged and sent down his two daughters to the north of the Kuei,[16] to be wives in (the family of) Yü. The Ti said to them, "Be reverent!"

Part II[17]

2   (Shun) carefully set forth the beauty of the five cardinal duties, and they came to be (universally) observed. Being appointed to be General Regulator, the affairs of every (official) department were arranged in their proper seasons. (Being charged) to receive (the princes) from the four quarters of the land, they were all docilely submissive. Being sent to the great plains at the foot of the mountains, notwithstanding the tempests of wind, thunder, and rain, he did not go astray.

The Ti said, "Come, you Shun. I have consulted you on (all) affairs, and examined your words, and found that they can be carried into practice;—(now) for three years. Do you ascend the seat of the Ti." Shun wished to decline in favour of some one more virtuous, and not to consent to be (Yao's) successor. On the first day of the first month, (however), he received (Yao's) retirement (from his duties) in the temple of the Accomplished Ancestor.[18]

3   He examined the pearl-adorned turning sphere, with its transverse tube of jade, and reduced to a harmonious system (the movements of) the Seven Directors.[19]

16. A small stream in Shansi which flows into the Yellow River.
17. Here begins the "Canon of Shun." Its initial paragraph (here omitted) is now known to have been added in the fifth century A.D.
18. The Accomplished Ancestor was presumably the progenitor of the family of Yao.
19. Probably the seven stars of the [constellation of the] Great Bear. (Tr.)

Thereafter, he sacrificed specially, but with the ordinary forms, to God; sacrificed with reverent purity to the Six Honoured Ones[20]; offered their appropriate sacrifices to the hills and rivers; and extended his worship to the host of spirits.[21]

He called in (all) the five jade-symbols of rank; and when the month was over, he gave daily audience to (the President of) the Four Mountains, and all the Pastors,[22] (finally) returning their symbols to the various princes.

In the second month of the year he made a tour of inspection eastwards, as far as T'ai-chung,[23] where he presented a burnt-offering to Heaven, and sacrificed in order to the hills and rivers. Thereafter he gave audience to the princes of the east. He set in accord their seasons and months, and regulated the days; he made uniform the standard-tubes, with the measures of length and of capacity, and the steel-yards; he regulated the five (classes of) ceremonies, with (the various) articles of introduction,—the five symbols of jade, the three kinds of silk, the two living (animals) and the one dead one. As to the five instruments of rank, when all was over, he returned them. In the fifth month he made a similar tour southwards, as far as the mountain of the south,[24] where he observed the same ceremonies as at T'ai. In the eighth month he made a tour westwards, as far as the mountain of the west, where he did as before. In the eleventh month he made a tour northwards, as far as the mountain of the north, where he observed the same ceremonies as in the west. He (then) returned (to the capital), went to (the temple of) the Cultivated Ancestor,[25] and sacrificed a single bull.

In five years there was one tour of inspection, and there were

20. Probably spirits who were believed to rule over certain natural phenomena.
21. This paragraph describes Shun as exercising the religious prerogatives of a sovereign.
22. Literally, "shepherds of the people," meaning the princes of the various states.
23. Mount T'ai in Shantung, one of the "four mountains" marking the boundary of his realm.
24. The southern boundary of the country, etc.
25. Presumably identical with the "Accomplished Ancestor" mentioned previously.

four appearances of the princes at court. They gave a report (of their government) in words, which was clearly tested by their works. They received chariots and robes according to their merits.

He instituted the division (of the land) into twelve provinces, raising altars upon twelve hills in them. He (also) deepened the rivers.

He exhibited (to the people) the statutory punishments, enacting banishment as a mitigation of the five (great) inflictions[26]; with the whip to be employed in the magistrates' courts, the stick to be employed in schools, and money to be received for redeemable offences. Inadvertent offences and those which could be ascribed to misfortune were to be pardoned, but those who transgressed presumptuously and repeatedly were to be punished with death. "Let me be reverent! Let me be reverent!" (he said to himself.) "Let compassion rule in punishment!"

He banished the Minister of Works to Yü island[27]; confined Huan-tao on mount Ch'ung;[28] drove (the chief of) San-miao[29] (and his people) into San-wei,[30] and kept them there; and held Kun a prisoner till death on mount Yü.[31] These four criminals being thus dealt with, all under heaven acknowledged the justice (of Shun's administration).

4   After twenty-eight years the Ti [Yao] deceased, when the people mourned for him as for a parent for three years. Within the four seas all the eight kinds of instruments of music were stopped and hushed. On the first day of the first month (of the) next year, Shun went to (the temple of) the Accomplished Ancestor.[32]

---

26. The five punishments were branding on the forehead, cutting off the nose, cutting off the feet, castration, and death.
27. In the north, not far from modern Peking.
28. In the far south (Hunan).
29. San-miao was a territory in southern China embracing parts of Hupei, Hunan, and Kiangsi.
30. San-wei was a district around a mountain of the same name in the extreme west (Kansu).
31. In Shantung.
32. I.e., after governing jointly with Yao for twenty-eight years, Shun now became ruler in his own right. Tradition holds that he reigned for an additional fifty years.

Introduction to The Numerous Regions

"The Numerous Regions" (*To Fang*) is one of the fifteen genuinely pre-Confucian documents of the *Book of History*. Written not long after the events it describes, it deals with the Chou conquest of the Shang state (traditional date: 1122 B.C.). The Chous—a relatively uncultured people from the west of China—had overthrown the Shangs by means of superior military prowess. They now faced the much more difficult task of consolidating their rule over a population more civilized than themselves which resented its political subjection. The object of "The Numerous Regions" is clearly to justify the Chou conquest over the Shang state; its thesis is that this victory conformed to a higher law of Heaven.

In this document (and in several others of comparable date from the *Book of History*) there appears for the first time in Chinese literature the famous theory of the Mandate of Heaven. According to this theory—later given wide currency by Mencius and implicitly accepted by Chinese sovereigns until the present century—the right to rule is conferred by Heaven. Because Heaven prefers virtue to vice, it will withdraw its mandate from an evil ruler and bestow it upon one more worthy. Thus the mere existence of a well-functioning state proves that the reigning dynasty holds the Mandate of Heaven; its overthrow demonstrates that it has lost Heaven's favor. In accordance with this concept, "The Numerous Regions" paints the last of the Shang kings in the darkest possible hues, contrasting sharply with the alleged modesty and forbearance of the Chou conqueror. Moreover, its account of the Shang dynasty's previous conquest of the Hsia (1766 B.C.)—an event of doubtful historicity which the Chous quite possibly invented—establishes a precedent for the Chou overthrow of the Shang. Like the final Shang sovereign, the last of the Hsia is described as utterly evil and depraved; therefore Heaven transferred its mandate to Kings Wen and Wu, the founders of the imperial Chou house.*

* Although Wen and Wu are frequently mentioned together, King Wen actually ruled only a small principality. His son, King Wu, revolted against the Shang and inaugurated the imperial Chou dynasty.

In the later centuries of Chou rule* it was assumed that both the Hsias and the Shangs had governed the entire area of Chinese civilization—which in those days meant the north China plain.† But whether a Hsia dynasty ever existed at all is questionable; and its reputed successor, the Shang, certainly never held sway over more than a small area of present-day Honan and Shansi provinces. The Chou rulers were the first to organize a larger area of China through the delegation of authority to feudal vassals. By Confucius' time the authority of the Chou emperor had long since declined, and the origins of the dynasty were largely forgotten. The myth arose that until the recent disorders all of China had been ruled by a single dynasty, and that the Mandate of Heaven applied to the entire country. Ever since, in periods of political fragmentation as well as of union, the Chinese have regarded the unity of their country under a single government as the natural and rightful state of affairs.

* The Chou era is usually considered to have ended in 403 B.C., with the beginning of the "Warring States" period. But a small Chou state, ruled by the descendants of the former emperors, persisted until 256 B.C.
† China south of the Yangtze River remained a largely uncultivated wilderness until the occupation of the north by barbarians in the Six Dynasties period (A.D. 222-589).

FROM THE NUMEROUS REGIONS (TO FANG)

1   In the fifth month, on the day Ting-hai, the king arrived from Yen,¹ and came to (Hao), the honoured (capital of) Chou. The duke of Chou² said, "The king speaks to the following effect: 'Ho! I make an announcement to you of the four states, and the numerous (other) regions. Ye who were the officers and

From *The Sacred Books of China*, Part I, *The Shu King* (also known as *The Sacred Books of the East*, Vol. III), trans. by James Legge, Oxford: At the Clarendon Press, 1899, pp. 214-19. (All parentheses inserted by translator.)
1. Yen was an area of the northeast (north Shansi and south Manchuria). Evidently the king had just returned from suppressing a rebellion there.
2. This was Tan, the famous Duke of Chou who was Confucius' favorite ancient worthy. He was a brother of King Wu, the first Chou emperor of China. When Wu died, leaving only a minor son as heir, the newly conquered territories threatened to fall away from their allegiance to the Chou house. The Duke of Chou then took power as regent and spent seven years restoring order. His virtue was demonstrated in that he refrained from seizing the throne for himself, but after the seven years returned the empire to his nephew, the legitimate heir.

people of the prince of Yin,[3] I have dealt very leniently as regards your lives, as ye all know. You kept reckoning greatly on (some) decree of Heaven,[4] and did not keep with perpetual awe before your thoughts (the preservation of) your sacrifices.[5]

" 'God[6] sent down correction on Hsia,[7] but the sovereign[8] (only) increased his luxury and sloth, and would not speak kindly to the people. He showed himself dissolute and dark, and would not yield for a single day to the leadings of God:—this is what you have heard. He kept reckoning on the decree of God (in his favour), and did not cultivate the means for the people's support. By great inflictions of punishment also he increased the disorder of the states of Hsia. The first cause (of his evil course) was the internal misrule, which made him unfit to deal well with the multitudes. Nor did he endeavour to find and employ men whom he could respect, and who might display a generous kindness to the people; but where any of the people of Hsia were covetous and fierce, he daily honoured them, and they practised cruel tortures in the cities. Heaven on this sought a (true) lord for the people, and made its distinguished and favouring decree light on T'ang the Successful, who punished and destroyed the sovereign of Hsia. Heaven's refusal of its favour (to Hsia) was decided. The righteous men of your numerous regions were not permitted to continue long in their posts of enjoyment, and the many officers whom Hsia's (last sovereign) honoured were unable intelligently to maintain the people in the enjoyment (of their lives), but, on the contrary, aided one another in oppressing them, till of the hundred ways of securing (prosperity) they could not promote (one).

3. Yin was the name used by the Chous for the Shang people. The word never appears on literary remains of the Shang period, indicating that the Shangs did not apply the term to themselves.

4. I.e., that Heaven would not withdraw support from a long-established dynasty.

5. The non-observance of sacrifices to the founder and other ancestors of the ruling house marked the extinction of a state. Either no one remained alive to perform the sacrifices, or the new rulers did not permit them.

6. The word here translated as "God" means literally "Supreme Ruler." It is often used interchangeably with T'ien ("Heaven"), a more abstract term denoting the supreme, but impersonal, power of the universe.

7. The Hsia dynasty.

8. Chieh, the last Hsia monarch, famed for his extreme wickedness.

" 'In the case indeed of T'ang the Successful, it was because he was the choice of your numerous regions that he superseded Hsia, and became the lord of the people. He paid careful attention to the essential virtue (of a sovereign), in order to stimulate the people, and they on their part imitated him and were stimulated. From him down to Ti Yi,[9] the sovereigns all made their virtue illustrious, and were cautious in the use of punishments; —thus also exercising a stimulating influence (over the people). When they, having examined the evidence in criminal cases, put to death those chargeable with many crimes, they exercised the same influence; and they did so also when they liberated those who were not purposely guilty. But when the throne came to your (last) sovereign, he could not with (the good will of) your numerous regions continue in the enjoyment of the favouring decree of Heaven.'

2   "Oh! the king speaks to the following effect:—'I announce and declare to you of the numerous regions, that Heaven had no set purpose to do away with the sovereign of Hsia or with the sovereign of Yin. But it was the case that your (last) ruler, being in possession of your numerous regions, abandoned himself to great excess, and reckoned on the favouring decree of Heaven, making trifling excuses for his conduct. And so in the case of the (last) sovereign of Hsia; his plans of government were not of a tendency to secure his enjoyment (of the kingdom), and Heaven sent down ruin on him, and the chief of the territory (of Shang) put an end (to the line of Hsia). In truth, the last sovereign of your Shang was luxurious to the extreme of luxury, while his plans of government showed neither purity nor progress, and thus Heaven sent down such ruin on him.

" 'The wise, through not thinking, become foolish, and the foolish, by thinking, become wise. Heaven for five years waited kindly, and forbore with the descendant (of T'ang), to see if he would indeed prove himself the ruler of the people; but there was nothing in him deserving to be regarded. Heaven then sought among your numerous regions, making a great impression by its terrors to stir up some one who would look (reverently) to it, but in all your regions there was not one deserv-

9. Ti Yi, the next-to-last ruler of the Hsia line.

ing of its favouring regard. But there were the kings of our Chou, who treated well the multitudes of the people, and were able to sustain the burden of virtuous (government). They could preside over (all services to) spirits and to Heaven. Heaven thereupon instructed us, and increased our excellence, made choice of us, and gave us the decree of Yin, to rule over your numerous regions.

3   " 'Why do I now presume to make (these) many declarations? I have dealt very leniently as regards the lives of you, the people of these four states. Why do you not show a sincere and generous obedience in your numerous regions? Why do you not aid and co-operate with the kings of our Chou, to secure the enjoyment of Heaven's favouring decree? You now still dwell in your dwellings, and cultivate your fields;—why do you not obey our kings, and consolidate the decree of Heaven? The paths which you tread are continually those of disquietude;— have you in your hearts no love for yourselves? do you refuse so greatly to acquiesce in the ordinance of Heaven? do you triflingly reject that decree? do you of yourselves pursue unlawful courses, scheming (by your alleged reasons) for the approval of upright men? I simply instructed you, and published my announcement[10]; with trembling awe I secured and confined (the chief criminals):—I have done so twice and for three times. But if you do not take advantage of the leniency with which I have spared your lives, I will proceed to severe punishments, and put you to death. It is not that we, the sovereigns of Chou, hold it virtuous to make you untranquil, but it is you yourselves who accelerate your crimes (and sufferings).'

4   "The king says, 'Oh! ho! I tell you, ye many officers of the various regions, and you, ye many officers of Yin, now have ye been hurrying about, doing service to my overseers for five years. There are among you the inferior assistants, the chiefs, and the numerous directors, small and great:—see that ye all attain to the discharge of your duties. Want of harmony (in life) rises from (the want of it in) one's (inner) self:—strive to

10. Presumably this refers to "The Great Announcement" (*Ta Kao*), another document of the *Book of History* dating from the early decades of Chou rule.

be harmonious. Want of concord in your families (arises from the want of it in your conduct);—strive to be harmonious. When intelligence rules in your cities, then will you be proved to be attentive to your duties. Do not be afraid, I pray you, of the evil ways (of the people); and moreover, by occupying your offices with a reverent harmony you will find it possible to select from your cities individuals on whose assistance you can calculate. You may thus long continue in this city of Lo,[11] cultivating your fields. Heaven will favour and compassionate you, and we, the sovereigns of Chou, will greatly help you, and confer rewards, selecting you to stand in our royal court. Only be attentive to your duties, and you may rank among our great officers.'

"The king says, 'Oh! ye numerous officers, if you cannot exhort one another to pay a sincere regard to my charges, it will further show that you are unable to honour your sovereign; and all the people will (also) say, "We will not honour him." Thus will ye be proved slothful and perverse, greatly disobedient to the royal charges. Throughout your numerous regions you will bring on yourselves the terrors of Heaven, and I will then inflict on you its punishments, removing you far from your country.'

5   "The king says, 'I do not (wish to) make these many declarations, but it is in a spirit of awe that I lay my commands before you.' He further says, 'You may now make a (new) beginning. If you cannot reverently realize the harmony (which I enjoin), do not (hereafter) murmur against me.' "

11. The wording seems to indicate that the announcement was made in Lo; some critics have argued that Lo was the "honoured capital" of the first sentence of the document. However that may be, the Chou rulers did enfeoff the descendants of the Shang kings as rulers of the region of Sung in eastern Honan, thus enabling them to continue the sacrifices to their ancestors.

Introduction to the Spring and Autumn Annals (Ch'un Ch'iu) and the Tso Commentary (Tso Chuan)

The first professional historians in China were the *shih*—scribes and chroniclers at the various state courts. Inscriptions on archaeological objects suggest that their functions evolved out of score-keeping at the archery contests, which were a favorite diversion among the nobility of feudal times. Subsequently these same officials became associated with divination—the selection of lucky days for undertaking particular activities—by being assigned to record significant predictions. The *shih* was a sort of seer, an advisor to the ruler who illustrated his advice by reference to historical precedent. As the states expanded and interstate relations became more complex, a permanent record of diplomatic transactions also became necessary. The *shih*—who as a scribe was present at official meetings—kept records of such proceedings. Eventually it became customary in the various states to keep systematic accounts, arranged by day and year, of all the events which the governments considered worth remembering; and permanent officials were appointed to look after the archives. By the eighth century B.C. and perhaps even before, at least some of the Chinese courts maintained regular chronicles; apparently most of them did so eventually. Today the only such chronicles still extant come from Ch'in (the state which first unified China) and from Confucius' native state of Lu, together with fragments of a Wei chronicle preserved through quotations in other works. Most of the rest disappeared in the book-burning of 213 B.C., because they tended to exalt the individual states which the Ch'in emperor had so recently destroyed.

The *Spring and Autumn Annals (Ch'un Ch'iu)*—"spring and autumn" being an abbreviated reference to the four seasons of the year—is the chronicle of Lu. It is a year-by-year account of politically significant events occurring not only in Lu itself, but in many of the other Chinese states between 722 and 481 B.C. This book gave its name to the period of history with which it deals (the so-called Spring and Autumn period), and with its commentaries has exercised a profound influence upon all subsequent Chinese historical writing. Allegedly compiled by Confucius himself, it was greatly revered by the Confucian school and raised to Classic status in Han times. Dry and laconic in style, often nearly unintelligible in its brevity, this chronicle in itself provides few clues as to why it was held in such esteem. To all appearances it is merely an outline account of diplomatic exchanges, important battles, state marriages, court rituals, and occasional natural events such as floods, eclipses, or allegedly supernatural portents. But the presumption that Confucius must have had good reason for devoting his attention to this book gave rise to an enormous exegetical tradition. Generations of Chinese scholars pored over the text of the *Annals*, seeking through analysis of its exact wording, inclusions, or omissions to determine Confucius' supposed judgment about the events it relates. Most of these interpretations are patently forced; often they are also self-contradictory. But it is conceivable that they drew upon an interpretative tradition actually going back to Confucius. Though it is unlikely that Confucius had anything to do with compiling the *Annals*, he may possibly have used it as a text to illustrate his views on political morality. Occasional references in the *Mencius* and elsewhere suggest that its connection with Confucius is not entirely a later invention.

Such was the reputation of the *Annals* that an ancient work of quite separate origin was cast in the form of an explanation of it. This was the *Tso Commentary (Tso Chuan)*—today the principal source for the Spring and Autumn period of Chinese history. The *Tso Commentary* is a compilation of miscellaneous materials which in effect fill out the bare bones of the *Annals*, providing much background information and relevant detail. The text is arranged to correspond with the reigns and year-periods of the dukes of Lu—a procedure which frequently interrupts the continuity of narration. However, some of the entries have no corresponding passage in the *Annals*, just as certain paragraphs of the *Annals* lack any commentary in the *Tso*—indicating that originally the two works were not related.

The traditional author of the *Tso Commentary* is one Tso Ch'iu-ming, of whom nothing whatever is known except his name. But scholars generally agree that the work attributed to him was put together mainly in the third century B.C., with a few sections being added in early Han times. Like the *Book of History*, the *Tso Commentary* consists very largely of conversations and speeches which

—with their rhythmic and formal style and obvious Confucian moralizing—are clearly no more than literary fictions. In contrast to the *History*, the *Tso* also contains narrative passages of considerable length, which make it the oldest work of this type in Chinese literature. This narrative portion—though employed by the compilers mainly to set the scene for the speeches—is actually much older, and of far greater historical importance. Analysis of its archaic style and vocabulary has shown strong affinities between it and the bronze inscriptions dating from the early and middle Chou period. Scholars have accordingly concluded that the *Tso* narrative —despite some reworking by later editors—is by origin a genuine product of pre-Confucian times.

The Spring and Autumn period was an age of continual armed conflict, and the *Tso Commentary* is justly famous for its descriptions of warfare. However, its battle scenes generally focus on the deeds of individual heroes rather than the broad sweep of the fighting. For the most part, much more attention is paid to the preparations and discussions before the battle and to the fate of the participants afterward than to the action itself. War in those times was still in many respects a knightly sport—an opportunity to demonstrate individual courage and skill. Hostilities were conducted according to a code of conduct respected by both sides. The gentleman-soldier did not massacre noncombatants, strike elderly men, or kill opponents already wounded; he considered it unfair to employ deceptive tactics or lay ambushes. Long campaigns were rare; most issues were decided by a single battle. Typically, the two opposing armies encamped opposite one another and waited for several days while the commanders conducted sacrifices and the diviners studied the portents. When the agreed-upon moment for action arrived, the attackers threw themselves upon the enemy, and confused hand-to-hand fighting ensued. A decision was reached quickly. The stronger side broke through its opponents' formations, killed those who still resisted, and pursued the remainder for a short distance. The victorious soldiers picked up any articles of value which had been dropped and returned to their camp or went home. Victory was not exploited. The winning prince did not expect to destroy his enemy or even to annex his territory; the spoils of war were the tribute imposed by the victor upon the vanquished.

Although warfare in the Spring and Autumn period was more or less constant, its ravages were limited by the small number of participants. Only the rulers of states, their nobles, and their feudal retainers engaged in actual combat; the peasant masses were not directly affected. The potential ferocity of battle was restricted by a primitive technology. Armament was rudimentary. The nobles and their principal retainers carried shields of bamboo or oxhide; the main body of soldiery wore padded jackets. The weapons of war were daggers and short, bronze-tipped swords, supplemented by hooking and cutting blades. When iron weaponry came into general use about 400 B.C., the era of knightly warfare came to an end. The conflicts of the ensuing Warring States period (403-221 B.C.) bore a professional character quite foreign to the warfare of the Spring and Autumn: battles were more complex, less localized, and more destructive.

The Chinese have never regarded history as a recital of facts for their own sake. The *Tso Commentary* provides not only an invaluable fund of information on the Spring and Autumn period; it is also a classic illustration of knightly ethics. Taking the stark outline of fact or legend, it supplies appropriate moral interpretations. According to the *Tso*, history is the arena for the demonstration of ethical principles. Righteous conduct brings reward, while defiance of propriety inevitably results in failure. Thus war must be justified if it is to succeed: generals should be less concerned with purely military questions than with the ethical imperatives governing a situation. Implicit in this attitude is the assumption that history is not the product of impersonal factors, but of conscious decisions by human actors who are responsible for their deeds. This presumed correlation between intentions and results serves to give history its moral significance. The *Tso Commentary* is a monument to the Confucian conviction that ethics and politics are inseparable, and that history is a series of moral examples for the instruction of humanity.

FROM THE SPRING AND AUTUMN ANNALS
(CH'UN CH'IU)

Duke Hsüan. Year XII

[Duke Hsüan of Lu reigned from 607 to 590 B.C. The following seven paragraphs constitute the complete text for the twelfth year of

From *The Chinese Classics*, Vol. V, Part I, *The Ch'un Ts'ew, with the Tso Chuen*, trans. by James Legge, Hongkong: Lane, Crawford & Co.; London: Trübner & Co., 1872, p. 316. (Words added by translator are indicated by parentheses; words added by present editors appear in square brackets.)

his reign (596-595 B.C.). In style, content, and length, "Year XII" is typical of the entries in the *Annals* as a whole.]

1 In the duke's twelfth year, in spring, there was the burial of duke Ling of Ch'en.
2 The viscount of Ch'u laid siege to (the capital of) Cheng.
3 In summer, in the sixth month, on [the day] I-mou, Hsün Lin-fu of Chin led a force, and fought with the viscount of Ch'u at Pi, when the army of Chin was disgracefully defeated.
4 It was autumn, the seventh month.
5. In winter, in the twelfth month, on [the day] Mou-yin, the viscount of Ch'u extinguished Hsiao.
6 An officer of Chin, one of Sung, one of Wei, and one of Ts'ao, made a covenant together at Ch'ing-ch'iu.
7 An army of Sung invaded Ch'en, (but) a body of men from Wei relieved it.

FROM THE TSO COMMENTARY (TSO CHUAN)
Duke Hsüan. Year XII

[The small state of Cheng, in central China, was the victim of its unfortunate geographical position between two of the most powerful states of the period—Chin in the northwest, Ch'u in the south. Both Chin and Ch'u wished to make Cheng their vassal, while Cheng sought to maintain its independence by playing off its two great neighbors against each other.

Three years prior to the events related here (Year IX of Duke Hsüan of Lu), Ch'u invaded Cheng; but Chin came to Cheng's assistance and Ch'u was defeated. The following year Cheng recognized its submission to Chin; Ch'u invaded Cheng once again but was repulsed by Chin a second time. A year later (Year XI), Ch'u once again invaded Cheng; Cheng saw fit to submit, but at the same time made overtures to Chin. Ch'u regarded this as treachery, and in the year of our narrative (Year XII) invaded Cheng for the fourth year in succession . . .]

From *The Chinese Classics*, Vol. V, Part I, *The Ch'un Ts'ew, with the Tso Chuen*, trans. by James Legge, Hongkong: Lane, Crawford & Co.; London: Trübner & Co., 1872, p. 316. (Words added by translator are indicated by parentheses; words added by present editors appear in square brackets.)

COMMENTARY TO PARAGRAPH 2

. . . In spring, the viscount of Ch'u had held the capital of Cheng in siege for seventeen days, when the people divined whether it would be well for them to accept conditions of peace, but the answer was not favourable. They then divined whether they should weep in the grand temple, and bring forth their chariots into the streets (*i. e.*, probably, to be ready for removing where Ch'u might direct); and the reply was favourable. The people of the city then made a great weeping, and the keepers of the parapets all cried aloud, so that the viscount of Ch'u withdrew his men, till the people repaired the wall. He then advanced and renewed the siege, when the place was reduced at the end of three months. He entered the city by the Huang gate, and proceeded to the principal street, where he was met by the earl of Cheng, with his flesh exposed, and leading a sheep. "Uncared for by Heaven," said the earl, "I could not serve your lordship, and aroused your anger, till it has been discharged upon my city. The offence is all mine; and I dare do nothing now but wait for your commands. If you carry us away to the south of the [Yangtze] Kiang, to occupy the land by the shores of the sea, be it so. If you take the State and give it to some other as its ruler, to whom I shall be as in the position of a handmaid, be it so. If you kindly regard former relations of friendship between our States, and . . . you do not extinguish our altars, so that I may change my course, and serve your lordship equally with the governors of the nine (new) districts (which you have established), that will be your kindness, and it is my desire, but it is what I do not dare to hope for. I have presumed to disclose to you all my heart; your lordship will take your measures accordingly."

His attendants urged the viscount not to grant (the earl's request), urging that, having got the State, he ought not to forgive him; but the king replied, "Since the ruler of Cheng can humble himself thus, he must be able to secure the faith of his people; how can I hope to obtain the State?" With this he retired 30 *li* and granted peace. . . .

COMMENTARY TO PARAGRAPH 3

In summer, in the 6th month, the armies of Chin (marched to) relieve Cheng. . . .

. . . When they reached the [Huang] Ho, they heard that Cheng had made peace with Ch'u, and Hsün Lin-fu [commander of the Chin army of the centre] wished to return, saying, "We are too late for the relief of Cheng; what will be the use now of perilling the lives of our people? Let us wait till Ch'u has retired, and then make a movement (against Cheng)."

Shih Hui [commander of the Chin first army] approved of this view, and said, "According to what I have heard, military enterprizes should be undertaken only when there is an opportunity of prosecuting them with advantage. An enemy who cultivates, without changing, kindness in his virtue, justice in his punishments, the ordering of his government, the right regulation of different affairs, and the statutes and rules of his State, is not to be contended with; it is not against such an one that we conduct punitive expeditions. Now when the army of Ch'u punished Cheng, there was anger because of [Cheng's] double dealing, and compassion when the earl [of Cheng] humbled himself. When (Cheng) revolted from (Ch'u), (the viscount [of Ch'u]) invaded it. When it submitted, he forgave it:—his kindness and justice were established. There was the justice of punishment in the attack of revolt; there was the kindness of virtue in the gentle dealing with submission. Both these things were shown.

(Again), last year Ch'u entered the capital of Ch'en, and this year it entered that of Cheng, but its people have not complained of the fatigue and toil, nor murmured against their ruler:— showing how well its government is ordered. (Then), throughout Ch'u, when its forces are called out according to its system, its travelling merchants, husbandmen, mechanics, and stationary traders, have not their several occupations injuriously interfered with, and the footmen and chariot-men act in harmony with one another:—showing how collision is avoided in its ordering of affairs.

(Further), when Wei Go became chief minister, he selected the best statutes of Ch'u. When the army is marching, the (footmen of the) right keep on either side of the chariot, and those of the left go in quest of grass and rushes. The bearers of the standards . . . keep in advance, looking out anxiously that nothing occur for which there is not preparation. The troops in the centre are ready to act as occasion may require, while behind them is the strength of the army. The different officers move according to the signals displayed, and the ordering of the army is ready for any emergency, without special orders for it being given. Thus is Ch'u able to carry out its statutes.

(Lastly), When the viscount of Ch'u raises individuals to office, they are of the same surname with himself, chosen from among his relatives, and of other surnames, chosen from the old servants of the State. But offices are given with due respect to the necessary qualifications, and rewards are conferred according to the service performed, while at the same time additional kindness is shown to the aged. Strangers receive gifts, and enjoy various exemptions. Officers and the common people have different dresses to distinguish them. The noble have a defined standard of honour; the mean have to comport themselves according to different degrees. Thus are the rules of propriety observed in Ch'u.

Now why should we enter on a struggle with a State which thus manifests kindness, carries out justice, perfects its government, times its undertakings, follows its statutes, and observes so admirably the rules of propriety? To advance when you see advance is possible, and withdraw in face of difficulties, is a good way of moving an army; to absorb weak States, and attack those that are wilfully blind, is a good rule of war. Do you for the present order your army accordingly, and follow that maxim. There are other States that are weak and wilfully blind; why must you deal with Ch'u, (as if it were so)? . . .

Hsien Huo [assistant to Lin-fu] then said, "This counsel is not good. Chin obtained the leadership of the States by the prowess of its armies and the strength of its leaders. But now it is losing the States, and its strength cannot be spoken of. If, when the enemy is before us, we do not follow him, we cannot be said to have prowess. If we are to lose our chief place among the States, the best thing we can do is to die. Moreover, we marched out with our armies in array; if, because the enemy is strong, we retire, we shall not be men. To begin with our ruler's charge to a command in the army, and to end with not being a man:—you all may play that part, but I will not do so." Upon this with (the portion of) the army of the centre (under his command), he crossed the Ho. . . .

Han Chüeh [marshal of the host] said to Hsün Lin-fu, "Hsien Huo with his portion of the army has committed a grave offence. But you are commander-in-chief;—whose offence is it that the generals do not obey your orders? You have lost our subject State [Cheng]; and if you lose that army, your offence will indeed be heavy;—you had better advance. If the affair do not prove successful, there will be others to share the blame. Will it not be better for you to bear the blame as one of six than to bear it alone?"

The whole army then crossed the Ho. . . .

(In the meantime), Hsü-po of Ch'u drove [his subordinate] Yüeh-po, with She-shu on the right of the chariot, to flout and provoke the army of Chin. Hsü-po said, "I have heard that when an army is flouted, the driver urges his chariot, with the flag shaking, close to the entrenchments, and then returns." Yüeh-po said, "I have heard that the archer on the left discharges a strong arrow, and then takes the reins, while the charioteer descends, dusts the horses, and adjusts the martingales, and then they return." She-shu said, "I have heard that the spearman on the right enters the entrenchments, cuts off an ear, takes another man prisoner, and returns." They all three did as they had heard, and were returning, pursued by the men of Chin, who came after them like two horns, from the left, and the right. Yüeh-po shot the horses on the left, and the men on the right, so that the pursuers could not advance. He had but one arrow left, when a stag rose up before the chariot, which he shot right in the hump. Pao Kuei of Chin was right behind him, when he made She Shu [of Ch'u] take the stag, and present it to the pursuer, saying, "It is not the season of the year for such a thing, the time for presenting animals has not arrived, but I venture to offer this to feast your followers." Pao Kuei stopped the pursuit, saying, "He on the left shoots well; he on the right speaks well;—they are superior men." So they got off. . . .

[After this incident, two dissatisfied officers of Chin (Wei I and Chao Chan) wished to provoke a battle with Ch'u. Though their commanders refused permission, the two officers were nonetheless allowed to approach the Ch'u army with messages.]

. . . (Meanwhile), being afraid in the camp of Chin that the two officers would enrage the army of Ch'u, they had sent some large chariots to meet them. P'an Tang [of Ch'u], seeing at a distance the dust raised by these, sent a horseman with all speed to tell the [Chin] king that the army of Chin was advancing. The men of Ch'u (on their side), were also afraid lest the king should enter the army of Chin, and issued from their camp in order of battle. Sun Shu [of Ch'u] said, "Let us advance. It is better that we set upon them than let them set upon us. . . . Let us press on them." Accordingly he hurried on the army. The carriages dashed along, and the footmen seemed to fly; and so they fell on the army of Chin. Hsün Lin-fu [the Chin commander] did not know what he was doing, but ordered the drums to be beaten in the army, crying out. "A reward to those who first recross the river!" The army of the centre and the third army struggled for the boats, till the fingers (of those trying to get in, and that were cut off by those who had already got possession) could be taken up with both hands at once. The other armies moved to the right of the first, which alone held its place without moving. Ch'i, Minister of Works [in Ch'u], led the troops which had occupied the left front to pursue the third army . . . [The viscount of Ch'u] ordered P'an Tang . . . to act on the left by following the first army (of Chin). Hsi K'e [assistant to the commander of the first army] said, "Shall we await their onset?" Chi of Sui replied, "The army of Ch'u is in the flush of its might. If it now collect around us, we are sure to be destroyed. Our best plan is to gather in our troops, and retreat. We shall share the reproach of the other armies, but we shall save the lives of the people." He then placed his own troops in the rear of the retreating forces, and retired without being defeated. . . .

(In the flight), a chariot belonging to Chin sank in a rut, and could not proceed. A man of Ch'u told its occupant to take out the frame for weapons. After this, it advanced a little, and then the horses wanted to turn. The same man advised to take out the large flag-staff, and lay it crosswise. When this was done, the carriage got out of the hole, when its occupant turned round and said to his helper, "We are not so accustomed to fly as the soldiers of your great State!"

Chao Chan [the Chin officer] gave his two best horses to assist his elder brother and his uncle, and was going back with the others, when he met the enemy, and was unable to escape them. He abandoned his chariot therefore, and ran into a wood. The great officer Feng [of Ch'u] was driving past with his two sons, and (catching sight of Chan), he told them not to look round. They did so, however, and said, "The old great officer Chao [Chan] is behind us." He was angry with them, and made them dismount, pointing to a tree, and saying, "Let me find your bodies there." He then gave the reins to Chao Chan, who thus made his escape. The other, next day, found his sons' bodies at the spot which he had marked.

. . . When it was dusk, the army of Ch'u encamped in Pi, while what remained of that of Chin could not encamp anywhere, but kept crossing the Ho all the night, the noise of its movements never ceasing.

On [the day] Ping-ch'en, the heavy waggons of Ch'u were brought to Pi, and the viscount [of Ch'u] went on to Hengyung. P'an Tang said to him, "Why should your lordship not signalize your triumph by making a mound, and collect in it the bodies of the Chinites so as to form a grand monument? I have heard that successful battles should be shown to posterity, so that the prowess of them may not be forgotten." The viscount said, "You do not know what you are talking about . . .

"Military prowess is seen in the repression of cruelty, the calling in of the weapons of war, the preservation of the great appointment [of heaven], the firm establishment of one's merit, the giving response to the people, the harmonizing all [the States], and the enlargement of the general wealth. . . . Now I have caused the bones of the soldiers of two States to lie bleaching on the earth:—an act of cruelty; I display my weapons of war to awe the States:—thus unable to call them in. Cruel and not calling in the weapons of war, how can I preserve the great appointment? And while still the State of Chin remains, how can I firmly establish my merit? There are many things by which I oppose what the people desire, and how can they get repose from me? Without the practice of virtue, striving by force for supremacy among the States, how can I produce harmony among them? I have made my gain from the perils of others, and found my safety in their disorders;—these things are my glory, but what enlargement of the general wealth is there in them? Not one of the seven virtues belonging to military prowess attaches to me;—what have I to display to my posterity? Let us simply make here a temple for the tablets of my predecessors, and announce to them our success. The merit of military prowess does not belong to me.

(Moreover), in ancient times, when the intelligent kings punished disrespectful and disobedient States, they took the greatest criminals among them, and buried them under a mound as the greatest punishment. Thus it was that grand monuments were made for the warning of the unruly and bad. But now when it is not certain to whom the guilt can positively be ascribed, and the people have all with the utmost loyalty died in fulfilling their ruler's commands, what grounds are there for rearing a grand monument?"

After this the viscount offered sacrifice at the Ho, reared a temple for the tablets of his predecessors, announced to them the successful accomplishment of his enterprise, and returned to Ch'u.

.   .   .   .

Introduction to Ssu-ma Ch'ien

Ssu-ma Ch'ien (ca. 145-90 B.C.) was the founder of the great Chinese tradition of historical scholarship, which remained a highly influential part of his country's intellectual life until modern times. By profession he was a court astronomer (i.e., regulator of the calendar)* serving the Han emperor Wu Ti (r. 140-87 B.C.). But his chief attention was devoted to the writing of his masterwork, the *Historical Records* (*Shih Chi*), which deals with Chinese history from the earliest period down to his own day. The idea for a work of this scope—the first of its type to be attempted in China—apparently originated with the historian's father, Ssu-ma Tan, though all evidence indicates that Ssu-ma Ch'ien was its principal, if not its sole author. The complete *Historical Records* consists of some 700,000 Chinese characters—the equivalent of perhaps four thousand-page English volumes. Though of necessity treating mainly of China—the only major civilization which the Chinese then knew existed—it is in concept, if not in fact, a history of the whole world, including chapters on the principal lands and peoples beyond the Chinese frontiers.

Prior to the time of Ssu-ma Ch'ien, the *Book of History* and the several commentaries upon the *Spring and Autumn Annals*† represented the dominant Chinese approach to history. In all of these works, factual narrative is decidedly subordinate to the purpose of moral instruction. Measured against such a standard, the quality of the *Historical Records* is truly extraordinary. Ssu-ma Ch'ien did not arrange his sources to draw a moral; and he cherished a high ideal of historical accuracy. His method was to quote, almost verbatim, those ancient books and documents which he considered significant

---

* His title was actually "Grand Historian," though in view of the nature of his duties this is somewhat misleading.
† Three of these exist today: the *Tso Commentary* (*Tso Chuan*), the *Kung-yang* commentary and the *Ku-liang* commentary. The latter two consist of questions and answers about the meaning of the *Annals*. For the *Tso Commentary* see the preceding selection.

and reliable, sometimes summarizing their contents or adding connecting narrative.* He did not always attempt to resolve inconsistencies in his sources: on doubtful points he reserved judgment, merely setting down the conflicting accounts side by side. His own opinions—clearly identified as such—appear for the most part at the beginning or end of a chapter and form a minor proportion of the work as a whole.

Not all sections of the *Historical Records* are of equal value as history. For the period of the earliest Chinese dynasties Ssu-ma Ch'ien accepted the traditional—and largely mythological—accounts. For the Spring and Autumn period (722-481 B.C.) he quoted extensively from the *Tso Commentary* and another work known as *Conversations from the States (Kuo Yü)* which covers much of the same material. For the period between the end of Spring and Autumn and the unification of China (in 221 B.C.), he referred to a book called *Intrigues of the Warring States (Chan-kuo Ts'e)*. But the portion of the *Historical Records* covering the century or so before his own time is largely his own. Here he drew upon documents selected from the imperial archives, writings of contemporary authors, and reports of eyewitnesses to events. It is this portion of his work which provides the greatest detail and is most valuable as a historical source.

The organization of the *Historical Records* is startlingly different from that of comparable Western histories. The whole is divided into five sections, called "Basic Annals," "Chronological Tables," "Treatises," "Hereditary Houses," and "Memoirs." Information pertaining to a particular person or period is not all presented in one place, but scattered widely throughout the essays of the various categories. This arrangement has a logic of its own, for the *Historical Records* is meant to be read as a whole, not piecemeal.

The first section of the *Historical Records*, "Basic Annals," is a chronological account of political affairs concerning the governments of China as a whole. Unlike his successor, Pan Ku, Ssu-ma Ch'ien here included all those rulers whom he considered to have wielded *de facto* power over a large section of the country.† The second section, "Chronological Tables"—an invention of Ssu-ma Ch'ien—lists for cross-reference the dates of important events both

* The practice of quoting long passages from existing sources was followed by most Chinese historians. This was not considered plagiarism: it was a sign of respect for one's predecessors and an assurance that the transmitted information was accurate.

† Later historians criticized him for placing "usurpers" reside real emperors.

in the separate states and under the empire. The mere determination of such dates was a difficult and complex matter; for each of the former states had followed its own system of time-reckoning according to the reigns of its rulers; and most of the state chronicles were destroyed in the book-burning of 213 B.C. Ssu-ma Ch'ien was thus the first historian to provide a unified chronological framework for the whole of Chinese history.

The third section of the *Historical Records*, "Treatises," consists of essays on specialized subjects of interest to governments, such as official religious ceremonies, economic policy, the maintenance of rivers and canals. The fourth part, "Hereditary Houses," deals with the principal noble families of China; it is similar in form to the "Basic Annals" except that it concerns the separate states which preceded the unification of the empire. The last and longest section —comprising seventy of the one hundred and thirty chapters of the *Historical Records*—consists of "Memoirs" (or "Biographies"). These are collections of illustrative anecdotes about persons or groups who were important in Chinese society—not only statesmen and generals, but also poets, imperial concubines, merchants, non-Chinese tribes, and so forth. The political aspects of these people's lives, if any, are generally dealt with under "Basic Annals" or "Hereditary Houses"; the "Memoirs" record more private incidents concerning the family, writings, and character of a person, or the salient characteristics of groups.

No consistent philosophy of history is attributable to Ssu-ma Ch'ien. Especially when discussing events close to his own time, his judgments were flexible and non-dogmatic. He was not predisposed toward any of the philosophical schools of his day, as for instance Pan Ku later favored Confucianism. Ssu-ma Ch'ien's notion of causation emphasized the personalities of great men and, to a lesser extent, natural circumstances; he paid little attention to supernatural influences. His primary interest was in political, rather than social, economic, or intellectual history; in this he was at one with most historians everywhere until recent times. His most obvious departure from rational analysis was his acceptance of the traditional Chinese concept of dynastic decline. According to this theory—embodied in the *Book of History*—the mystic virtue or force (*te*) of the founder of a ruling house flows on through his descendants, gradually weakening until his final successor has forfeited the Mandate of Heaven.

Few would dispute that Ssu-ma Ch'ien ranks among the great

historians of the world. His rationalism and realism, objectivity and scholarly approach to history were unique in his own time, and admirable even by modern standards. For a thousand years after him, no one else even attempted to write a comprehensive account of Chinese history from the beginning until the present. The structure of the *Historical Records* was copied by all subsequent dynastic histories of China until modern times; and the work itself stood as a model of solid scholarship and literary excellence for Chinese historians through two millennia. Apart from the Classics themselves, few books have been so influential in China for so long a period of time—or so often committed to memory. With its citations from documents which have long since disappeared, its careful distinctions between archival materials and opinion, its clear and vivid style, the *Historical Records* is even today a highly readable work, as well as the best single extant source for early Chinese history.

LETTER OF SSU-MA CH'IEN TO
HIS FRIEND JEN AN

[In the year 99 B.C. Ssu-ma Ch'ien incurred the displeasure of the emperor Wu Ti by speaking in defense of a famous Chinese general who had surrendered to the barbarians. As a penalty for this indiscretion he was condemned to be castrated. Though it was usual in such circumstances to save one's honor by committing suicide, Ssu-ma Ch'ien resolved to suffer this punishment in order to continue his historical work. The following letter describes his feelings:]

A man has only one death. That death may be as weighty as Mount T'ai, or it may be as light as a goose feather. It all depends upon the way he uses it. . . .

It is the nature of every man to love life and hate death, to think of his relatives and look after his wife and children. Only when a man is moved by higher principles is this not so. Then there are things which he must do. . . .

Records of the Grand Historian of China, Vol. I, trans. from the *Shih Chi* of Ssu-ma Ch'ien by Burton Watson, New York and London: Columbia University Press, 1961, n.p. Reprinted by permission of Columbia University Press.

Yet the brave man does not necessarily die for honor, while even the coward may fulfill his duty. Each takes a different way to exert himself. Though I might be weak and cowardly and seek shamelessly to prolong my life, yet I know full well the difference between what course ought to be followed and what rejected. How could I bring myself to sink into the shame of ropes and bonds? If even the lowest slave and scullion maid can bear to commit suicide, why should not one like myself be able to do what has to be done? But the reason I have not refused to bear these ills and have continued to live, dwelling in vileness and disgrace without taking my leave, is that I grieve that I have things in my heart which I have not been able to express fully, and I am shamed to think that after I am gone my writings will not be known to posterity. . . .

Before I had finished my rough manuscript, I met with this calamity. It is because I regretted that it had not been completed that I submitted to the extreme penalty without rancor. When I have truly completed this work, I shall deposit it in the Famous Mountain archives. If it may be handed down to men who will appreciate it, and penetrate to the villages and great cities, then though I should suffer a thousand mutilations, what regret would I have?

Introduction to the Hsiung-nu

Prior to the advent of European sea-power in the nineteenth century, the chief external threat to China came from beyond her northwest frontiers. The steppes of western Manchuria, Inner Mongolia, and Chinese Turkestan (Sinkiang) harbored various nomadic peoples who lived in an uneasy relationship with the Chinese state. When the central government of China was weak, the nomads encroached upon the frontier provinces, raiding settlements and demanding tribute. At other times they engaged in peaceful trade across the border or served as military auxiliaries in Chinese service. These nomads were of diverse origins: they spoke a variety of languages belonging to the Mongol, Turkic, and Tungusic families. A wide gap in life-style as well as in language separated them from the Chinese. The harsh climate and barren land of the steppe demanded of its inhabitants great skill in the control and utilization of animals. The nomads relied upon their herds—sheep and cattle, horses, perhaps also camels, goats, or yaks—to supply all the necessities of life: food and clothing, shelter, fuel, and transport.

Conflicts of Chinese with nomad "barbarians" are mentioned in Chinese sources as far back as the early Chou period (began 1122 B.C.). But nomadism entered upon a new phase with the employment of cavalry in warfare. In Chou times the nomads had possessed horses, but they fought on foot, while the Chinese aristocrats fought from chariots. In the fourth century B.C. the invention of the stirrup made it possible for horsemen to shoot straight even while riding; and cavalry became a formidable military instrument. The technique of cavalry warfare reached China via the steppe; its obvious effectiveness soon forced the Chinese to adopt it for themselves. The great mobility of mounted warriors and their ability to fight on rough terrain soon put an end to chariot warfare in China. Cavalry was first employed as an integral part of a Chinese army in 320 B.C. by the ruler of Chao, a state on the northwest frontier; in the third century B.C. it became the dominant arm of all Chinese forces. Indeed, the adeptness of the mounted warriors of Ch'in— who were partly nomad in origin—contributed substantially to Ch'in's eventual victory over the other Chinese states.

But even when the Chinese learned cavalry techniques, the nomads possessed certain clear advantages in mounted warfare. Except in periods of prolonged conflict, they were far more practiced horsemen than the Chinese. Their mobility permitted them great freedom of attack and maneuver; when hard-pressed they could retreat into the steppe. While the cultivated fields and complex irrigation works of China were highly vulnerable to attack and easily damaged, the nomads carried all their wealth with them. On the other hand, Chinese civilization exerted an attractive force upon the nomads which tended to modify their style of life. The steppe offered few of the amenities available in the settled regions of China. Nomads who conquered agricultural populations soon acquired a taste for the luxuries of civilization. The collection of tribute tied them to the tributary region and thus limited their mobility; attempts to settle down and rule the subjugated peoples did

so even more. Becoming progressively less nomadic, the steppe warriors tended to lose the habits on which their original military advantage was based.

The Great Wall of China was an attempt to prevent the incursions of nomads into the empire. Completed by the First Emperor,
Shih Huang-ti, (r. 221-210 B.C.), it linked up various sections of
"Little Wall" built in the fourth and third centuries B.C. by individual border states. From the military standpoint, such walls
served to hold up the advance of hostile cavalry until the defenders
could bring their strength to bear on the point of attack. But its
value depended upon constant watchfulness and the presence of
loyal government troops on the frontiers. In periods of disorder
within China, when the central power broke down, the Great Wall
was virtually useless as a factor in Chinese defense.

The line of the Great Wall marked the approximate natural
limits of both Chinese and nomad expansion. Beyond that line, Chinese settlement and political control were subject to the law of
diminishing returns; within it, nomad intruders tended to become
assimilated to Chinese society. Whereas in China a dense agricultural population produced high yields per unit of land, the steppe
could support only a sparse population with a pastoral or semi-pas-
toral economy. As the well-watered lands of China proper faded
away into the sparsely watered steppe, Chinese-style agriculture became less and less feasible, and dependence upon animals progressively greater. Chinese and nomadic social forms diverged corre-
spondingly. Chinese agriculture required a hierarchy of educated
officials and bureaucrats to keep accounts, regulate water supply to
the fields, and direct the maintenance of canals and embankments.
Conversely, conditions of life on the steppe produced a relatively
egalitarian "barbarian" society. The characteristic social order of
China could not adequately be transported into the steppe, nor that
of the steppe into China. No vital economic interests drew the two
regions together. Commerce between them was normally restricted
to a few luxury products exchanged between rulers: fine horses,
hides, precious stones from the nomads; bolts of silk cloth from the
Chinese.

The traditional view of China's relations with the steppe is one
of civilized Chinese being forced to defend themselves against barbarian aggressiveness. No doubt this was sometimes the case. But
Ssu-ma Ch'ien's account makes evident that the problem for China
was not so much nomad incursions as the questionable loyalty of

Chinese border commanders. The mere existence of the nomads provided Chinese generals in the frontier provinces with an alternative to submission to the emperor of China. In times when the central government was weak, such men were tempted to set up their own semi-independent border states in alliance with nomad leaders. The number of nomads in relation to Chinese was never large—nor could it be, given the conditions of steppe life. But the centrifugal tendency among border commanders was a distinct threat to Chinese unity. Throughout the history of China, successful defense of the northwest frontiers has always depended upon the ability of the central government to control its own subordinates.

In Ch'in and Han times the principal nomad threat to China came from the Hsiung-nu—groups of Turkic-speaking peoples who ranged over the steppe country north of the great bend of the Yellow River. These scattered tribes formed a confederation at about the same time as the unification of China, and their leader dealt on almost equal terms with the Chinese emperor. The essay on the Hsiung-nu by Ssu-ma Ch'ien is the earliest known analysis of China's relations with the steppe. By means of (presumably imaginary) conversations between nomad leaders and the Chinese envoys, he makes clear the mutual exclusiveness of Chinese and nomad culture and the unprofitability of Chinese advance into the steppe. He asserts a clear cause-and-effect relationship between nomad incursions and weak Chinese governments. Indeed, the dynamics of China's steppe relations, as described by Ssu-ma Ch'ien, maintained itself with little change until modern times. Though strong Chinese emperors sometimes advanced into Central Asia, their purpose was rather to secure bases against the nomads than to annex territory. Conversely, the nomads were unable permanently to rule China except by confirming the established social structure, with all that this involved in terms of gentry dominance.

This ancient pattern was changed only in the eighteenth century with the advent of effective hand guns for infantrymen. The horse thereby became obsolete as an instrument of war, and the nomads lost their military importance. In the nineteenth century the building of railroads made commercial agriculture profitable on the steppe. Chinese farmers poured into Manchuria and (to a lesser extent) Inner Mongolia; and nomadism as a way of life was doomed. As the navies of predatory European powers descended upon China in the nineteenth century, the sea replaced the land frontier as the principal focus of China's foreign policy.

FROM THE HISTORICAL RECORDS (SHIH CHI) OF SSU-MA CH'IEN

The Account of the Hsiung-nu/Chapter 110

The ancestor of the Hsiung-nu was a descendant of the rulers of the Hsia dynasty[1] by the name of Ch'un-wei. As early as the time of Emperors Yao and Shun[2] and before, we hear of these people, known as Mountain Barbarians, Hsien-yün or Hun-chu, living in the region of the northern barbarians and wandering from place to place pasturing their animals. The animals they raise consist mainly of horses, cows, and sheep, but include such rare beasts as camels, asses, mules, and the wild horses known as *t'ao-t'u* and *t'o-chi*. They move about in search of water and pasture and have no walled cities or fixed dwellings, nor do they engage in any kind of agriculture. Their lands, however, are divided into regions under the control of various leaders. They have no writing, and even promises and agreements are only verbal. The little boys start out by learning to ride sheep and shoot birds and rats with a bow and arrow, and when they get a little older they shoot foxes and hares, which are used for food. Thus all the young men are able to use a bow and act as armed cavalry in time of war. It is their custom to herd their flocks in times of peace and make their living by hunting, but in periods of crisis they take up arms and go off on plundering and marauding expeditions. This seems to be their inborn nature. For long-range weapons they use bows and arrows, and swords and spears at close range. If the battle is going well for them they will advance, but if not, they will retreat, for they do not consider it a disgrace to run away. Their only con-

Records of the Grand Historian of China, Vol. II, trans. from the *Shih Chi* of Ssu-ma Ch'ien by Burton Watson, New York and London: Columbia University Press, 1961, pp. 155-6, 160-63, 165-72. Reprinted by permission of Columbia University Press.

1. Traditional dates: 2205-1766 B.C.
2. Yao and Shun were the mythological sage-kings who supposedly preceded the Hsia dynasty.

cern is self-advantage, and they know nothing of propriety or righteousness.[3]

From the chiefs of the tribe on down, everyone eats the meat of the domestic animals and wears clothes of hide or wraps made of felt or fur. The young men eat the richest and best food, while the old get what is left over, since the tribe honors those who are young and strong and despises the weak and aged. On the death of his father, a son will marry his stepmother, and when brothers die, the remaining brothers will take the widows for their own wives. They have no polite names[4] but only personal names, and they observe no taboos in the use of personal names.

[An account follows of China's relations with the barbarians in Hsia, Shang, and Chou times.]

Finally Ch'in overthrew the other six states, and the First Emperor of the Ch'in dispatched Meng T'ien[5] to lead a force of a hundred thousand men north to attack the barbarians. He seized control of all the lands south of the Yellow River[6] and established border defenses along the river, constructing forty-four walled district cities overlooking the river and manning them with convict laborers transported to the border for garrison duty. He also built the Direct Road from Chiu-yüan to Yün-yang.[7] Thus he utilized the natural mountain barriers to establish the border defenses, scooping out the valleys and constructing ramparts and building installations at other points where they were needed. The whole line of defenses stretched over ten thousand li[8] from Lin-t'ao to Liao-tung[9] and even ex-

3. The Chinese regarded propriety (li) and righteousness (i)—i.e. civilized behavior—as the fundamental difference between themselves and barbarians.

4. I.e., names used to avoid the appearance of over-familiarity.

5. His principal general.

6. I.e., south of the great northern loop of the Yellow River, which encloses the Ordos steppe—a region not normally part of Chinese territory.

7. This road extended along the northern frontier, from the middle of the Yellow River loop eastward to a point north of modern Peking.

8. The exact length of the ancient li is uncertain; probably it was equivalent to about one-third of a mile. Under the Ch'in dynasty the Great Wall extended for some 1400 miles (or ca. 4200 li).

9. I.e., from Kansu to eastern Manchuria.

tended across the Yellow River and through Yang-shan and Pei-chia.

At this time the Eastern Barbarians[10] were very powerful and the Yüeh-chih[11] were likewise flourishing. The *Shan-yü*[12] or chieftain of the Hsiung-nu was named T'ou-man. T'ou-man, unable to hold out against the Ch'in forces, had withdrawn to the far north, where he lived with his subjects for over ten years. After Meng T'ien died and the feudal lords revolted against the Ch'in, plunging China into a period of strife and turmoil, the convicts which the Ch'in had sent to the northern border to garrison the area all returned to their homes. The Hsiung-nu, the pressure against them relaxed, once again began to infiltrate south of the bend of the Yellow River until they had established themselves along the old border of China.

[Ssu-ma Ch'ien now relates that T'ou-man wished to set up a younger son as heir; but through a ruse the eldest son, Mo-tun, had his father killed.]

At this time the Eastern Barbarians were very powerful and, hearing that Mo-tun had killed his father and made himself leader, they sent an envoy to ask if they could have T'ou-man's famous horse that could run a thousand *li* in one day. Mo-tun consulted his ministers, but they all replied, "The thousand-*li* horse is one of the treasures of the Hsiung-nu people. You should not give it away!"

"When a neighboring country asks for it, why should I begrudge them one horse?" he said, and sent them the thousand-*li* horse.

After a while the Eastern Barbarians, supposing that Mo-tun was afraid of them, sent an envoy to ask for one of Mo-tun's consorts. Again Mo-tun questioned his ministers, and they replied in a rage. "The Eastern Barbarians are unreasoning beasts

10. I.e., the nomads of eastern Manchuria, the Tunghu.
11. The Yüeh-chih were nomad tribes who apparently spoke an Indo-European language. Until driven out by the Hsiung-nu, they occupied territories in Kansu.
12. *Shan-yü* means "Great Son of Heaven"—a close approximation to the title of the emperor of China.

to come and request one of the *Shan-yü's* consorts. We beg to attack them!"

But Mo-tun replied, "If it is for a neighboring country, why should I begrudge them one woman?" and he sent his favorite consort to the Eastern Barbarians.

With this the ruler of the Eastern Barbarians grew more and more bold and arrogant, invading the lands to the west. Between his territory and that of the Hsiung-nu was an area of over a thousand *li* of uninhabited land; the two peoples made their homes on either side of this wasteland.[13] The ruler of the Eastern Barbarians sent an envoy to Mo-tun saying, "The Hsiung-nu have no way of using this stretch of wasteland which lies between my border and yours. I would like to take possession of it!"

When Mo-tun consulted his ministers, some of them said, "Since the land is of no use you might as well give it to him," while others said, "No, you must not give it away!"

Mo-tun flew into a rage. "Land is the basis of the nation!" he said. "Why should I give it away?" And he executed all the ministers who had advised him to do so.[14]

Then he mounted his horse and set off to attack the Eastern Barbarians, circulating an order throughout his domain that anyone who was slow to follow would be executed. The Eastern Barbarians had up until this time despised Mo-tun and made no preparations for their defense; when Mo-tun and his soldiers arrived, they inflicted a crushing defeat, killing the ruler of the Eastern Barbarians, taking prisoner his subjects, and seizing their domestic animals. Then he returned and rode west, attacking and routing the Yüeh-chih,[11] and annexed the lands of the ruler of Lou-fan and the ruler of Po-yang south of the Yellow River. Thus he recovered possession of all the lands which the Ch'in general Meng T'ien had taken away from the Hsiung-nu; the border between his territory and that of the Han empire now followed the old line of defenses south of the Yellow River, and

13. The Gobi Desert.
14. This part of the account is probably taken from current tradition among the Hsiung-nu. Mo-tun's alleged statement that "land is the basis of the nation" presumably refers to the fact that each nomad group had its own territory within which it migrated.

from there he marched into the Ch'ao-na and Fu-shih districts and then invaded Yen and Tai.[15]

At this time the Han forces were stalemated in battle with the armies of Hsiang Yü,[16] and China was exhausted by warfare. Thus Mo-tun was able to strengthen his position, massing a force of over three hundred thousand skilled crossbowmen.

[A description follows of the Hsiung-nu system of government.]

Shortly after the period described above, Mo-tun launched a series of campaigns to the north, conquering the tribes of Hun-yü, Ch'ü-she, Ting-ling, Ko-k'un, and Hsin-li. Thus the nobles and high ministers of the Hsiung-nu were all won over by Mo-tun, considering him a truly worthy leader.

At this time Kao-tsu, the founder of the Han,[17] had just succeeded in winning control of the empire and had transferred Hsin, the former king of Hann,[18] to the rulership of Tai,[19] with his capital at Ma-i. The Hsiung-nu surrounded Ma-i and attacked the city in great force, whereupon Hann Hsin surrendered to them.[20] With Hann Hsin on their side, they then proceeded to lead their troops south across Mount Chü-chu and attack T'ai-yüan,[21] marching as far as the city of Chin-yang. Emperor Kao-tsu led an army in person to attack them, but it was winter and he encountered such cold and heavy snow that two or three out of every ten of his men lost their fingers from frostbite. Mo-tun feigned a retreat to lure the Han soldiers on to an attack. When they came after him in pursuit, he concealed

15. Yen and Tai were south of the Great Wall (in Hopei).
16. Hsiang Yü was one of the principal rebels to contend for the throne after the death of the First Emperor, Shih Huang-ti, in 210 B.C. Hsiang was subsequently defeated by Liu Pang (later the Emperor Kao-tsu), founder of the Han dynasty, who had once been one of his generals.
17. Kao-tsu reigned 206-195 B.C.
18. Hann Hsin had been a companion of Kao-tsu in the wars leading to the foundation of the Han dynasty. Hann (in Honan) was formerly one of the smaller Chinese states.
19. Tai was a region in the far north bordering on the lands of the Hsiung-nu. Formerly held by the frontier state of Chao, it was disputed for centuries between herdsmen from Inner Asia and cultivators from China, though it did not provide the optimum environment for either way of life.
20. In 200 B.C.
21. T'ai-yüan was in central Shansi—a long way within the Chinese borders.

all of his best troops and left only his weakest and puniest men to be observed by the Han scouts. With this the entire Han force, supplemented by three hundred and twenty thousand infantry, rushed north to pursue him; Kao-tsu led the way, advancing as far as the city of P'ing-ch'eng.[22]

Before the infantry had had a chance to arrive, however, Mo-tun swooped down with four hundred thousand of his best cavalry, surrounded Kao-tsu on White Peak, and held him there for seven days. The Han forces within the encirclement had no way of receiving aid or provisions from their comrades outside, since the Hsiung-nu cavalry surrounded them on all sides, with white horses on the west side, greenish horses on the east, black horses on the north, and red ones on the south.[23]

Kao-tsu sent an envoy in secret to Mo-tun's consort, presenting her with generous gifts, whereupon she spoke to Mo-tun, saying, "Why should the rulers of these two nations make such trouble for each other? Even if you gained possession of the Han lands, you could never occupy them. And the ruler of the Han may have his guardian deities as well as you. I beg you to consider the matter well!"

Mo-tun had previously arranged for the troops of Wang Huang and Chao Li, two of Hann Hsin's generals, to meet with him, but though the appointed time had come, they failed to appear and he began to suspect that they were plotting with the Han forces. He therefore decided to listen to his consort's advice and withdrew his forces from one corner of the encirclement. Kao-tsu ordered his men to load their crossbows with arrows and hold them in readiness pointed toward the outside. These preparations completed, they marched straight out of the encirclement and finally joined up with the rest of the army.

Mo-tun eventually withdrew his men and went away, and Kao-tsu likewise retreated and abandoned the campaign, dispatching Liu Ching to conclude a peace treaty with the Hsiung-nu instead.

22. Near the Great Wall.
23. The Chinese considered these four colors as symbolic of the four directions of the compass. This account suggests that the Hsiung-nu held similar beliefs.

After this Hann Hsin became a general for the Hsiung-nu, and Chao Li and Wang Huang violated the peace treaty by invading and plundering Tai and Yün-chung. Shortly afterwards, Ch'en Hsi[24] revolted and joined with Hann Hsin in a plot to attack Tai. Kao-tsu dispatched Fan K'uai to go and attack them; he recovered possession of the provinces and districts of Tai, Yen-men, and Yün-chung, but did not venture beyond the frontier.[25]

At this time a number of Han generals had gone over to the side of the Hsiung-nu, and for this reason Mo-tun was constantly plundering the region of Tai and causing the Han great worry. Kao-tsu therefore dispatched Liu Ching to present a princess of the imperial family to the *Shan-yü* to be his consort.[26] The Han agreed to send a gift of specified quantities of silk floss and cloth, grain, and other food stuffs each year, and the two nations were to live in peace and brotherhood. After this Mo-tun raided the frontier less often than before. Later Lu Wan, the king of Yen,[27] revolted and led his party of several thousand followers across the border to surrender to the Hsiung-nu; they roamed back and forth in the region from Shang-ku[28] to the east, causing considerable disturbance.

After Emperor Kao-tsu passed away, Emperor Hui and Empress Lü in turn ruled the country.[29] At this time the Han had just come to power and the Hsiung-nu, unimpressed by its strength, were behaving with great arrogance. Mo-tun even sent an insulting letter to Empress Lü.[30] She wanted to launch a campaign against him, but her generals reminded her that "even Emperor Kao-tsu, with all his wisdom and bravery, encountered great difficulty at P'ing-ch'eng," and she was finally persuaded

24. A Chinese vassal.
25. I.e., beyond the Great Wall.
26. I.e., as a condition of peace.
27. Yen was a region of southern Manchuria and extreme northwestern China.
28. Shang-ku was a place along the Great Wall (in Hopei).
29. Kao-tsu died in 195 B.C. and Empress Lü, as mother of the heir to the throne (who was a minor), became the real ruler of China.
30. Mo-tun proposed marriage—which was considered presumptuous of a barbarian.

to give up the idea and resume friendly relations with the Hsiung-nu.

When Emperor Wen came to the throne[31] he renewed the peace treaty with the Hsiung-nu. In the fifth month of the third year of his reign [177 B.C.], however, the Hsiung-nu Wise King of the Right[32] invaded the region south of the Yellow River, plundering the loyal barbarians of Shang Province,[33] who had been appointed by the Han to guard the frontier, and murdering and carrying off a number of the inhabitants. Emperor Wen ordered the chancellor Kuan Ying to lead a force of eighty-five thousand carriages and cavalry to Kao-nu, where they attacked the Wise King of the Right. The latter fled beyond the frontier. The emperor in person visited T'ai-yüan,[34] at which time the king of Chi-pei revolted. When the emperor returned to the capital he disbanded the army which Kuan Ying had used in the attack on the barbarians.

The following year the *Shan-yü* sent a letter to the Han court which read:

The great *Shan-yü* whom Heaven has set up respectfully inquires of the emperor's health. Formerly the emperor broached the question of a peace alliance, and I was most happy to comply with the intentions expressed in his letter. Certain of the Han border officials, however, imposed upon and insulted the Wise King of the Right, and as a result he heeded the counsel of Hou-i, Lu-hou, Nan-chih, and others of his generals and, without asking my permission, engaged in a skirmish with the Han officials, thus violating the pact between the rulers of our two nations and rupturing the bonds of brotherhood that joined us. The emperor has twice sent letters complaining of this situation and I have in turn dispatched an envoy with my answer, but my envoy has not been allowed to return, nor has any envoy come from the Han. As a result, the Han has broken off peaceful relations and our two neighboring countries are no longer bound in alliance.

Because of the violation of the pact committed by the petty offi-

31. Emperor Wen reigned 180-157 B.C.
32. The Wise King of the Right and Wise King of the Left were the Shan-yü's highest-ranking subordinates.
33. Shang province was in the Ordos region, within the northern loop of the Yellow River.
34. In Shang province.

cials, and the subsequent events, I have punished the Wise King of
the Right by sending him west to search out the Yüeh-chih people
and attack them. Through the aid of Heaven, the excellence of his
fighting men, and the strength of his horses, he has succeeded in
wiping out the Yüeh-chih, slaughtering or forcing to submission
every member of the tribe. In addition he has conquered the Lou-
lan, Wu-sun, and Hu-chieh tribes, as well as the twenty-six states
nearby, so that all of them have become a part of the Hsiung-nu
nation. All the people who live by drawing the bow are now united
into one family and the entire region of the north is at peace.

Thus I wish now to lay down my weapons, rest my soldiers, and
turn my horses to pasture; to forget the recent affair and restore
our old pact, that the peoples of the border may have peace such as
they enjoyed in former times, that the young may grow to manhood, the old live out their lives in security, and generation after
generation enjoy peace and comfort.

However, I do not as yet know the intentions of the emperor.
Therefore I have dispatched my palace attendant Hsi-hu-ch'ien to
bear this letter. At the same time I beg to present one camel, two
riding horses, and eight carriage horses. If the emperor does not
wish the Hsiung-nu to approach his frontier, then he should order
the officials and people along the border to withdraw a good distance back from the frontier. When my envoy has arrived and delivered this, I trust that he will be sent back to me.

The envoy bearing the letter arrived in the region of Hsin-
wang during the sixth month. When it was delivered to the emperor, he began deliberations with his ministers as to whether it
was better to attack or make peace. The high officials all stated,
"Since the *Shan-yü* has just conquered the Yüeh-chih and is riding on a wave of victory, he cannot be attacked. Moreover, even
if we were to seize the Hsiung-nu lands, they are all swamps and
saline wastes, not fit for habitation. It would be far better to
make peace."

The emperor agreed with their opinion and in the sixth year
of the former part of his reign [174 B.C.] he sent an envoy to
the Hsiung-nu with a letter which read as follows:

The emperor respectfully inquires about the health of the great
Shan-yü. Your palace attendant Hsi-hu-ch'ien has brought us a
letter which states:

[Here the contents of the Shan-yü's letter are repeated.]

We heartily approve these words. This indeed is the way the sage rulers of antiquity would have spoken.

The Han has made a pact of brotherhood with the Hsiung-nu, and for this reason we have sent generous gifts to you. Any violations of the pact or ruptures of the bonds of brotherhood have been the work of the Hsiung-nu. However, as there has been an amnesty since the affair of the Wise King of the Right occurred,[35] you need not punish him too severely. If your intentions are really those expressed in your letter, and if you will make them clearly known to your various officials so that they will henceforth act in good faith and commit no more violations of the pact, then we are prepared to honor the terms of your letter.

Your envoy tells us that you have led your troops in person to attack the other barbarian nations and have won merit, suffering great hardship on the field of battle. We therefore send you from our own wardrobe an embroidered robe lined with patterned damask, an embroidered and lined underrobe, and a brocaded coat, one each; one comb; one sash with gold ornaments; one gold-ornamented leather belt; ten rolls of embroidery; thirty rolls of brocade; and forty rolls each of heavy red silk and light green silk, which shall be delivered to you by our palace counselor I and master of guests Chien.

Shortly after this, Mo-tun died and his son Chi-chu was set up with the title of Old *Shan-yü*. When Chi-chu became *Shan-yü*, Emperor Wen sent a princess of the imperial family to be his consort, dispatching a eunuch from Yen named Chung-hsing Shuo[36] to accompany her as her tutor. Chung-hsing Shuo did not wish to undertake the mission, but the Han officials forced him to do so. "My going will bring nothing but trouble to the Han!" he warned them.

After Chung-hsing Shuo reached his destination, he went over to the side of the *Shan-yü*, who treated him with the greatest favor.

35. Chinese sources fail to mention any amnesty actually occurring at this time. The emperor's statement is evidently an attempt to assert Chinese sovereignty over the Hsiung-nu.
36. As a native of the old border kingdom of Yen, this eunuch was presumably familiar with barbarian ways.

The Hsiung-nu had always had a liking for Han silks and food stuffs, but Chung-hsing Shuo told them,[37] "All the multitudes of the Hsiung-nu nation would not amount to one province in the Han empire. The strength of the Hsiung-nu lies in the very fact that their food and clothing are different from those of the Chinese, and they are therefore not dependent upon the Han for anything. Now the *Shan-yü* has this fondness for Chinese things and is trying to change the Hsiung-nu customs. Thus, although the Han sends no more than a fifth of its goods here, it will in the end succeed in winning over the whole Hsiung-nu nation. From now on, when you get any of the Han silks, put them on and try riding around on your horses through the brush and brambles! In no time your robes and leggings will be torn to shreds and everyone will be able to see that silks are no match for the utility and excellence of felt or leather garments. Likewise, when you get any of the Han foodstuffs, throw them away so that the people can see that they are not as practical or as tasty as milk and kumiss!"[38]

He also taught the *Shan-yü's* aides how to make an itemized accounting of the number of persons and domestic animals in the country.

The Han letters addressed to the *Shan-yü* were always written on wooden tablets one foot and one inch in length and began, "The emperor respectfully inquires about the health of the great *Shan-yü* of the Hsiung-nu. We send you the following articles, etc., etc." Chung-hsing Shuo, however, instructed the *Shan-yü* to use in replying to the Han a tablet measuring one foot two inches, decorated with broad stamps and great long seals, and worded in the following extravagant manner: "The great *Shan-yü* of the Hsiung-nu, born of Heaven and Earth and ordained by the sun and moon, respectfully inquires about the health of the Han emperor. We send you the following articles, etc., etc."

37. The following speeches attributed to Chung-hsing Shuo probably represent current knowledge in China about the differences between the Chinese and the Hsiung-nu.

38. Even in the present century the use of milk and milk products—which the Chinese find intolerable—is a point of difference between the Chinese and their neighbors of the steppe.

When one of the Han envoys to the Hsiung-nu remarked scornfully that Hsiung-nu custom showed no respect for the aged, Chung-hsing Shuo began to berate him. "According to Han custom," he said, "when the young men are called into military service and sent off with the army to garrison the frontier, do not their old parents at home voluntarily give up their warm clothing and tasty food so that there will be enough to provide for the troops?"

"Yes, they do," admitted the Han envoy.

"The Hsiung-nu make it clear that warfare is their business. And since the old and the weak are not capable of fighting, the best food and drink are naturally allotted to the young men in the prime of life. So the young men are willing to fight for the defense of the nation, and both fathers and sons are able to live out their lives in security. How can you say that the Hsiung-nu despise the aged?"

"But among the Hsiung-nu," the envoy continued, "fathers and sons sleep together in the same tent. And when a father dies, the sons marry their own stepmothers, and when brothers die, their remaining brothers marry their widows! These people know nothing of the elegance of hats and girdles, nor of the rituals of the court!"

"According to Hsiung-nu custom," replied Chung-hsing Shuo, "the people eat the flesh of their domestic animals, drink their milk, and wear their hides, while the animals graze from place to place, searching for pasture and water. Therefore, in wartime the men practice riding and shooting, while in times of peace they enjoy themselves and have nothing to do. Their laws are simple and easy to carry out; the relation between ruler and subject is relaxed and intimate, so that the governing of the whole nation is no more complicated than the governing of one person. The reason that sons marry their stepmothers and brothers marry their widowed sisters-in-law is simply that they hate to see the clan die out. Therefore, although the Hsiung-nu encounter times of turmoil, the ruling families always manage to stand firm. In China, on the other hand, though a man would never dream of marrying his stepmother or his brother's widow, yet the members of the same family drift so far apart that they end

up murdering each other! This is precisely why so many
changes of dynasty have come about in China! Moreover, among
the Chinese, as etiquette and the sense of duty decay, enmity
arises between the rulers and the ruled, while the excessive
building of houses and dwellings exhausts the strength and resources of the nation. Men try to get their food and clothing by
farming and raising silkworms and to insure their safety by
building walls and fortifications. Therefore, although danger
threatens, the Chinese people are given no training in aggressive
warfare, while in times of stability they must still wear themselves out trying to make a living. Pooh! You people in your
mud huts—you talk too much! Enough of this blabbering and
mouthing! Just because you wear hats, what does that make
you?"

After this, whenever the Han envoys would try to launch into
any sermons or orations, Chung-hsing Shuo would cut them off
at once. "Not so much talk from the Han envoys! Just make sure
that the silks and grainstuffs you bring to the Hsiung-nu are of
the right measure and quality, that's all. What's the need for
talking? If the goods you deliver are up to measure and of good
quality, all right. But if there is any deficiency or the quality is
no good, then when the autumn harvest comes we will take our
horses and trample all over your crops!"

Day and night he instructed the *Shan-yü* on how to maneuver
into a more advantageous position.

.   .   .   .

Introduction to Pan Ku

Pan Ku (A.D. 32-92) ranks with Ssu-ma Ch'ien as one of the two
great Chinese historians of Han times. He was the principal author
of a work in one hundred chapters covering the period from the
founding of the Han dynasty (206 B.C.) through the death of the
usurper, Wang Mang (A.D. 23). This *History of the Former Han*

Dynasty (Han Shu) was actually begun by his father, Pan Piao, who had intended only to write a history of China from the point where Ssu-ma Ch'ien left off (*ca.* 100 B.C.). Pan Piao gathered materials for this work and in fact completed a number of chapters; but the project was incomplete at his death. Pan Ku then resolved to extend its scope by including the entire Former Han period, utilizing his father's previous work but adding a great deal of his own. Knowledge of Pan Ku's activities eventually reached the reigning emperor, Hsien-tsung, who—after some investigation—appointed him court historiographer, a position giving access to the imperial archives.

The work of Pan Ku differs from that of Ssu-ma Ch'ien in making no attempt at universality: it concerns itself only with the events of a single imperial dynasty. As such, it provided the model for Chinese official histories down to the twentieth century. The period from the foundation to the fall of a ruling house was believed to be a natural historical unit. In theory, each dynasty repeated essentially the same pattern as its predecessors and successors: there was no concept of continuous progression. This cyclic interpretation naturally stressed the repetitive factors in the history of any period at the expense of possibly unique elements; in essence it continued the ancient Chinese scheme of gradual decline from the founder to the final ruler of a dynasty. It likewise presupposed the Confucian notion that personal character is the chief moving force behind the unfolding of events.

To be sure, this periodization has some degree of validity. The founder of a ruling dynasty comes to power against formidable odds, and is necessarily a man of considerable ability and forcefulness. His successors, born to high position, tend to be corrupted by the luxury and intrigue of court life. The group surrounding the dynastic founder is usually small; most of its opponents have been eliminated or discredited; and various vested interests—with their claims upon the treasury—have been swept away. A period of order and prosperity ensues. But as time passes the ruling class becomes larger, and its mode of life ever more luxurious. The government incurs enormous expenses for great building projects and military expeditions. Financial difficulties inevitably follow. The tax burden upon the peasantry is increased, resulting in widespread discontent. Irrigation works fall into disrepair from lack of funds, causing floods and famines which lead to banditry. Frontier defenses are neglected, permitting barbarian incursions; and the armies of the bor-

dynastic cycle

der provinces renounce their loyalty to the central power. Rivals to
the imperial house arise: the result is a period of war and disorder.
The dynasty finally falls, and the whole cycle begins again.

Pan Ku followed the general pattern established by Ssu-ma
Ch'ien both in his method of procedure and his organization of materials. As was common practice among Chinese historians, he copied
extensively from his predecessors,* especially from Ssu-ma Ch'ien.
He also relied heavily upon documentary materials from the imperial archives. More than half of the *History of the Former Han
Dynasty* consists either of direct quotation from such documents or
skillful paraphrases. Like Ssu-ma Ch'ien also, he divided his work
into "Annals," "Chronological Tables," "Treatises," and "Memoirs." "Hereditary Houses" were omitted, since he was not concerned with the period before the unification of China; and his
"Annals" were reserved for those emperors whom the Confucian
scholars considered legitimate. Unlike Ssu-ma Ch'ien, Pan Ku was
a firm adherent of the orthodox Confucianism of his day. But he
upheld strict standards of historical accuracy and selected his documents to present a balanced study of his subjects. He was likewise
a literary artist of the first rank, whose prose as well as scholarship
has been lavishly admired by successive generations of educated
Chinese. Even today the *History of the Former Han Dynasty* is an
impressive work; and it remains the chief surviving primary source
for the latter half of its period through the reign of Wang Mang.

* As noted above ("Introduction to Ssu-ma Ch'ien," p. 133, n. *), this practice was considered perfectly normal and even admirable.

Introduction to Wang Mang

The reign of Wang Mang (A.D. 9-23) constitutes an extraordinary
episode in Chinese history—the first attempt of an emperor of
China to rule according to strictly Confucian ideals. Government
service had long been regarded as the proper culmination of a Confucian education: it signified the application of ethical values on the
widest possible scale. Confucius himself had set the example of

earnestly seeking political office; and his followers very commonly pursued government careers as the best means of realizing their principles. By the time of the Former Han dynasty (206 B.C.-A.D. 9), Confucianism was unquestionably the prevailing philosophy among the Chinese gentry; and certain of the emperors were notably influenced by it. But until the reign of Wang Mang, there had as yet been no example of an actual Confucian scholar on the throne.

Wang Mang became the beneficiary of a characteristic Confucian idea—that a virtuous man must honor his parents and favor his relatives. In Han times even the emperor was supposed to honor this principle, at least to some degree, in filling the great offices of state. Because an emperor's own brothers and paternal uncles—as potential rivals for the throne itself—were too dangerous to be trusted with great power, the practice developed of appointing the male relatives of the emperor's mother and of his wife to high government posts. Moreover, the respect for one's mother which was expected of a filial son gave to a widowed empress a position of enormous political influence. It was Wang Mang's good fortune to be the nephew of such a woman, the Empress Dowager Yüan, whose brothers held the chief offices of government during the reign of her son, Emperor Ch'eng (r. 33-7 B.C.).

Wang Mang managed his original rise to eminence by cleverly playing upon the Confucian sympathies of the principal class in Chinese society—the educated gentry. As a young man he carefully practiced the Confucian virtues in order to ingratiate himself with his powerful uncles. Appointed prime minister on their recommendation, he demonstrated a fine mastery of the arts of intrigue and propaganda, privately arranging the dismissal of all his chief rivals while at the same time winning a hitherto unprecedented public reputation. Wang Mang carried to a formerly unheard-of degree the Confucian principle of "declining and yielding," i.e. yielding precedence to others. By refusing most of the honors proffered him, he succeeded in creating an image of himself as the consummately modest Confucian gentleman. His great abilities were universally recognized; he was compared to Confucius' hero, the Duke of Chou. His eventual assumption of the imperial dignity was aided by an unusual concatenation of circumstances. Various occult popular beliefs enhanced his position: an old prophecy that the Han dynasty would end after two hundred and ten years; the notion that the imminent beginning of a new dynasty is heralded by supernatural portents (which duly appeared); the theory of the

Five Elements,* according to which the element identified with the Wang family (earth) was due to follow the element associated with the Han dynasty (fire) as the dominant principle of the universe. When Emperor P'ing became the third Han ruler in a row to die without direct heirs, popular opinion was overwhelmingly in favor of Wang Mang's taking his place.

Although he utilized Confucianism as a means to power, Wang Mang was also an accomplished scholar who genuinely believed in the efficacy of Confucian doctrine. As emperor, he avidly searched ancient texts for suitable classical precedents. The acid test of any proposal was whether it had been practiced in antiquity or recommended by recognized Confucian worthies. No doubt Confucius or Mencius would have disapproved of this exaggerated reverence for tradition; but Wang Mang thereby typified contemporary modes of thought. Confucianism in Han times was no longer the straightforward, pragmatic doctrine of its founders. It had become a vast corpus of precedents interpreted with extreme literalness. The rationalistic tendencies in early Confucianism—Confucius' own refusal to speak about spirits, or Hsün Tzu's attacks on superstition—were largely ignored by the Han scholars. Wang Mang, like most Confucians of his time, relied upon astrology and portents, practiced magic, and accepted a notion of fate which depended upon the succession of the "Five Elements."

Wang Mang's ultimate failure as emperor—he was overthrown by a military rebellion—was not unrelated to this concept of Confucianism. He instituted allegedly Confucian measures with little regard for practicality—i.e. the "well-field" system of land tenure which supposedly had prevailed in the early Chou period. At the same time, some of his supposed Confucianism was little more than a veneer concealing quite un-Confucian purposes. His devaluation of the currency was a clear case of sacrificing popular welfare to his desire for funds. His establishment of government monopolies was another. Wang Mang's colossal ego prompted him to undertake

* The Five Elements were wood, fire, earth, metal, and water. According to the theory most widely accepted in Wang Mang's lifetime, each of these elements produces its successor by a kind of natural process: thus wood produces fire, which produces earth (ashes), which produces metal (in mines), which produces (i.e. melts into) water (liquid), which produces (nourishes) wood (i.e. vegetation). Fire was the element of the Han dynasty because Kao-tsu, its founder, was supposedly descended from a mythical figure of antiquity known as the Red Lord. The Wang clan was believed to possess the power of earth because of the family's reputed descent from the Yellow Emperor (yellow being the color of earth).

grandiose and expensive projects—imperial tours, military expeditions, the construction of temples to his ancestors—which were in direct contradiction to the Confucian principle that government exists for the sake of the governed. Like other dictators before and since, he trusted nobody, refused to delegate responsibility, sacrificed his family to his ambition, and punished those who told him unpleasant truths. The result was a calamitous administrative breakdown with a concomitant loss to the emperor's once phenomenal popularity and reputation.

Even so, his errors were probably no worse than those committed by other emperors who suffered a better fate. Wang Mang was plagued by an extraordinary series of disasters not of his own making—droughts, pestilences, and floods. His reign coincided with the final breakdown of the irrigation system in the region around the capital, Ch'ang-an. Wang Mang's demoralized government was unable to cope with the resultant food scarcity and famine. To the common people, such misfortunes clearly demonstrated that Wang Mang had lost (or had never held) the Mandate of Heaven. Bandits became numerous; rebel troops arose to advance the claims to the throne of one or another scion of the Han house; and the imperial armies disintegrated. Wang Mang—who with better luck might have gone down in history as the honored founder of a dynasty—was reviled ever afterward in China as an unprincipled schemer who had usurped the throne of the Son of Heaven.

"The Memoir of Wang Mang," from Pan Ku's *History of the Former Han Dynasty,* is one of the masterpieces of Chinese literature. In it the story of this remarkable man gradually unfolds much as it must have appeared to his contemporaries. Wang Mang is first seen as the exceptionally able and upright public figure whose official eminence under the last of the Former Han emperors and subsequent assumption of the imperial dignity for himself is largely justified. Slowly his faults come to light; his errors bear their inevitable fruit. At last this once-exalted personage is a tired old man attempting to save himself with a divining board, then murdered in his palace by a common soldier. The historian Pan Ku was by no means an admirer of Wang Mang. But despite his critical appraisal of the man, his account stays close to the archival sources and is generally balanced in tone. Except for an occasional adjective and the historian's traditional summing-up at the end, "The Memoir of Wang Mang" is a notably objective study of one of the most remarkable figures in Chinese history.

FROM THE HISTORY OF THE FORMER
HAN DYNASTY (HAN SHU) BY PAN KU

The Memoir of Wang Mang/Part A

Wang Mang, whose courtesy given name was Chü-chün, was
the son of [Wang Wan], a younger [half]-brother of the Empress [nee Wang of Emperor] Hsiao-yüan.[1] The father, [Wang
Chin], and the [living] elder and younger brothers of the Empress [nee Wang of Emperor] Yüan were all enfeoffed as marquises[2] during the reigns of [Emperors] Yüan and Ch'eng.[3]
They occupied [high] positions and had important influence in
the government. In the clan there were nine marquises and five
Commanders-in-chief. . . .

Only [Wang] Mang's father, [Wang] Wan, who had died
young, was not made a marquis. The various elder and younger
cousins of [Wang] Mang were all the sons of Generals or of the
Five Marquises, so they took advantage of their opportunities
and were extravagant. In their equipages and horses, music and
women, idleness and gadding[4] they competed with one another.

[Wang] Mang alone was an orphan and in humble circumstances, hence he humbled himself and made himself courteous

From *The History of the Former Han Dynasty*, Vol. III, by Pan Ku, trans.
and ed. by Homer H. Dubs, Baltimore: Waverly Press, 1955, copyright by
the American Council of Learned Societies, pp. 125-7, 129, 140-43, 145-7,
149-50, 216-21, 253-7. Reprinted by permission of the American Council of
Learned Societies. Brackets within the text inserted by the translator.

1. Emperor Yüan reigned 49-33 B.C. The word *Hsiao* means "filial"; it
was added to the title of all the Han emperors beginning with the second.
2. At this time there existed only two noble ranks below that of emperor.
The title of king was reserved for members of the emperor's family on his
father's side. The title of marquis was granted to various maternal relatives
of the emperor and to certain imperial favorites.
3. Emperor Ch'eng reigned 33-7 B.C. The Empress Yüan (Wang Mang's
aunt) was his mother.
4. The phrase "idleness and gadding" is a quotation from the *Analects*,
XVI, 5.

and temperate. In studying the Classic of Rites [the *Yi-li*[5]], he rendered to Ch'en Ts'an, [a man] from P'ei Commandery, the services due to a teacher. [Wang Mang] fatigued himself and studied extensively, wearing garments like the Confucian masters. He served his mother and the widow of his elder brother, [Wang Yung], and reared [Wang Kuang], the orphaned son of his elder brother. Thus his conduct was quite perfect. Moreover, outside [his clan] he associated with eminent persons, and within [his clan] he served his various uncles, paying minute attention to the spirit of the rules of proper conduct. . . .

[Various officials], who were all gentlemen well-known in that age, all spoke in behalf of [Wang] Mang. Because of that, the Emperor esteemed [Wang] Mang. In the first year of [the period] Yung-shih,[6] he enfeoffed [Wang] Mang as Marquis of Hsin-tu with an estate of fifteen hundred households in the Tu District of Hsin-yeh [County] in Nan-yang [Commandery].[7] He was promoted to be Chief Commandant of Cavalry, Imperial Household Grandee, and Palace Attendant, and was careful as [an imperial] guard.

As his noble rank and position became more and more honorable, his conduct became more and more humble. He distributed equipages and horses, clothes, and fur garments, and bestowed them upon his guests, so that in his household there was no surplus [wealth]. He received and succored well-known gentlemen. He associated with a very large number of generals, chancellors, ministers, and grandees, hence those who occupied official positions in turn recommended him. Travelers talked about him; his empty fame flourished and spread, so that it overwhelmed that of his various uncles. He dared to do affected deeds which created a stir and performed them without shame. . . .

When [Wang] Mang had surpassed his equals and succeeded his four uncles, [Wang Feng, Wang Shang, Wang Yin, and

---

5. Or *I Li* (*Ceremonials and Rituals*), a book containing minute prescriptions for proper etiquette on various formal occasions. A work of this name (possibly the same one referred to here) was considered the fifth of the Five Confucian Classics in Han times (it was later supplanted by the *Li Chi* [*Book of Rites*]).

6. I.e., 16 B.C.

7. Nan-yang commandery was in central China on the middle Han River.

Wang Ken], as chief assistant in the government,[8] he wished to make his fame and reputation surpass that of his predecessors, hence he denied himself tirelessly and invited the Capable and Good [to come to him], making them Division Head Clerks.[9] He bestowed upon [other] gentlemen all of his grants [from the Emperor] and the income from his estate, being even more economical [in his personal expenses].

[Wang Mang was first appointed to the post of Commander-in-Chief (Prime Minister) a few months before the death of Emperor Ch'eng in 7 B.C. Shortly after the accession of Emperor Ai (reigned 7-1 B.C.), Wang Mang resigned to make way for the new emperor's maternal relatives.

When Emperor Ai died in 1 B.C., Wang Mang's aunt, the Grand Empress Dowager (Empress Yüan) was the senior imperial relative at court. She took charge of the government and recalled Wang Mang to power. The new emperor, P'ing, was a boy of eight; the Grand Empress Dowager became Regent.]

[Wang] Mang's appearance was severe and his speech was blunt. When he wanted to have something done, he subtly indicated it in his bearing; his clique took up his intentions and manifested them in a memorial,[10] [whereupon Wang] Mang bent his head to the earth with tears in his eyes, and firmly declined. On the one hand, he thereby misled the [Grand] Empress Dowager, and on the other, he thereby exhibited faithfulness to the mass of commoners.[11]

First, he had hinted that [the Governor of] Yi Province[12] should induce the barbarians outside the barrier to present a white pheasant, and, in the first year of [the period] Yüan-

8. His title was Commander-in-Chief (actually: Prime Minister).
9. I.e., he appointed good Confucians to office.
10. Court etiquette demanded that an imperial minister resign whenever the ruler (here: the Grand Empress Dowager) rejected an important proposal he had made. Wang Mang protected himself through the pretense that his suggestions originated with someone else.
11. The reference is to honors which Wang Mang desired for himself. In some instances he refused to accept grants of land or money and advised the Empress to bestow them upon the common people, thereby increasing his popularity.
12. Yi was a border province in present-day Szechuan.

shih, in the first month,[13] [Wang] Mang advised the [Grand] Empress Dowager to issue an imperial edict that the white pheasant should be offered in the [imperial] ancestral temples.[14] . . .

Thereupon various courtiers produced long expositions, [saying, "Wang] Mang's achievements and virtuous conduct have brought about the auspicious presage of a white pheasant [as at the time the Duke of] Chou [was minister to King] Ch'eng. That in a thousand years there are similarities is a law of the sage-kings. When a subject has great achievements, in his lifetime he should have a laudable title. Hence the Duke of Chou, during his lifetime, was given a title with [the name of] the Chou [dynasty in it. Wang] Mang has the great achievement of having given stability to the state and of having given tranquillity to the Han dynasty, so that it is proper that he should be granted the title, 'The Duke Giving Tranquillity to the Han [Dynasty],' that the [number of] households [in his noble estate] should be increased, and [his posterity should be given] the same noble title and estate [as the founder of their house]. On the one hand, [this appointment] will be in accordance with ancient principles, and on the other hand, it will take as its model past situations. Thereby it will accord with the mind of Heaven."

[Wang Mang presented a letter to the Empress refusing this honor; but she insisted that he accept.]

When [Wang] Mang again presented a letter excusing himself, the [Grand] Empress Dowager by an imperial edict ordered an Internuncio to lead [Wang] Mang to await [investiture] in the Eastern Wing of the [Palace] Hall. [But Wang] Mang pronounced himself ill and would not enter [the Palace Hall, so the Grand] Empress Dowager sent the Prefect of the Masters of Writing, [Yao] Hsün, with an imperial edict to [Wang Mang], saying, "Because you, sir, are humble, you have refused on account of illness. Your position, sir, is im-

13. February-March, A.D. 1.
14. Wang Mang here imitates a similar action which is recounted in the *Book of History*.

portant, and may not be left vacant. Arise promptly at this time."

When [Wang] Mang completely and firmly refused, the [Grand] Empress Dowager again sent the Grand Coachman at the Ch'ang-hsin [Palace, Wang] Hung, with an imperial decree summoning [Wang] Mang. [Wang] Mang [however] insistently pronounced himself ill. . . .

The [Grand] Empress Dowager thereupon issued an imperial edict, saying, "The Commander-in-chief, the Marquis of Hsin-tu, [Wang] Mang, has been one of the three highest ministers for three reigns and has performed the [same] duties [as those performed by] the Duke of Chou. He has established the plan [for the succession to the throne that is to endure for] ten thousand generations. In achievements and virtuous conduct he has been a model to palace officials. His influence has spread over [all] within the [four] seas, so that people of distant [regions] have thought with affection of right principles; a potentate of the Yüeh-shang, [whose speech must be] repeatedly interpreted [from one interpreter to another], presented a white pheasant as tribute.

"Let [Wang] Mang be additionally enfeoffed with [the income of] the twenty-eight thousand households in the two counties of Shao-ling and Hsin-hsi. His heirs who succeed him shall be exempted [from taxes and service] and their noble rank and estate shall be the same [as his]. . . . [Wang] Mang shall be the Grand Tutor and in charge of the business of the Four Coadjutors.[15] His title shall be the Duke Giving Tranquillity to the Han Dynasty. . . . Thereupon [Wang] Mang hypocritically feared that he had no alternative and so he arose and received his charter [of appointment]. . . .

When [Wang] Mang had pleased the mass of commoners, he also wanted the right to decide matters on his own authority.[16] He knew that the [Grand] Empress Dowager had no taste for governing, so he gave a hint to the ministers. They memorialized her, saying, ". . . It is not proper that the [Grand]

15. The coadjutors were the officials next in rank to the commander-in-chief; Wang Mang was now given control over their affairs.
16. I.e., without consulting the Grand Empress Dowager in each case.

Empress Dowager should in person supervise unimportant matters."

[Thus they] caused the [Grand] Empress Dowager to issue an imperial edict which said, "Since the Emperor is young in years, We are temporarily directing the government until he puts on the bonnet of virility.[17] Now most matters are complicated and detailed, while Our years are many and [Our] bodily vigor is insufficient. [If We attend to these matters], there is danger that [We] may not have the means of keeping [Our] body in health or of caring for the Emperor. . . .

. . . From this time and henceforth, except for enfeoffments of noble titles,[18] which shall nevertheless be reported [to Us], in all other matters, the Duke Giving Tranquillity to the Han Dynasty [Wang Mang] and the Four Coadjutors shall judge and decide. . . .

In the winter, when [the planet] Mars was occulted by the moon,[19] Emperor P'ing became ill. [Wang] Mang made a written declaration [to Heaven] in which he begged for [the Emperor's] life at the altar to the Supreme [One]. He had a jade circlet hung on his person, carried jade insignia, and [declared] that he was willing in person to take the place [of the dying Emperor]. The declaration was stored in a "metal-bound coffer"[20] and placed in the Front Hall [of the Palace].[21] He ordered the various highest ministers not to presume to speak [to him about government business, in order that he might concentrate on caring for the Emperor's illness].

In the twelfth month,[22] Emperor P'ing died. . . .

17. This bonnet (or cap) was assumed at a solemn ceremony marking a boy's transition to manhood.
18. Enfeoffment involved granting someone the right to draw income from state-owned lands; it was among the most important prerogatives of the throne.
19. November 29, A.D. 5.
20. "The Metal-Bound Coffer" is the title of a chapter of the *Book of History*. Wang Mang here repeats an act said to have been performed by the Duke of Chou.
21. Since Wang Mang was later reputed to have murdered Emperor P'ing, this incident—with its magical connotations—is significant as evidence of the opposite. Wang Mang was superstitious; presumably he would have feared the wrath of the spirits if he had violated such a solemn declaration.
22. February 3, A.D. 6.

At that time, the line of descent from Emperor Yüan had been ended, but of the great-grandsons of Emperor Hsüan[23] there were living: five kings and forty-eight full marquises, [including] the Marquis of Kuang-chi, [Liu] Hsien. [Wang] Mang hated it that they were adults, so advised, "A cousin is not permitted to be the successor [to his cousin of the same generation]." So he selected the very youngest among [Emperor Hsüan's] great-great-grandsons, [Liu] Ying, the son of the Marquis of Kuang-chi, [Liu] Hsien. He was in the second year of his age. [Wang Mang] took as a pretext that when he was divined about and physiognomized, he was the most auspicious [of all].

In this month, the Displayer of Splendor in the South, Hsieh Hsiao, memorialized that the Chief of Wu-kung [prefecture], Meng T'ung, while a well was being dug, had secured a white stone, round above the square below, with red writing on the stone. The writing said, "An instruction to the Duke Giving Tranquillity to the Han Dynasty, [Wang] Mang, that he should become the Emperor." The coming of mandates [from Heaven] through portents began indeed with this one.

[Wang] Mang had the various highest ministers advise the [Grand] Empress Dowager [nee Wang] of it. The [Grand] Empress Dowager said, "This [thing] is trumped up to deceive the empire. [Its message] cannot be put into practise." The Grand Guardian, [Wang] Shun, said to the [Grand] Empress Dowager that when matters have already reached such [a condition as they had], there was nothing that could be done [about it],[24] that if she wished to check it, she did not have the strength to stop it; and also that [Wang] Mang would not presume to have any other [intentions], but merely desired to be entitled the Regent, in order to make his power greater and to settle the empire and make it obedient. The [Grand] Empress Dowager listened to him and promised [to do so].

[Wang] Shun and others thereupon together had the [Grand]

23. Emperor Hsüan ruled 74-48 B.C. Four reigns had intervened since his death; but there were now no living descendants of the Emperors Yüan, Ch'eng, Ai, and P'ing.
24. I.e., Wang Mang's popularity and reputation were such that he could not be dismissed.

Empress Dowager issue an imperial edict which said, ". . . Let it be ordered that the Duke Giving Tranquillity to the Han Dynasty should occupy [the post of] Regent and should [be permitted to] mount the eastern [master's] steps [at the altar to Heaven],[25] as in the former case [was done by] the Duke of Chou. Let the prefecture of Wu-kung become the territory whose revenue is allocated to the Duke Giving Tranquillity to the Han Dynasty, and let its name be the town of Han-kuang (the Han [dynasty's] brilliance). Let there be prepared a memorial concerning the ceremonial [for the above]."

[Wang Mang's newest honor was not universally applauded, however. The imperial general, Chai Yi, claiming that Wang Mang had murdered Emperor P'ing, led a popular revolt of considerable proportions. It was suppressed by troops loyal to Wang Mang (A.D. 7-8).]

The mass of commoners knew [what was Wang Mang's] motive in receiving respectfully the mandate [given through] the portents. The courtiers discussed it extensively and memorialized separately in order to indicate the gradual [steps] by which he should take [the throne as] the actual [Emperor]. . . .

Ai Chang, a man of Tzu-t'ung, had been doing elementary studying in Ch'ang-an.[26] Heretofore he had no distinction but loved to boast. When he saw that [Wang] Mang was acting as Regent, he immediately made a bronze casket with two envelope covers. He wrote on one of them, "The design in the metal casket [with] the Seal of the Lord of Heaven's Act." On the other he wrote, "The written metal charter [with] the Seal of the Red Lord's Act,[27] which a certain person [Emperor Kao] trans-

---

25. This was a ceremonial act permitted only to the emperor.
26. The city of Ch'ang-an was the capital of the empire under the Former Han dynasty, located near the site of the former capital of Ch'in, Hsien-yang.
27. These phrases imitate the legends on the imperial seals. "Red Lord" is the honorific title given by Kao-tsu, the first Han emperor (r. 206-195 B.C.), to his father. Though the father never actually reigned, filial piety demanded that he be referred to as the founder of the dynasty. Ai Chang's inscription is meant to suggest that the founder of the previous (Han) dynasty transmits his mandate to the founder of the next, Wang Mang.

mits to the Yellow Emperor,[28] [Wang Mang]" . . . The writ-ing said that Wang Mang should be the actual Son of Heaven and the [Grand] Empress Dowager [should act] according to the mandate of Heaven. Both on the design and the writing were written [the names of] eight persons who were [Wang] Mang's high officials. It also named two fine names,[29] Wang Hsing (Wang Rises) and Wang Sheng (Wang Prospers); [Ai] Chang, taking advantage [of this opportunity, also] inserted his own surname and personal name amongst [them, so that] altogether there were eleven persons. For all of them there were written official [titles] and noble ranks as [Wang Mang's] coadjutors and assistants.

When [Ai] Chang heard that the matters of the well in Ch'i [Commandery] and of the stone ox[30] had been referred [to the officials], on that very day,[31] at dusk, he put on yellow clothes, took the casket, went to the Temple of [Emperor] Kao, and thereupon delivered it to the Supervisor [of the Temple]. The Supervisor thereupon reported it.

On [the day] *mou-ch'en*[32] [Wang] Mang went to the Temple of [Emperor] Kao, bowed, and received the metal casket and the resignation [of the Han dynasty, which] the gods had [com-manded]. Wearing the royal hat, he visited the [Grand] Em-press Dowager, returned, seated himself in the Front Hall of the Wei-yang Palace, and issued a written message, which said:

"I possess no virtue, [but] I rely upon [the fact that] I am a descendant of my august deceased original ancestor, the Yellow Lord, and a distant descendant of my august deceased first an-cestor, the Lord of Yü, [Shun], and the least of the Grand Em-press Dowager's relatives. August Heaven and the Lords on High have made abundantly apparent their great assistance, so that the mandate [of Heaven] has been completed and the suc-cession [to the imperial rule] has been set in order. By portents

28. The Yellow Emperor was a legendary king of antiquity. Referring to Wang Mang by this name was intended to be flattering.
29. I.e., two names selected for their auspicious meanings.
30. Two previously reported portents which foretold the rise of Wang Mang.
31. January 8, A.D. 9.
32. January 10, A.D. 9. *Mou-ch'en* is the name of a day in the Chinese sixty-day cycle.

and credentials, designs and writings, a metal casket and a written charter, the gods have proclaimed that they entrust me with the myriad common people of the empire.

"The Red Lord is the genius of Emperor Kao of the Han dynasty. He has received a mandate from Heaven and has transmitted the state [to me by] a writing on a metal charter. I have been extremely reverent and awed—[how could I] presume not to receive it respectfully? On [the day] *mou-ch'en*, which is a day for founding, I wear the royal hat and ascend the throne as the actual Son of Heaven. It is fixed that the title [of my dynasty] in possessing the empire shall be Hsin.[33]

33. This dynastic title was adopted from Wang Mang's fief of Hsin-tu, just as the title of Kao-tsu (Han) was derived from that of his previous kingdom.

IV

Religion

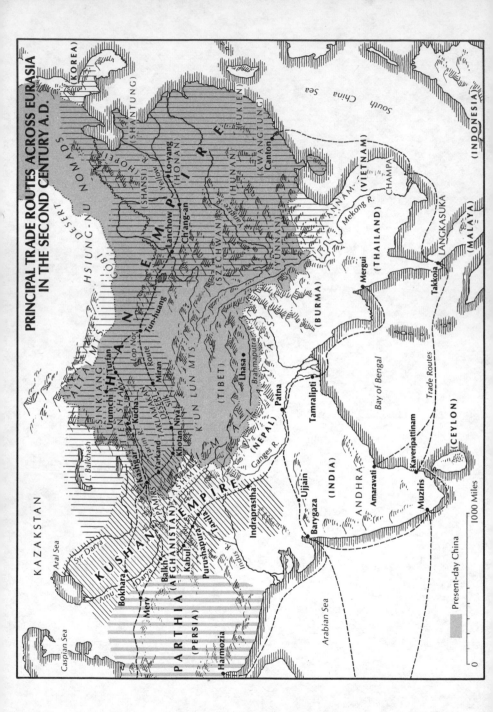

PRINCIPAL TRADE ROUTES ACROSS EURASIA IN THE SECOND CENTURY A.D.

(KOREA)

South China Sea

KAZAKSTAN

Caspian Sea

Aral Sea

L. Balkhash

Syr Darya

Amu Darya

HSIUNG-NU NOMADS

GOBI DESERT

ALTAI MTS.

SINKIANG

TIEN SHAN

Urumchi

Turfan

Kucha

Kashgar

Yarkand

TAKLAMAKAN DESERT

Tarim R.

Khotan

Niya

PAMIRS

Merv

Bokhara

Balkh

Kabul

(AFGHANISTAN)

Purushapura

Taxila

KASHMIR

KUSHAN EMPIRE

PARTHIA (PERSIA)

Harmozia

Arabian Sea

Muziris

(CEYLON)

Kaveripattinam

Amaravati

ANDHRA

(INDIA)

Ujjain

Barygaza

Indraprastha

Ganges R.

(NEPAL)

Patna

Tamralipti

Bay of Bengal

Brahmaputra R.

KUN LUN MTS.

(TIBET)

Lhasa

HIMALAYAS

Lop Nor

Miran

Route

Tunhuang

North Route

Lanchow

Ch'ang-an

Yellow

(SHANSI)

(HONAN)

Lo-yang

(HOPEI)

(SHANTUNG)

H A N   E M P I R E

(SZECHWAN)

Yangtze R.

(HUPEH)

(HUNAN)

(YUNNAN)

(KWANGTUNG)

Canton

(FUKIEN)

BURMA

Mergui

(THAILAND)

Mekong R.

ANNAM (VIETNAM)

CHAMPA

LANGKASUKA

Takkola

(MALAYA)

(INDONESIA)

Trade Routes

Present-day China

0   1000 Miles

Confucianism

Introduction

The Confucian way of thought was human-centered rather than other-worldly, viewing human beings primarily as members of society rather than in their relationship to the beyond. Indeed, Confucianism recognized no supreme, personal Deity. Heaven (*T'ien*) was the highest power of the universe—a kind of overruling providence more closely resembling the Western concept of Nature than a God capable of direct relationship with man. The standard of Confucian ethics was harmony with the Way of Heaven—which meant righteousness and propriety—not obedience to the will of God. The worship of ancestral spirits was an important aspect of Confucianism; but such spirits were numerous and had once been human themselves. They demanded respect, but scarcely inspired the reverence which a single, transcendent Deity would have done.

At an earlier period of history, however, the Chinese did worship a more personalized high god. Oracle bones from Anyang indicate that a deity named Ti or Shang Ti was the most important of the various gods worshipped by the Shang people.* In Chou times† the chief deity was called T'ien; he was pictured in the Chinese script of that time as a large, and therefore important, man. Apparently T'ien was originally a collective divinity representing the ancestors of the race—the former kings who resided in Heaven (the sky). Aided perhaps by the fact that the Chinese language does not distinguish between singular and plural nouns, T'ien eventually came to be regarded as a rather abstract, impersonal force in the sky. By Confucius' time the names T'ien and Ti were being used interchangeably, with Ti denoting the supreme Power in a rather more personalized way.

* Traditional dates of the Shang dynasty: 1765-1123 B.C.
† 1122-403 B.C.

Confucius himself never used the term Ti, though he sometimes spoke of T'ien (Heaven). He invoked Heaven in an occasional ancient turn of phrase, or alluded to Heaven's Way as identical with his own ethical ideas. But although popular opinion in his day held that the earth is full of ghost-like beings—spirits of deceased persons, spirits inhabiting natural phenomena like trees, rocks, or rivers— Confucius categorically refused to discuss such matters. Whether he secretly doubted the existence or the powers of spirits and refrained from saying so out of respect for contemporary belief is no longer possible to say. In any case, he regarded living human beings as more important than supernatural ones: spirits should be served according to proper ritual forms, but without excess. In the third century B.C. the highly influential Hsün Tzu explicitly denied the powers of spirits, though he, too, continued to value the ritual of worship. Despite such important precedents, spirit worship, magic, occultism, divination, and supernatural portents retained their hold on the Chinese mind. In Han times such practices were followed even by educated people with impeccable Confucian credentials (e.g., Wang Mang); and they remained an important element of the Chinese outlook on life until modern times.

FROM THE ANALECTS OF CONFUCIUS (LUN YÜ) *

III, 11   Someone asked for an explanation of the Ancestral Sacrifice.[1] The Master said, "I do not know. Anyone who knew the explanation could deal with all things under Heaven as easily as I lay this here;" and he laid his finger upon the palm of his hand.[2]

III, 12   Of the saying, "The word 'sacrifice' is like the word 'present'; one should sacrifice to a spirit as though that spirit

From *The Analects of Confucius*, trans. by Arthur Waley, London: George Allen & Unwin, 1958. Reprinted by permission of George Allen & Unwin, Ltd.
* For Introduction to Confucius see above, pp. 3-6.
  1. This was the sacrifice supposedly performed by the emperors of ancient times. In Confucius' day the power of the emperor was merely nominal; and the ancient imperial rites were no longer performed correctly.
  2. The imperial rites, if properly performed, were believed to have enormously beneficent effects throughout society.

was present," the Master said, "If I am not present at the sacrifice, it is as though there were no sacrifice."[3]

III, 13   Wang-sun Chia[4] asked about the meaning of the saying,

> Better pay court to the stove
> Than pay court to the Shrine.[5]

The Master said, "It is not true. He who has put himself in the wrong with Heaven has no means of expiation left."

V, 12   Tzu-kung said, "Our Master's views concerning culture and the outward insignia[6] of goodness, we are permitted to hear; but about Man's nature[7] and the ways of Heaven he will not tell us anything at all."

VI, 20   Fan Ch'ih asked about wisdom. The Master said, "He who devotes himself to securing for his subjects what it is right they should have, who by respect for the Spirits keeps them at a distance,[8] may be termed wise."

VII, 20   The Master never talked of prodigies, feats of strength, disorders[9] or spirits.

VII, 34   When the Master was very ill, Tzu-lu asked leave to perform the Rite of Expiation. The Master said, "Is there such a thing?"[10] Tzu-lu answered saying, "There is. In one of the Dirges it says, 'We performed rites of expiation for you, calling

3. I.e., the important thing is the sacrificer's state of mind, not whether the spirits are actually "present" or not.
4. Wang-sun Chia was an army commander in the service of Duke Ling of Wei, a contemporary of Confucius.
5. I.e., it is better to be on good terms with the hearth-god than with the ancestral spirits.
6. Lit., the insignia denoting rank; metaphorically, proper behavior.
7. I.e., human nature prior to the acquisition of culture and education.
8. I.e., when the spirits receive their proper sacrifices they refrain from "possessing" human beings, causing sickness, madness, etc.
9. Strange natural occurrences (which were commonly regarded as portents), e.g., the birth of deformed creatures, snow in summer, etc.
10. I.e., is there any ancient authority for such a rite? (Tr.)

upon the sky-spirits above and the earth-spirits below. The Master said, "My expiation began long ago!"[11]

XI, 11   Tzu-lu asked how one should serve ghosts and spirits. The Master said, "Till you have learnt to serve men, how can you serve ghosts?" Tzu-lu then ventured upon a question about the dead. The Master said, "Till you know about the living, how are you to know about the dead?"[12]

11. I.e., his entire life is his justification before Heaven.
12. Whether or not the dead possessed consciousness was a much-debated point. It was sometimes suggested that if the spirits of the dead were unconscious, it was useless to sacrifice to them.

FROM THE HSÜN TZU[*]

Heaven's[1] ways are constant. It does not prevail because of a sage like Yao[2]; it does not cease to prevail because of a tyrant like Chieh.[3] Respond to it with good government, and good fortune will result; respond to it with disorder, and misfortune will result. If you encourage agriculture and are frugal in expenditures, then Heaven cannot make you poor. If you provide the people with the goods they need and demand their labor only at the proper time, then Heaven cannot afflict you with illness. If you practice the Way[4] and are not of two minds, then Heaven cannot bring you misfortune. Flood or drought cannot make your people starve, extremes of heat or cold cannot make them fall ill, and strange and uncanny occurrences cannot cause them harm. But if you neglect agriculture and spend lavishly, then Heaven cannot make you rich. If you are careless in your provisions and slow to act, then Heaven cannot make you whole.

From *Hsün Tzu: Basic Writings,* trans. by Burton Watson, New York and London: Columbia University Press, 1963, pp. 79-85. Reprinted by permission of Columbia University Press.
* For Introduction to Hsün Tzu see above, pp. 31-3.
1. In Hsün Tzu's usage, "Heaven" (T'ien) corresponds closely to the Western concept of Nature or natural law.
2. The virtuous ancient sage-king often praised by the Confucians.
3. Chieh was the wicked final sovereign of the Hsia dynasty, which according to tradition ruled 2205-1766 B.C.
4. *Tao.*

If you turn your back upon the Way and act rashly, then Heaven cannot give you good fortune. Your people will starve even when there are no floods or droughts; they will fall ill even before heat or cold come to oppress them; they will suffer harm even when no strange or uncanny happenings occur. The seasons will visit you as they do a well-ordered age, but you will suffer misfortunes that a well-ordered age does not know. Yet you must not curse Heaven, for it is merely the natural result of your own actions. Therefore, he who can distinguish between the activities of Heaven and those of mankind is worthy to be called the highest type of man.

To bring to completion without acting, to obtain without seeking[5]—this is the work of Heaven. Thus, although the sage has deep understanding, he does not attempt to exercise it upon the work of Heaven; though he has great talent, he does not attempt to apply it to the work of Heaven; though he has keen perception, he does not attempt to use it on the work of Heaven. Hence it is said that he does not compete with Heaven's work. . . .

When [the wise man] turns his thoughts to Heaven, he seeks to understand only those phenomena which can be regularly expected. When he turns his thoughts to earth, he seeks to understand only those aspects that can be taken advantage of. When he turns his thoughts to the four seasons, he seeks to understand only the changes that will affect his undertakings. When he turns his thoughts to the yin and yang,[6] he seeks to understand only the modulations which call for some action on his part. The experts may study Heaven; the ruler himself should concentrate on the Way.

Are order and disorder due to the heavens? I reply, the sun and moon, the stars and constellations revolved in the same way in the time of Yü[7] as in the time of Chieh. Yü achieved order:

5. This formulation shows the influence of Taoist philosophy.
6. The theory of Yin-Yang was an attempt to explain the changes in the world in terms of two fundamental but opposed natural principles. Yin stood for the passive, negative, feminine, dark, cold qualities; Yang for the active, positive, masculine, bright, warm, etc. The dominance of the Yin or the Yang in the universe at any given time was supposed to explain the condition of natural phenomena as well as human events.
7. The ancient sage-king, supposed founder of the Hsia dynasty.

Chieh brought disorder. Hence order and disorder are not due to the heavens.

Are they then a matter of the seasons? I reply, the crops sprout and grow in spring and summer, and are harvested and stored away in autumn and winter. It was the same under both Yü and Chieh. Yü achieved order; Chieh brought disorder. Hence order and disorder are not a matter of the seasons.

Are they due to the land? I reply, he who acquires land may live; he who loses it will die. It was the same in the time of Yü as in the time of Chieh. Yü achieved order; Chieh brought disorder. Hence order and disorder are not due to the land. . . .

The king of Ch'u[8] has a retinue of a thousand chariots, but not because he is wise. The gentleman must eat boiled greens and drink water, but not because he is stupid. These are accidents of circumstance. To be refined in purpose, rich in virtuous action, and clear in understanding; to live in the present and remember the past—these are things which are within your own power. Therefore the gentleman cherishes what is within his power and does not long for what is within the power of Heaven alone.[9] The petty man, however, puts aside what is within his power and longs for what is within the power of Heaven. Because the gentleman cherishes what is within his power and does not long for what is within Heaven's power, he goes forward day by day. Because the petty man sets aside what is within his power and longs for what is within Heaven's power, he goes backward day by day. The same cause impels the gentleman forward day by day, and the petty man backward. What separates the two originates in this one point alone.

When stars fall or trees make strange sounds,[10] all the people in the country are terrified and go about asking, "Why has this happened?" For no special reason, I reply. It is simply that, with the changes of Heaven and earth and the mutations of the yin and yang, such things once in a while occur. You may wonder at them, but you must not fear them. The sun and moon are

8. Ch'u was the southernmost of the major Chinese states.

9. I.e., good luck.

10. Hsün Tzu is probably referring in particular to the sacred trees planted around the altar of the soil, whose rustlings and creakings were believed to have deep significance. (Tr.)

subject to eclipses, wind and rain do not always come at the proper season, and strange stars occasionally appear. There has never been an age that was without such occurrences. If the ruler is enlightened and his government just, then there is no harm done even if they all occur at the same time. But if the ruler is benighted and his government ill-run, then it will be no benefit to him even if they never occur at all. Stars that fall, trees that give out strange sounds—such things occur once in a while with the changes of Heaven and earth and the mutations of the yin and yang. You may wonder at them, but do not fear them.

Among all such strange occurrences, the ones really to be feared are human portents. When the plowing is poorly done and the crops suffer, when the weeding is badly done and the harvest fails; when the government is evil and loses the support of the people; when the fields are neglected and the crops badly tended; when grain must be imported from abroad and sold at a high price, and the people are starving and die by the roadside —these are what I mean by human portents. When government commands are unenlightened, public works are undertaken at the wrong season, and agriculture is not properly attended to, these too are human portents. When the people are called away for *corvée* labor at the wrong season, so that cows and horses are left to breed together and the six domestic animals produce prodigies; when ritual principles are not obeyed, family affairs and outside affairs are not properly separated, and men and women mingle wantonly, so that fathers and sons begin to doubt each other, superior and inferior become estranged, and bands of invaders enter the state—these too are human portents. Portents such as these are born from disorder, and if all three types occur at once, there will be no safety for the state. The reasons for their occurrence may be found very close at hand; the suffering they cause is great indeed. You should not only wonder at them, but fear them as well.

An old text says, "Strange occurrences among the creatures of nature are not discussed in the *Documents*."[11] Useless distinctions, observations which are not of vital importance—these

11. I.e., the *Book of History*.

may be left aside and not tended to. But when it comes to the
duties to be observed between ruler and subject, the affection
between father and son, and the differences in station between
husband and wife—these you must work at day after day and
never neglect.

You pray for rain and it rains. Why? For no particular reason, I say. It is just as though you had not prayed for rain and
it rained anyway. The sun and moon undergo an eclipse and
you try to save them;[12] a drought occurs and you pray for rain;
you consult the arts of divination before making a decision on
some important matter. But it is not as though you could hope
to accomplish anything by such ceremonies. They are done
merely for ornament. Hence the gentleman regards them as ornaments, but the common people regard them as supernatural.
He who considers them ornaments is fortunate; he who considers them supernatural is unfortunate.

From Sec. 17, "A Discussion of Heaven"

12. By beating drums to drive it away. This practice is mentioned in the
Tso Commentary (Duke Wen, Year XV).

Taoism

Introduction

The system of thought known as Taoism constitutes one of the two
chief molds in which ancient Chinese civilization was formed. A
philosophy, a religion, and a science all at once, it is outranked
only by Confucianism in its influence upon the Chinese mind. Philosophical Taoism—especially as embodied in the two great Taoist
classics, the *Tao Te Ching* (*Lao Tzu*) and the *Chuang Tzu*—is a
doctrine of great subtlety and profundity. It concerns itself with the
ultimate questions—the origin and meaning of life, the nature of

the universe—and culminates in the mystic union of the individual with Tao. This so-called classical Taoism appealed to people who sought a private, individualistic philosophy of life rather than the socially oriented ethic of Confucianism, and a tranquil (often rural) existence apart from the larger concerns of society. Its adherents were necessarily the members of an educated elite, those with the leisure for contemplation and sufficient income to free them from manual labor. Religious, or "popular" Taoism, on the other hand, was a technique for attaining salvation and an organized Church with a wide mass appeal. Its doctrine included moral injunctions as well as a regime of dietary regulations and breathing exercises, the object of which was to prolong life. Popular Taoism boasted a large pantheon of gods and spirits who were worshipped in ceremonies of great complexity. It became a significant force in China in the final decades preceding the fall of the Han dynasty (in A.D. 220) and attained its greatest influence in the centuries of disunion known as the Six Dynasties period (A.D. 222-589).

The starting point of the Taoist system is not a supreme, personal Deity, but the impersonal law of the universe, which is called Tao. Tao (usually translated as "Way") is a common word in Chinese, denoting the inner principle of a thing. Confucius equated Tao with the Way of proper human behavior, which he defined as righteousness and propriety. To the Taoists, however, it is the essence and the operating principle of all the phenomena of the universe. It is the Chaos at the beginning and at the end of the world, from which all things arise and to which they will return. It is the unique One which is dependent on nothing else, and also the totality of all separate things. In Tao all contrasts are blended and all opposites united. It is simple, formless, and without qualities—thus the assertion that it has no name. It is the law which governs change, but is itself eternal and unchangeable. To understand Tao is to grasp the natural and inevitable order of the universe—the course of physical nature and of human affairs.

The fundamental ethical idea of Taoism is generally stated as conduct in harmony with Tao. The reasoning behind this is that the human body is the cosmos in miniature: the microcosm which contains the macrocosm. The various parts of the body—head, feet, eyes, veins, hair, etc.—are said to correspond to the sky, the sun and moon, rivers, stars, and planets. Now the universe is a giant mechanism which automatically produces its effects. The gods and spirits have no vital role in its government: they merely preside over its various divisions. The birth, life-span, and death of living creatures, the four seasons, the five elements, and the Yin and the Yang all proceed naturally in an eternal, ever-recurring cycle. Nature produces its effects without effort, and requires no external direction. Indeed, natural catastrophes such as floods, droughts, poor harvests, and so on, are the result of human interference with the normal unfolding of events: Nature works best if let alone. Similarly in human affairs, harmony with Tao signifies the absence of all exertion and striving. The Taoist ethic is summed-up in the word "non-action" (*wu-wei*). Whereas Confucians pictured the ideal gentleman as constantly active in promoting the general welfare, Taoists thought of him as doing nothing.

Given the centrality of the physical universe in the Taoist conception, it is hardly surprising that this philosophy is pervaded by a kind of nature-mysticism. The figures of Taoist legend are frequently persons living in close contact with the elements—fishermen, farmers, hermits. The Taoist attitude is one of sympathy for all living and growing things, and encouragement of a life close to unspoiled nature. Harmony with Tao also means responsiveness to one's own inner nature—conduct in accordance with one's *te*. This word *te* is a key Taoist concept, usually translated as "power" or "virtue"; it denotes the potential or latent force in a person or thing or sometimes one's accumulated stock of merits.* Taoism stresses spontaneity and intuition, recognizing that the highest skill is one which has become "second nature." The simplicity of rural life is preferred to the complexity of cities. Man-made institutions, fame, laws, and comforts are all unnatural and artificial; striving for them brings merely conflict and misery. Book-learning, too, means a departure from simplicity and naturalness. Knowledge pertains to artificial things, to the means of winning possessions and power or of satisfying sensuous desires; its effect is to alienate the individual from Tao. Thus Taoist literature praises ignorance, which sometimes means the innocence of a child, but more often a "forgetting" of things once known. The "empty" mind is one which has become receptive to the rhythm of the universe by ridding itself of prejudice and egoistic desires. Knowledge of Tao cannot be gained through logic or from books; it can only be grasped intuitively.

Taoism thus reverses the usual scale of values and rejects most of the objects for which men ordinarily strive. From the standpoint

---

* Thus *Tao Te Ching* may be translated as *Classic of the Way and the Power*.

of the Absolute Tao, all opinions and standards are limited and flawed, and at least partially false. Taoist philosophy thus points up the relativity of all phenomena and fosters skepticism toward established opinions and institutions. This attitude is also the prime source of Taoist humor, which is largely based upon paradox. At its best, the literature of classical Taoism is delightfully witty and subtle, the point of its anecdotes more often implied than openly expressed. Taoist stories exalt the lowly, the imperfect, even the grotesque, at the expense of those whom the world generally admires. They poke fun at the earnest Confucian, who gravely discusses questions of propriety and righteousness; they ridicule his pretensions and denigrate the rank and office which he regarded as suitable rewards of virtue. Taoist literature likes to point out how the same thing can be either high or low, beautiful or ugly, right or wrong, merely according to the observer's point of view.

The Taoist paradoxes may also inspire the sort of sudden enlightenment which later became a hallmark of Zen (in Chinese: Ch'an) Buddhism, requiring a leap from absurd reality into the mystic comprehension of the Ultimate. The goal of Taoism at its highest is mystic union—consciousness of the individual's oneness with Tao. Mystic union is the ideal enshrined in the great Taoist classics, the *Tao Te Ching* and the *Chuang Tzu*. Taoism asserts that the supreme and omnipresent reality of the universe is ordinarily hidden from mankind by the multiplicity of visible phenomena. Knowledge of Tao is always present in us; but it is vague and confused by our involvement in the external world. Through a long apprenticeship in the techniques of contemplation, the seeker after Tao may experience this knowledge in its original purity. He becomes a Taoist sage—one who through union with Tao has attained the wisdom of Tao.

For the majority of practicing Taoists the goal was less exalted. They sought to prolong life on earth, or at least to avoid sudden death; their ultimate object was personal immortality. The eternal life they sought, however, was not that of a pure spirit residing in another world. The Chinese never presupposed a duality between matter and spirit, or body and soul. Rather, they imagined the universe as a continuum alternately dominated by the Yin and Yang principle and the succession of the Five Elements. In any event, souls were vague and undefined beings. Each person had ten of them—three superior ones, or *hun*, corresponding to the Yang, or heavenly principle; seven inferior ones, or *p'o*, corresponding to the

Yin, or earthly principle. When the body died these souls dispersed; what became of them in the other world was disputed; but in any case they did not remain together. The body, on the other hand was a unity, and therefore the only entity capable of continuing the human personality after death.

Though there is no supreme God in Taoism—only the impersonal Tao—the popular concept of Tao eventually became personalized. By the fourth or fifth century A.D., it was generally believed that the Tao had at one time assumed human form. As such he was known as the "Lord of Tao," or Lord Huang-Lao—a combination of the mythological Yellow Emperor (Huang Ti) and the ancient sage Lao Tzu, supposed author of the *Tao Te Ching*. Lord Huang-Lao was the highest of the Taoist deities, but he was scarcely unique. Popular Taoism was characterized by a host of immortals whose function it was to instruct believers in the way to eternal life. Some of the immortals originated as indigenous nature-deities or demons; the Taoist church took over the sacrifices in their honor. But the influence of Mahayana Buddhism is also evident, with its vast hierarchy of Buddhas and Bodhisattvas; and the Lord of Tao corresponds to the Buddha-principle in its periodic incarnations.

By the end of the second century A.D., Taoism had become the first large-scale, organized religion in Chinese history. Its prominence is closely linked to the rise of the Yellow Turbans—the Taoist-led secret society which established branches throughout much of China and, in A.D. 184, instigated a great popular rebellion. Though the revolt of the Yellow Turbans collapsed, it fatally weakened the Han dynasty. But the Taoist church survived them both. Several centuries afterward it still retained many of the organizational forms given it by the leaders of the Yellow Turbans. The fundamental unit of the Taoist church was the parish, which was locally supported by the contributions of members. Its head was called Instructor; his position was hereditary in the families of the original Taoist missionaries to the district; and his function was to conduct religious services. The ranks of the church were open to men and women both. Believers were classed either as initiates— those sufficiently advanced in the faith to aspire to eternal life— and ordinary laymen, to whom the religion promised health, happiness, progeny, and long life. Initiates and laymen followed similar regimes of diet and meditation, though less rigorously in the case of laymen. The festivals of the Taoist church were many and varied; they were the occasions for great outpourings of religious feeling and included public confession and penitence. As Buddhism gained influence in China, the Taoist church adopted many Buddhist organizational forms and rites. Taoist temples, monasteries, and convents sprang up; Taoist scriptures appeared which in many cases were imitations of Buddhist texts. The distinctions between the popular forms of Buddhism and Taoism tended to disappear; and the two became an almost indistinguishable mass of mythology and magic.

The decades following the fall of the Han dynasty (in A.D. 220) witnessed a renewed interest in philosophical Taoism. Neo-Taoism, as this movement is sometimes known, was not a church, but rather an intellectual tendency among members of the gentry class. Its adherents were just those persons who in quieter times would normally have sought careers in government service. Amid the disorders and uncertainties of the third century A.D., many of these gentlemen preferred to cultivate personal relationships, private tastes, and aloofness from social involvement. At princely courts as well as among friends, groups were organized to promote the study of literary, aesthetic, or philosophical (but not political) subjects. Their discussions were known as *ch'ing-t'an*, or "purity debates," meaning that they were uncontaminated by contact with mundane matters. Their favorite texts were the *Tao Te Ching, Chuang Tzu*, and *Book of Changes*. The most famous practitioners of *ch'ing-t'an* were the so-called Seven Sages of the Bamboo Grove, several of them noted poets, who met frequently together to enjoy the pleasures of nature, philosophy, music, and wine. The Neo-Taoist movement also produced some scholars with genuine scientific curiosity who conducted useful investigations into the nature of the physical universe. Eventually, however, *ch'ing-t'an* degenerated into barren discussion, hedonism, and an attitude of indifference to everything except one's own private concerns.

The Taoist church enjoyed its greatest influence in the Six Dynasties period (A.D. 222-589). Thereafter it gradually declined, though it never disappeared altogether. Its many superstitious practices and ignorant practitioners gave it an ill repute among sophisticated and educated people; and the religious impulses which once found expression in Taoism now turned increasingly to Mahayana Buddhism—a more highly developed faith. But the great Taoist literary works, above all the *Tao Te Ching* and the *Chuang Tzu*, never lost their attraction for persons of mystical bent and subtle intellect. Taoist relativism and skepticism have left their mark on the Chinese character; the Taoist love of spontaneity and feeling for nature have given strong impetus to pictorial art and lyric poetry. The political influence of Taoism, however, was largely indirect. The Taoist church was decentralized, lacking any all-embracing organization which might have rivalled the power of the state bureaucracy. From time to time, Chinese rulers or their close associates fell under the spell of Taoist initiates who claimed to possess the secret of bodily immortality. Certain emperors were fascinated by the notion of the perfect Taoist sage (i.e., the sovereign) as beyond good and evil, untouchable and impregnable; and they interpreted the unity of Tao in a political sense.

Taoism and its rival, Confucianism—in contrast to the warring creeds of Europe or the Near East—were never regarded as mutually exclusive. Indeed, many ideas of Taoist origin found their way even into Confucian Classics like the *Book of Rites* or the appendices to the *Book of Changes*. The Taoist encouragement of individuality and the inner, spiritual life in fact provided a necessary complement to the Confucian concern with man in his public aspect. While Confucianism is straightforward and commonsensical, Taoism is mystical and otherworldly. Throughout history, innumerable Chinese have practiced Confucianism in their public life and cherished Taoism privately. Amid the complex demands of Confucian society with its elaborate ritual prescriptions, Taoist philosophy provided a welcome refuge where the individual could call his soul his own.

Introduction to the Tao Te Ching (Lao Tzu)

The most famous name in Taoist philosophy is that of Lao Tzu ("Old Master"), reputed author of the earliest Taoist classic, the *Lao Tzu* or *Tao Te Ching* (meaning *Classic of the Way and the Power*). According to tradition he was a slightly older contemporary of Confucius; and legend records a meeting between them. But whether a person known as Lao Tzu even existed in the sixth century B.C. is open to question. If he did, he cannot have written the *Tao Te Ching*, which contains ideas that became current only several centuries later. The book presupposes a significant prior development of the characteristic Taoist techniques for the attainment of immortality and mystic union; in part it is also a polemic against Confucians and Legalists. The work may tentatively be dated as originating in the third century B.C.; it probably assumed final form a century or so afterward. Whether its author was one person or several is not certain; no reliable evidence exists as to his possible identity.

The *Tao Te Ching* is a work of great philosophical depth and literary power. Its concern is with the obscure springs of life, the nature of the universe and of man. It seeks to evoke a mystic Truth which can only be suggested, not explained, and does so in language of compelling imagery. The statements of the *Tao Te Ching* are poetic in form, full of symbol and metaphor and striking paradoxes; their meaning is often obscure and elusive. The style is formal, the structure rhythmic and parallelistic. The entire work consists of eighty-one brief stanzas or chapters, setting forth what appear to be ancient proverbs interspersed with interpretative comment in both poetry and prose.

Because of its cryptic and ambiguous language, the *Tao Te Ching* is open to various interpretations. Most commonly it is regarded as an exaltation of the private, individually lived existence as opposed to the ethic of social involvement. It might also be given political meaning as a defense of laissez-faire government as against the Confucian or Legalist impulse to planning and regulation. Certain Western scholars have found in it echoes of Christianity; in the past century it has repeatedly been translated into Western languages. However interpreted, the *Tao Te Ching* is a work of almost universal appeal which has had a profound effect upon educated Chinese through more than two millennia. Its depth of thought as well as its literary excellence place it unquestionably among the religious classics of the world.

FROM THE TAO TE CHING (LAO TZU)

Chapter I

The Way that can be told of is not an Unvarying Way;[1]
The names that can be named are not unvarying names.

From Arthur Waley, *The Way and Its Power, A Study of the Tao Te Ching*, London: George Allen & Unwin, 1934. Reprinted by permission of George Allen & Unwin, Ltd.
    1. I.e., if it can be described in words, it is not the ultimate Tao.

It was from the Nameless that Heaven and Earth sprang;

The named is but the mother that rears the ten thousand creatures, each after its kind.

Truly, "Only he that rids himself forever of desire[2] can see the
Secret Essences";

He that has never rid himself of desire can see only the Outcomes.[3]

These two things[4] issued from the same mould, but nevertheless
are different in name.

This "same mould" we can but call the Mystery,

Or rather the "Darker than any Mystery,"

The Doorway whence issued all Secret Essences.

Chapter II

It is because every one under Heaven recognizes beauty as
beauty, that the idea of ugliness exists.

And equally if every one recognized virtue as virtue, this would
merely create fresh conceptions of wickedness.[5]

For truly "Being and Not-being grow out of one another;

Difficult and easy complete one another.

Long and short test one another;

High and low determine one another.

The sounds of instrument and voice give harmony to one another.

Front and back give sequence to one another."

Therefore the Sage[6] relies on actionless activity,

Carries on wordless teaching,

But the myriad creatures are worked upon by him; he does not
disown them.

He rears them, but does not lay claim to them,

Controls them, but does not lean upon them,

2. Desire for worldly rewards: fame, power, pleasures, possessions, etc.
3. The visible and tangible manifestations of the Essences.
4. I.e., the Essences and the Outcomes.
5. On the assumption of universal relatedness, opposites cause each other,
as for instance in the Yin-Yang philosophy.
6. In Taoist literature, the Sage is the person who comprehends the nature
of Tao, and thereby becomes one with Tao. Being one with Tao, he possesses
the all-embracing powers of Tao; he is the microcosm in the macrocosm.

Achieves his aim, but does not call attention to what he does;
And for the very reason that he does not call attention to what
    he does
He is not ejected from fruition of what he has done.[7]

Chapter III

If we stop looking for "persons of superior morality" (*hsien*) to
put in power, there will be no more jealousies among the people.
If we cease to set store by products that are hard to get, there
will be no more thieves. If the people never see such things as
excite desire, their hearts will remain placid and undisturbed.
Therefore the Sage rules

By emptying their hearts[8]
And filling their bellies,
Weakening their intelligence[9]
And toughening their sinews   '
Ever striving to make the people knowledgeless and
    desireless.

Indeed he sees to it that if there be any who have knowledge,
they dare not interfere.[10] Yet through his actionless activity all
things are duly regulated.

Chapter IV

The Way is like an empty vessel[11]
That yet may be drawn from
Without ever needing to be filled.
It is bottomless; the very progenitor of all things in the
    world.
In it all sharpness is blunted,
All tangles untied,
All glare tempered,

7. I.e., because he does not claim credit for his achievements, credit cannot
be taken from him.
8. The expression "emptying the heart" in Chinese denotes open-mindedness and humility—signs of the cultured gentleman.
9. Particularly in the sense of "having ideas of one's own." (Tr.)
10. *Wei*, "to act" (the opposite of the Taoist principle of *wu-wei*, "non-
action"), is often used in Taoist literature in the sense of "interfere."
11. This can also be rendered as: "The Way is all-pervading" (or "filling
all space").

All dust[12] smoothed.
It is like a deep pool that never dries.
Was it too the child of something else? We cannot tell.
But as a substanceless image[13] it existed before the
    Ancestor.[14]

Chapter VIII

The highest good is like that of water. The goodness of water is
that it benefits the ten thousand creatures; yet itself does not
scramble, but is content with the places that all men disdain.[15]
It is this that makes water so near to the Way.
    And if men think the ground the best place for building a
        house upon,
    If among thoughts they value those that are profound,
    If in friendship they value gentleness,
    In words, truth; in government, good order;
    In deeds, effectiveness; in actions, timeliness—
    In each case it is because they prefer what does not lead to
        strife,
    And therefore does not go amiss.

Chapter IX

Stretch a bow[16] to the very full,
And you will wish you had stopped in time;
Temper a sword-edge to its very sharpest,
And you will find it soon grows dull.
When bronze and jade fill your hall
It can no longer be guarded.

12. Dust is the Taoist symbol for the noise and fuss of everyday life. (Tr.)
13. A *hsiang*, an image such as the mental images that float before us when
we think.
14. The Ancestor in question is almost certainly the Yellow Ancestor (or
Yellow Emperor) who, according to legend, separated the earth from Heaven
and thus destroyed the primal unity. In religious Taoism the Yellow Emperor (Huang Ti) was combined with Lao Tzu into a single figure, Lord
Huang-Lao, who became the principal Taoist deity.
15. I.e., the lowly places.
16. The [Chinese] expression used can also apply to filling a vessel to the
brim; but "stretching a bow" makes a better parallel to "sharpening a
sword." (Tr.)

Wealth and place breed insolence
That brings ruin in its train.
When your work is done, then withdraw!
Such is Heaven's Way.

Chapter XI

We put thirty spokes together and call it a wheel;
But it is on the space where there is nothing that the utility
    of the wheel depends.
We turn clay to make a vessel;
But it is on the space where there is nothing that the utility
    of the vessel depends.
We pierce doors and windows to make a house;
And it is on these spaces where there is nothing that the
    utility of the house depends.
Therefore just as we take advantage of what is, we should
    recognize the utility of what is not.

Chapter XII

The five colours confuse the eye,
The five sounds dull the ear,
The five tastes spoil the palate.
Excess of hunting and chasing
Makes minds go mad.
Products that are hard to get
Impede their owner's movements.
Therefore the Sage
Considers the belly[17] not the eye.
Truly, "he rejects that but takes this."

Chapter XIV

Because the eye gazes but can catch no glimpse of it,[18]
It is called elusive.

17. The belly in this instance means "what is inside him," his own inner
powers. (Tr.)
18. This is the traditional description of ghosts and spirits adopted as a description of the Way. (Tr.)

Because the ear listens but cannot hear it,[18]
It is called the rarefied.
Because the hand feels for it but cannot find it,
It is called the infinitesimal.
These three, because they cannot be further scrutinized,
Blend into one.
Its rising brings no light;
Its sinking, no darkness.
Endless the series of things without name
On the way back to where there is nothing.
They are called shapeless shapes;
Forms without form;
Are called vague semblances.
Go towards them, and you can see no front;
Go after them, and you see no rear.
Yet by seizing on the Way that was[19]
You can ride[20] the things that are now.
For to know what once there was, in the Beginning,
This is called the essence of the Way.

Chapter XVI

Push far enough towards the Void,[21]
Hold fast enough to Quietness,
And of the ten thousand things none but can be worked on
        by you.
I have beheld them, whither they go back.
See, all things howsoever they flourish
Return to the root from which they grew.
This return to the root is called Quietness;
Quietness is called submission to Fate;
What has submitted to Fate has become part of the
        always-so.
To know the always-so is to be Illumined;
Not to know it, means to go blindly to disaster.

19. I.e., the primeval beginnings.
20. I.e., dominate. (Tr.)
21. Or "emptiness," denoting humility.

He who knows the always-so has room in him for every-
    thing;[22]
He who has room in him for everything is without
    prejudice.
To be without prejudice is to be kingly;
To be kingly is to be of heaven;
To be of heaven is to be in Tao.
Tao is forever and he that possesses it,
Though his body ceases, is not destroyed.

Chapter XVIII

It was when the Great Way declined
That human kindness and morality arose;
It was when intelligence and knowledge appeared
That the Great Artifice[23] began.
It was when the six near ones[24] were no longer at peace
That there was talk of "dutiful sons";
Nor till fatherland was dark with strife
Did we hear of "loyal slaves."[25]

Chapter XIX

Banish wisdom, discard knowledge,
And the people will be benefited a hundredfold.
Banish human kindness, discard morality,
And the people will be dutiful and compassionate.
Banish skill, discard profit,
And thieves and robbers will disappear.
If when these three things are done they find life too plain
    and unadorned,
Then let them have accessories;

22. This is a play on words. "To have room in oneself for everything" is
cognate to "to be without prejudice" (kung)—a word which also means a
royal Duke.
23. Hypocrisy, artificiality.
24. The six family members included in the Confucian concept of the five
relationships: father, son, elder and younger brother, husband and wife.
25. As ministers called themselves. (Tr.)

Give them Simplicity[26] to look at, the Uncarved Block[27] to
    hold,
Give them selflessness[28] and fewness of desires.

Chapter XXV

There was something formless yet complete,
That existed before heaven and earth;
Without sound, without substance,
Dependent on nothing, unchanging,
All pervading, unfailing.
One may think of it as the mother of all things under
    heaven.
Its true name we do not know;
"Way" is the by-name that we give it.
Were I forced to say to what class of things it belongs I
    should call it Great (*ta*).
Now *ta* also means passing on,
And passing on means going Far Away,
And going far away means returning.[29]

Thus just as Tao has "this greatness" and as earth has it and as
heaven has it, so may the ruler also have it. Thus "within the
realm there are four portions of greatness," and one belongs to
the king. The ways of men are conditioned by those of earth.
The ways of earth, by those of heaven. The ways of heaven by
those of Tao,[30] and the ways of Tao by the Self-so.[31]

26. "Simplicity" (*su*) means literally "raw silk." It is the symbol of the
"attributeless" nature of Tao. (Tr.)
27. The Uncarved Block symbolizes the original unity underlying the apparent multiplicity of phenomena in the universe.
28. *Ssu* (the "self" element in the word translated "selflessness") is the opposite of *kung*, "public." It means absence of personal ambition. (Tr.)
29. I.e., returning to the primal beginnings.
30. The intention of this "chain-argument" (a rhetorical form very commonly used by early Chinese writers) is to show that a line of connection
may be traced between the ruler and Tao. This connection exists macrocos-
mically, in the line ruler, earth, heaven, Tao; but also microcosmically, in
that by passing on and on through successive stages of his own consciousnesss
back to the initial Unity he can arrive at the Way which controls the multi-
form apparent universe. The ecstasy called Far Away Wandering is also
known as the Far Away Passing On. (Tr.)
31. The "unconditioned"; the "what-is-so-of-itself." (Tr.)

Chapter XXVIII

"He who knows the male, yet cleaves to what is female
Becomes like a ravine,[32] receiving all things under heaven,"
And being such a ravine
He knows all the time a power that he never calls upon in
    vain.
This is returning to the state of infancy.
He who knows the white, yet cleaves to the black
Becomes the standard by which all things are tested;
And being such a standard
He has all the time a power that never errs,
He returns to the Limitless.
He who knows glory, yet cleaves to ignominy
Becomes like a valley that receives into it all things under
    heaven,
And being such a valley
He has all the time a power that suffices;
He returns to the state of the Uncarved Block.
Now when a block is sawed up it is made into implements;[33]
But when the Sage uses it, it becomes Chief of all Ministers.
Truly, "The greatest carver[34] does the least cutting."

Chapter XXX

He who by Tao purposes to help a ruler of men
Will oppose all conquest by force of arms;[35]
For such things are wont to rebound.[36]
Where armies are, thorns and brambles grow.
The raising of a great host
Is followed by a year of dearth.

32. I.e., lowly and receptive.
33. Play on the double sense of this word which also means "a subordinate,"
"an instrument of government." (Tr.)
34. Play on *chih* "to cut," "to carve," and *chih* "to rule." (Tr.)
35. This enigmatic line could be taken in the purely pacifist sense, as opposing all arms; it might also mean that conquest by an enemy ought to be
stopped by force of arms.
36. Lit., "to be reversed." He who overcomes by violence will himself be
overcome by violence. (Tr.)

Therefore a good general effects his purpose and then stops;
    he does not take further advantage of his victory.
Fulfils his purpose and does not glory in what he has done;
Fulfils his purpose and does not boast of what he has done;
Fulfils his purpose, but takes no pride in what he has done;
Fulfils his purpose, but only as a step that could not be
    avoided.[37]
Fulfils his purpose, but without violence;
For what has a time of vigour also has a time of decay.
This[38] is against Tao,
And what is against Tao will soon perish.

37. This is the principle of "action as a last resort" preached especially by
the Taoist Chuang Tzu.
38. Violence. (Tr.)

Introduction to the Lieh Tzu

The *Lieh Tzu* is a small collection of Taoist fables and anecdotes
traditionally attributed to a sage of that name who lived *ca.* 450-
375 B.C. Though the book cannot possibly have been written this
early, its actual date is disputed. It is sometimes regarded as a for-
gery of the third or fourth centuries A.D.—a view given credence by
the traces it shows of Buddhist influence. But many of its stories also
appear in the literature of early Han times; and some of its passages
are borrowed directly from the *Chuang Tzu*. In sum, it appears
most likely that the *Lieh Tzu* is a composite work derived from various sources and periods. The greater part of the text may go back to
the third or second centuries B.C., though certain sections undoubtedly were added at a later time.

    The *Lieh Tzu* consists of miscellaneous short episodes having little
intrinsic connection. On the whole, its ideas show strong affinities to
those of the *Tao Te Ching* and *Chuang Tzu*. Its style is somewhat
simpler, however, and the point of its stories generally more obvious.
Like all the classical Taoist literature, it makes much use of fantasy,
symbol, striking imagery, and paradox; and it frequently contra-

dicts conventional points of view. Its tone is often irreverent and witty; the underlying points profoundly serious.

One section of the *Lieh Tzu*, however, is distinctly out of harmony with the rest. This is the so-called "Yang Chu" chapter, which purports to set forth the philosophy of the famous hermit of the fourth century B.C. who was a precursor of classic Taoism. The use of Yang Chu's name, however, is presumably a literary device, since the chapter does not represent his actual opinions, as far as they are known. No original works by either Yang Chu or his school have survived, but he seems to have preached that worldly possessions and fame do not justify endangering life and health to acquire them. The "Yang Chu" chapter of the *Lieh Tzu* advocates something quite different—the unrestricted enjoyment of sensual pleasure and abolition of social conventions which hinder personal happiness. Quite possibly the Neo-Taoist gentry of the third and fourth centuries A.D. favored this attitude; but it is scarcely in accord with classic Taoism. The "Yang Chu" chapter is not by content a Taoist text at all, though it possesses an intrinsic interest as one of the rare hedonistic works in Chinese literature.

FROM THE LIEH TZU

Lieh-tzu said:

"Formerly the sages reduced heaven and earth to a system by means of the Yin and Yang.[1] But if all that has shape was born from the Shapeless, from what were heaven and earth born? I answer: There was a Primal Simplicity, there was a Primal Commencement, there were Primal Beginnings, there was a Primal Material. The Primal Simplicity preceded the appearance of the breath.[2] The Primal Commencement was the begin-

From *The Book of Lieh-tzu*, trans. by A. C. Graham, London: John Murray, 1960, pp. 18-19, 24, 27-31, 35-7, 65, 140-43. Reprinted by permission of John Murray, Ltd.

1. The passive and active, or earthly and heavenly principles of the universe.

2. According to Taoist concepts of physiology, breath (coming from without) was the giver of life. It combined with the "essences" inside a person to produce life.

ning of the breath. The Primal Beginnings were the breath beginning to assume shape. The Primal Material was the breath
when it began to assume substance. Breath, shape and substance
were complete, but things were not yet separated from each
other; hence the name "Confusion." "Confusion" means that the
myriad things were confounded and not yet separated from each
other.

"Looking you do not see it, listening you do not hear it, grop-
ing you do not touch it; hence the name "Simple." The Simple
had no shape nor bounds, the Simple altered and became one,
and from one altered to sevenfold, from sevenfold to ninefold.
Becoming ninefold is the last of the alterations of the breath.
Then it reverted to unity; unity is the beginning of the alterations of shape. The pure and light rose to become heaven, the
muddy and heavy fell to become earth, the breath which har-
moniously blended both became man. Hence the essences con-
tained by heaven and earth, and the birth and changing of the
myriad things."

When Confucius was roaming on Mount T'ai, he saw Jung
Ch'i-ch'i walking in the moors of Ch'eng, in a rough fur coat
with a rope round his waist, singing as he strummed a lute.
"Master, what is the reason for your joy?" asked Confucius.

"I have very many joys. Of the myriad things which heaven
begot mankind is the most noble, and I have the luck to be human; this is my first joy. Of the two sexes, men are ranked
higher than women, therefore it is noble to be a man. I have the
luck to be a man; this is my second joy. People are born who do
not live a day or a month, who never get out of their swaddling
clothes. But I have already lived to ninety; this is my third joy.
For all men poverty is the norm and death is the end. Abiding
by the norm, awaiting my end, what is there to be concerned
about?"

"Good!" said Confucius. "He is a man who knows how to
console himself."

There was a man of Ch'i country who was so worried that
heaven and earth might fall down, and his body would have

nowhere to lodge, that he forgot to eat and sleep. There was another man who was worried that he should be so worried about it, and therefore went to enlighten him.

"Heaven is nothing but the accumulated air; there is no place where there is not air. You walk and stand all day inside heaven, stretching and bending, breathing in and breathing out; why should you worry about it falling down?"

"If heaven really is accumulated air, shouldn't the sun and moon and stars fall down?"

"The sun and moon and stars are air which shines inside the accumulated air. Even if they did fall down, they couldn't hit or harm anyone."

"What about the earth giving way?"

"The earth is nothing but accumulated soil, filling the void in all four directions; there is no place where there is not soil. You walk and stand all day on the earth, stamping about with abrupt spurts and halts; why should you worry about it giving way?"

The man was satisfied and greatly cheered; and so was the man who enlightened him. . . .

When Lieh-tzu heard of it, he too smiled and said:

"It is nonsense to say either that heaven and earth will perish or that they will not. Whether they perish or not we can never know. However, from that side there is one point of view, from this side there is another. Hence the living do not know what it is like to be dead, the dead do not know what it is like to be alive. Coming, we do not know those who went before, going we shall not know those who come after. Why should we care whether they perish or not?"

Mr. Kuo of Ch'i was very rich. Mr. Hsiang of Sung, who was very poor, travelled from Sung to Ch'i to inquire about his methods.

"I am good at stealing," Mr. Kuo told him. "After I first became a thief, within a year I could keep myself, within two I was comfortable, within three I was flourishing, and ever since then I have been the benefactor of the whole neighbourhood."

Hsiang was delighted; he understood from what Kuo said that he was a thief, but misunderstood his Way of being a thief. So he climbed over walls and broke into houses, and grabbed any-thing in reach of his eye and hand. Before long, he was found guilty of possessing stolen goods, and lost his whole inheritance. Thinking that Kuo had deceived him, he went to him to complain.

"In what way have you been stealing?" Kuo asked him.

Hsiang described what had happened.

"Alas!" Kuo said. "Have you erred so far from the true Way of stealing? Let me explain. I have heard it said: 'Heaven has its seasons, earth has its benefits.' I rob heaven and earth of their seasonal benefits, the clouds and rain of their irrigating floods, the mountains and marshes of their products, in order to grow my crops, plant my seed, raise my walls, build my house. I steal birds and animals from the land, fish and turtles from the water. All this is stealing; for crops and seed, clay and wood, birds and animals, fish and turtles, are all begotten by heaven, and how can they become my possessions? Yet I suffer no retribution for robbing heaven. On the other hand precious things such as gold and jade, and commodities such as grain and silk, are collected by men, and how can we claim that it is heaven which provides them? When you steal them, why should you resent being found guilty?"

Hsiang was highly perplexed, and thought that Kuo was trapping him again. Happening to meet Master Tung-kuo, he questioned him and got this answer:

"Is not your very body stolen? When you must steal the Yin and Yang energies in harmonious proportions even to achieve your life and sustain your body, how can you take the things outside you without stealing them? In reality the myriad things of heaven and earth are not separate from each other; and to claim anything as one's own is always wrong-headed. Kuo's way of stealing is common to all, and so he escapes retribution; your motive for stealing is private, and so you were found guilty. Whether or not you distinguish between common and private, you are still stealing. It is the power of heaven and earth which makes the common common and the private private. For the man who understands the power of heaven and earth, what is stealing and what is not stealing?"

[The following tale demonstrates that the Taoists thought of simplicity and naturalness not as equivalent to ignorance or crudity, but rather as a state of mind going beyond ordinary knowledge.]

Lieh-tzu had Old Shang as teacher, and Po-kao-tzu as his friend. When he had nothing more to learn from either of them, he came home riding the wind.[3] Yin Sheng heard of him, joined his disciples, and for several months did not look for lodgings. Ten times, when Lieh-tzu was not busy, he took the opportunity to beg for his secrets; and each time Lieh-tzu turned him away and would not tell him. Yin Sheng was indignant and took his leave; Lieh-tzu made no objection.

A few months after Yin Sheng withdrew he had not renounced his aim, and went to join Lieh-tzu again.

"Why do you keep coming and going?" Lieh-tzu asked him.

"Not long ago I made a request to you, but you would not tell me. It is true that I felt some rancour against you, but now it is all gone. So I have come again."

"I used to think you intelligent; are you really as vulgar as all that? Here, I will tell you what I learned from my own Master. Three years after I began to serve the Master and befriend a certain man, my mind no longer dared to think of right and wrong, my mouth no longer dared to speak of benefit and harm; and it was only then that I got as much as a glance from the Master. After five years, my mind was again thinking of right and wrong, my mouth was again speaking of benefit and harm; and for the first time the Master's face relaxed in a smile. After seven years, I thought of whatever came into my mind without any longer distinguishing between right and wrong, said whatever came into my mouth without any longer distinguishing between benefit and harm; and for the first time the Master pulled me over to sit with him on the same mat. After nine years, I thought without restraint of whatever came into my mind and said without restraint whatever came into my mouth without knowing whether the right and wrong, benefit and harm, were mine or another's, without knowing that the Master was my teacher and the man I have mentioned was my friend.

3. This was one of the feats commonly attributed to Taoist magicians.

Only then, when I had come to the end of everything inside me and outside me, my eyes became like my ears, my ears like my nose, my nose like my mouth; everything was the same. My mind concentrated and my body relaxed, bones and flesh fused completely, I did not notice what my body leaned against and my feet trod, I drifted with the wind East or West, like a leaf from a tree or a dry husk, and never knew whether it was the wind that rode me or I that rode the wind.

"Now you come to be my disciple, and before even a year has gone round, you are indignant and resentful time and again. The air will refuse your slip of a body, the earth will refuse to carry one joint of your finger; can you hope to tread the void and ride the wind?"

Yin Sheng was deeply ashamed, held his breath for a long time,[4] and did not dare to speak again.

Lao-ch'eng-tzu studied magic under Master Yin Wen, who told him nothing for three years. Lao-ch'eng-tzu asked what he had done wrong and offered to leave. Master Yin Wen bowed him into the house, shut the door on his attendants, and talked with him.

"Formerly, as Lao-tzu was setting out for the West, he looked back and told me: The breath of all that lives, the appearance of all that has shape, is illusion. What is begun by the creative process, and changed by the Yin and Yang, is said to be born and to die; things which, already shaped, are displaced and replaced by a comprehension of numbers and understanding of change, are said to be transformed, to be illusions of magic. The skill of the Creator is inscrutable, his achievement profound, so that it is long before his work completes its term and comes to an end. The skill of the magician working on the shapes of things is obvious but his achievement shallow, so that his work is extinguished as soon as it is conjured up. It is when you realise that the illusions and transformations of magic are no different from birth and death that it becomes worthwhile to study magic with you. You and I are also illusion; what is there to study?"

4. Holding the breath was one of the principal Taoist ascetic practices; its object was to "nourish the body."

Lao-ch'eng-tzu went home to practise Master Yin Wen's teaching, and after pondering deeply for three months, was able to appear and disappear at will and turn round and exchange the four seasons, call up thunder in winter, create ice in summer, make flying things run and running things fly. He never disclosed his arts all his life, so that no one handed them down to later generations.

From the "Yang Chu" Chapter

Yang Chu said:

"It is in life that the myriad things of the world are different; in death they are all the same. In life, there are clever and foolish, noble and vile; these are the differences. In death, there are stench and rot, decay and extinction; in this we are all the same. . . .

"Some in ten years, some in a hundred, we all die; saints and sages die, the wicked and foolish die. In life they were Yao and Shun, in death they are rotten bones; in life they were Chieh and Chou, in death they are rotten bones. Rotten bones are all the same, who can tell them apart? Make haste to enjoy your life while you have it; why care what happens when you are dead?"

Yang Chu said:

"Yüan Hsien grew poor in Lu, Tzu-kung grew rich in Wei.[5] Yüan Hsien's poverty injured his life, Tzu-kung's wealth involved him in trouble."

"If that is so, wealth and poverty are both bad; where is the right course to be found?"

"It is to be found in enjoying life, in freeing ourselves from care. Hence those who are good at enjoying life are not poor, and those who are good at freeing themselves from care do not get rich."

[The phrase *yang sheng* ("tending life," "tending the living") had different meanings for different schools. For individualists of the fourth century B.C. (deriving from the historical Yang Chu him-

5. Yüan Hsien and Tzu-kung were two of Confucius' disciples.

self) it meant the satisfaction of personal needs without injuring health and life. For Confucians, "tending the living" and "taking leave of the dead" were the filial duties of supporting and decently burying one's parents. The present passage gives the Confucian terms a hedonist reinterpretation. (Tr.)]

Yen-tzu asked Kuan Chung about "tending life." Kuan Chung answered:

"It is simply living without restraint; do not suppress, do not restrict."

"Tell me the details."

"Give yourself up to whatever your ears wish to listen to, your eyes to look on, your nostrils to turn to, your mouth to say, your body to find ease in, your will to achieve. What the ears wish to hear is music and song, and if these are denied them, I say that the sense of hearing is restricted. What the eyes wish to see is the beauty of women, and if this is denied them, I say that the sense of sight is restricted. What the nostrils wish to turn to is orchids and spices, and if these are denied them, I say that the sense of smell is restricted. What the mouth wishes to discuss is truth and falsehood, and if this is denied it, I say that the intelligence is restricted. What the body wishes to find ease in is fine clothes and good food, and if these are denied it, I say that its comfort is restricted. What the will wishes to achieve is freedom and leisure, and if it is denied these, I say that man's nature is restricted.

"All these restrictions are oppressive masters. If you can rid yourself of these oppressive masters, and wait serenely for death, whether you last a day, a month, a year, ten years, it will be what I call 'tending life.' If you are bound to these oppressive masters, and cannot escape their ban, though you were to survive miserably for a hundred years, a thousand, ten thousand, I would not call it 'tending life.' "

Then Kuan Chung in his turn questioned Yen-tzu:

"I have told you about 'tending life.' What can you tell me about taking leave of the dead?"

"It does not matter how we take leave of the dead. What is there to say about it?"

"I insist on hearing."

"Once I am dead, what concern is it of mine? It is the same to me whether you burn me or sink me in a river, bury me or leave me in the open, throw me in a ditch wrapped in grass or put me in a stone coffin dressed in a dragon-blazoned jacket and embroidered skirt. I leave it to chance."

Kuan Chung turned to Pao Shu-ya and Huang-tzu, and said:

"Between the two of us, we have said all that there is to say about the Way to live and to die."

Introduction to Ko Hung: The Pao-p'u Tzu

The Taoist search for eternal life gave rise to a vast number of hygienic and ascetic practices, known respectively as "nourishing the body" and "nourishing the spirit." According to Taoist conviction, "nourishing the body" slowed down the aging process in the mortal body and at the same time produced within it an immortal body. The process was long and laborious: only through years of effort would the embryo of the immortal body grow to maturity. But the adept who finally attained such a body did not die: he only seemed to do so. In fact, he mounted bodily to Heaven to dwell with the other Immortals. The method of "nourishing the body" was diet, drugs, and breathing exercises. Because the body was believed to contain three voracious worms which cause sickness, old age, and death, certain foods had to be eliminated from the diet: cereals were considered especially pernicious because the worms fed on them. The principal Taoist drug was cinnabar (mercuric sulfide), which had to be purified through a long and expensive series of transformations. Taoist practitioners experimented with mixing chemical substances to produce an elixir which would grant immortality—incidentally gaining much useful knowledge of drugs and anesthetics. Breathing exercises had as their object retention of the breath for as long a time as possible. The breath, entering the body from without, was considered the giver of life; it united with the body's interior essences to produce the spirit—the directing spirit of man and the source of his personality.

"Nourishing the spirit" involved various contemplative practices somewhat akin to the Indian Yoga. It is these which provide the chief link between classical and popular Taoism; for the same techniques which supposedly prolonged life might also lead to the mystic unity. The immediate object of "nourishing the spirit" was to establish control over the immortal beings inhabiting the body. Because each person was believed to be a microcosm of the universe, these included not only the ten souls, but all the 36,000 gods of the cosmos. Taoists supposed that these interior spirits constantly tended to leave the body; their departure, however, caused the person's death. The attempt to retain them within was called "guarding the One"—i.e., maintaining their unity and preventing the dispersion which occurred at death.* The basic method was concentration upon one of the interior spirits in order to perceive its presence; this was known as the "interior vision" and necessarily required long practice. However, nothing could force the spirits to remain in a body against their will; it was necessary to appeal to their benevolence. Various foods were considered offensive to their sensibilities; thus the seeker after immortality did not eat meat or onions or drink wine. Even more, the spirits approved of a pure life and good works. Thus the Taoist quest for immortality began with the practice of virtue.

The most famous exponent of this type of Taoism was Ko Hung (A.D. 253-333?), who called himself Pao-p'u Tzu ("Philosopher Embracing Simplicity"). A native of the region which is now Kiangsu province, he came from a family of officials; but his paternal granduncle was said to have become a Taoist immortal. Ko Hung himself conformed to both family traditions. He spent many years in official posts, and received high honors for his part in suppressing a military rebellion. He was learned in the Confucian Classics. But magic and alchemy were his primary interests, and he preferred the hermit's life to any other. Ko Hung describes himself as an antisocial and uncommunicative person who would go to extraordinary lengths to procure books on occult subjects, or to discuss their contents with informed persons. To judge from the variety and detail of his chemical formulas, he was a practiced alchemist. In old age he retired to a mountain near Canton, where he lived quietly for many years and wrote books. At age eighty he died, and is said to have become a Taoist immortal.

---

* Cf. ch. X of the *Tao Te Ching:* "Can you keep the unquiet physical-soul (*p'o*) from straying, hold fast to the Unity, and never quit it?"

Ko Hung was an enormously prolific writer. His works include collections of his official correspondence, eulogies for dead persons, inscriptions suitable for tombstones, and biographies of famous immortals, spirits, and hermits. He also copied out many books on medicine, divination, astrology, and history. His reputation for wide learning was unmatched south of the Yangtze. The *Pao-p'u Tzu*, his most famous work, consists of twenty "inner" and fifty "outer" chapters on the subject of earthly immortality. It includes an astounding number of detailed formulas for producing and purifying the medicines and metals (primarily gold and cinnabar) which were believed to prolong life. Ko Hung also addressed himself to skeptics, offering many proofs for the existence of immortals, and propounding a merit system according to which specified numbers of good deeds were rewarded with additional years of life. All these ideas became accepted doctrines of popular Taoism in the following centuries.

FROM THE PAO-P'U TZU

Discussion on Immortality/From Chapter 2

Somebody asked: Is it really possible that the *Shen-hsien* [spirit-immortals] do not die? Pao-p'u tzu answered: Even though one has a very keen sight, there are nevertheless forms that cannot be all seen. Though one is, by nature, gifted with a very good ear, there are nevertheless tones that cannot be all heard. . . . The Universe shows a great variety of things, what is there that could not exist? Still more, those who have attained immortality, fill up historical records; why, therefore, reject the way of immortality as non-existing?

Upon this the questioner burst into loud laughter and said: What has a beginning, must have an end; what has existence, must undergo decay. . . . Death is an unchangeable principle of the laws of human beings and the great end which must come to us.

From "Pao-P'u Tzu Nei P'ien," trans. and ed. by Eugene Feifel (*Monumenta Serica*, Vol. VI, 1941; Vol. IX, 1944, Peking, China: Catholic University of Peking, Henri Vetch), VI, 132-5, 139, 146, 155-6, 158-61, 172-3, 209-11; IX, 5, 10-12, 14-16, 18, 26-7. Reprinted by permission of Monumenta Serica Institute, University of California at Los Angeles. Words in brackets are supplied by the present editors.

However, what I have heard is this, that there are plants which wither even before the hoar-frost forms; that even during summer the verdure fades away; that the leaf-sheath includes the grain which, however, never ripens; that the fruit, before it has formed, has already dried up and fallen down. I never heard of anyone who enjoyed a long life of ten thousand years and lived for an endless time. . . .

Pao-p'u tzu answered: When the faculty of hearing has gone, the rumbling of the thunder cannot make men hear it. When the faculty of seeing has gone, the three lights cannot make men see them. Is it perhaps, that the noise of the rumbling carts is fine, and the light of the sun and of the moon hanging in the sky dim? However the deaf man calls it toneless, and the blind man says there is no object. . . . If darkness has filled up one's heart and mind, one does not believe that in olden times lived two men named Chou (Kung) [the Duke of Chou] and K'ung-tzu [Confucius]; still less, if one is told of the way of the *Shen-hsien* [spirit-immortals].

Existence and decay, beginning and end, are indeed the great laws of the world. Yet there are dissimilarities and uniformities; differences in length and shortness (show limitless variety), now thus, now otherwise; changes and transformations into a thousand forms occur; curious and strange things show infinite variety; things are equal, but their details (qualities and conditions) are different; their origin is uniform but their end dissimilar: things cannot be all spoken of in one way.

Suppose there is a wise and greatly talented man. He admirably leaves the world and quits employment,[1] he conceals his eminence and covers his decorations; he does away with all feigned appearance and quits his harassing occupation; he preserves his simple nature within his most refined substance and he forgets the mean affairs outside in the ordinary world. Only seldom would the common people be able to recognize him as an outstanding man, a genius in the world of namelessness; only seldom would they grasp his high mind when it appears in a shabby body. How much more is this the case, when a *Hsien-jen* [true immortal] is in question! Their interests are unlike, their

1. Reference to a passage in the *Book of Changes,* hexagram 33 ("Retreat").

ways are different. They consider wealth and nobility as misfortune, glory and splendour as filth and dirt, objects of art as dust and rubbish, reputation and honour as morning dew. They walk on the blast of flames and are not burned; they stride across dark waves and lightly pass along; they mount on wings and fly up to the azure fields; they drive with the wind, clouds are their carts; they lift up their eyes and rise up to the utmost heights, they look down and settle upon the K'un-lun.[2] How could the walking corpses see them?

Suppose the *Shen-hsien* [spirit-immortals] amuse themselves by walking among men. They conceal their true nature and hide their extraordinary qualities; their outward appearance is like that of all other common people; they walk along with them, shoulder to shoulder, keeping pace with them. Who then has the power to recognize them? . . .

The reason why people do not believe that the way to immortality can be learned and do not admit that one can lengthen one's life, is just because [the emperors] Ch'in (Shih-)huang and Han Wu (-ti)[3] sought for it, but did not obtain it. . . . [However,] among people who rush forward, there are those who do not reach the goal. Among farmers, there are likewise those who have no harvest. Among merchants or trades-people, there are those who obtain no gain. Among warriors, there are those who earn no merits. Still more is it so with the difficult enterprise of aiming at the practices for gaining immortality! Must all those succeed who practise it? . . .

The rules of immortality demand an earnest desire for quietness, loneliness, non-activity and forgetfulness of one's own body. But the ruler strikes the bell of a thousand *tan*; he beats the thunder-clap drum; boom boom, bang bang, it sounds clamorously; so his soul is in a flurry, his mind is uneasy. The countless varieties of play and amusement make him lose the refinement of his mind and choke his ears. He lightly and quickly flies

2. K'un-lun is the place where strange beings are born, where saints and *Shen-hsien* have their pleasure. (Tr.) The K'un-lun is a high mountain range between Tibet and Sinkiang and extending into central China.

3. Ch'in Shih-huang (the "First Emperor" of China) reigned 221-210 B.C.; Han Wu Ti reigned from 141 to 87 B.C. Both were strongly influenced by Taoist magicians who claimed to possess the secret of eternal life.

along in his carriages, he angles in the depths and sends his arrow up to the heights.

The rules of immortality require that one extend his love to the creeping worm and do no harm to beings with the life-fluid; however, the ruler has his majestic wrath[4] and mows people down as one mows grass.[5] The great yellow halberd[6] once brandished, the sharp axe[7] handed over for a time, then corpses are lying over a distance of a thousand li, blood flows like water, and in the city, the heads are continually falling.

The rules of immortality require that one entirely abstain from flesh, give up cereals and purify one's interior.[8] However, the ruler cooks fat meat and slaughters fat animals. He slays and cuts up all living beings. The eight delicacies, the hundred kinds of savoury dishes are in heaps and abundantly spread before him and he stews and boils and agreeably spices them,[9] he tastes of the delicious meal and eats the delicacies till he is perfectly satisfied.

The rules of immortality demand universal love for the whole world, that one regard one's neighbor as one's own self. But the ruler absorbs the weak States and attacks those which are in dark conditions. He takes their States away when they are in disorder and throws down those which are beginning to decline. He opens up new land and extends his frontiers to form new territories. He annihilates other States, he drives the inhabitants along in hordes and throws them on the fields of death. The lonely ghosts err about in those distant places; the bleached bones

4. Reference to a line in the *Book of Songs:* "the king rose majestic in his wrath." ("Greater Odes," Mao text #241)

5. Reference to a statement in the *Tso Commentary* (Duke Yin, Year VI), which, however, makes a somewhat different point: "The head of a State or of a clan looks upon evil relations as a husbandman looks upon weeds or grass, which must be removed. He cuts down, kills them, heaps them up . . ." etc. (Legge trans.)

6. Or golden halberd, used by the emperor. (Tr.)

7. The axe is the sign of the ruler, holding the sway over the empire, the people and the army. If there was any danger imminent against the State, the emperor took the sharp axe from the temple and set out to restore peace and order. (Tr.)

8. Taoists found the odor of flesh offensive. Cereals were believed to nourish the internal worms which cause bodily decay.

9. Spices were considered offensive to the gods within the body.

lie on the fields of (in) putrefaction. . . . Ch'in (Shih-)huang caused nine families out of ten to think of revolt. Han Wu(-ti) brought the empire into an uproar; the population decreased by fifty per cent. The prayers offered up for the rulers are of some benefit, but the curses of the people will injure them in return. . . .

The *kuei* [demons] and *shen* [spirits][10] often do puzzling tricks and make eccentric performances among men, and what is written in the books and records are likewise many evidences for the *kuei* and *shen*. If the common man still does not believe in the existence of the *shen* and *kuei* on earth, all the more does he not believe that the *Hsien-jen* [true immortals] dwell in high places and abide in remote regions, that as the clear and the muddy (river) flow in different currents,[11] they rise up to heaven, go straight on their way and never return into this world. He who has not obtained the Tao, how can he see and hear them? The Confucianists and the Mohists, however, are convinced that such practices cannot be made a subject of teaching. So they never admit that such things happened. Hence it is easy to understand that the common man does not believe in them. Only those who are already acquainted with the truth, after having tested all recipes, obtain a clear verification and understand perfectly that those things cannot but exist: those alone can know it, this knowledge cannot be forced (upon the common people). So one cannot say that there are no *Hsien-jen* on earth, because one has seen neither a *kuei* nor a *shen* nor a *Hsien-jen*. . . .

Answer to Common Belief/From Chapter 3

Somebody asked: Is it really true that those who practise the Tao should first earn merits? Pao-p'u tzu answered: Yes, it is so. The [Taoist book] *Yü-ch'ien Ching*[12] says: To have merits, comes first; next comes, getting rid of one's faults. He who prac-

10. Of the ten souls within the human body, the three *hun* (heavenly souls) were believed to become *shen* (spirits); the seven *p'o* (earthly souls) became *kuei* (demons).
11. Signifying the enlightened *hsien-jen* and the common blind people. (Tr.)
12. Now nonexistent.

tises the Tao obtains high merits by rescuing people from danger, by helping them to avoid misfortune, by guarding men against sickness and preventing them from dying unjustly and unnecessarily.

He who aspires after immortality should, above all, regard as his main duties: loyalty, filial piety, friendship, obedience, goodness, fidelity. If one does not lead a virtuous life but exercises himself only in magical tricks, he can by no means attain long life. If one does evil, should this be of grave nature, the god of the fate[13] would take off one *chi* [300 days], and for a small sin he would take off a *suan* [three days] of one's life, all according to the light or grave character of the deed. Thus the lifetime he takes away is not of the same length. There is naturally a fixed number of life-years for all who have received destiny and life. The number of life-years of those who have received a great one, cannot easily be exhausted by subtraction of *chi* and *suan*, and so they die of old age. If their natural gift is small and their offences many, then their lifetime is soon exhausted by the subtractions of *chi* and *suan*, and they die young.

Again the book says: If somebody wants to become an earthly immortal, he must have done three hundred good deeds; if he wants to become a heavenly immortal, he must have done one thousand and two hundred good deeds. If he has only one thousand one hundred and ninety-nine good deeds and carelessly falls back into a sin, he will lose all his former good deeds and he has to start again from the very beginning with good deeds. Therefore, a deed is good though it is of unimportant nature, and a deed is bad though it is a trifle. Even if he does nothing bad, but speaks about his practices[14] or demands a reward for his charity, then he loses the good deed of this one action, but he does not lose all the others.

Moreover the book says: If the number of good actions is not yet completed, he will have no profit from them, although he takes the elixir of immortality. If he does not drink the elixir of

13. Ssu-ming is the god who is responsible for the life of men. Later on he became popular under the name of Tsao Wang, kitchen god. (Tr.)
14. Compare the statement in the *Chuang Tzu*, ch. 3: "If you do good, stay away from fame"; and the anecdote in which the Taoist patriarch Lao Tzu is criticized for having become famous.

immortality, but keeps on performing good actions, he will not be visited by the misfortune of a sudden death, though he will not, on this account, attain immortality. I still doubt whether people like Old P'eng[15] have yet performed sufficient good deeds and for this very reason could not soar up to heaven.

Gold and Cinnabar, or the Elixir of Life/From Chapter 4

Naturally, after having eaten delicious sweets, one feels the insipidity of duckweed. After having seen the K'un-lun, one will realize the extreme smallness of an ant-hill. After having learned of the way of gold and cinnabar, one will not be inclined to look any more at petty recipes. But as it is difficult to prepare the great medicine on a sudden, we have to fall back on the use of lesser medicines to preserve our life. If we take ten thousand of the latter kind, it will be of some small benefit, but they will not bring us immortality. That is why Lao-tzu in his secret tradition said: "Unless you obtain transformed cinnabar and gold juice, your labour will be of no avail."[16] Even the five cereals are capable of supporting human life. With them man lives, without them he dies. How could it be otherwise than that the divine medicine of first quality would be ten thousand times better for man than the five cereals!

Now the substance of cinnabar is such, that the more it is heated the more exquisite are its sublimations. Yellow gold, if put in fire and melted a hundred times, will not be spoiled nor will it rot until the end of the world, though it is buried in the ground. If these two substances are eaten, they will strengthen our body so as to stop old age and effect immortality. Thus we derive strength for ourselves from an external substance just as lard feeds fire and so it cannot die out. If we smear vertigris on our feet before going into water, we borrow the strength of the copper to protect our flesh. Gold and cinnabar, however, upon entering our body, permeate our blood-system in a way different from the external application of vertigris. . . .

The first kind of cinnabar is called *Tan-hua* (flower of cinna-

15. The Chinese Methuselah.
16. The *Tao Te Ching*, of course, says no such thing; but its various obscure and symbolic statements made possible farfetched interpretations.

bar). First prepare the *hsüan-huang* [a heated mixture of nine catties of mercury and one catty of lead]. Then use a solution of realgar [arsenic sulfide] and of alum, then use crystal salt, *Lu*-salt [native lake salt], *yü-shih*, [white arsenic ore] oyster shell, red *shih-chih* [red siliceous clay], soapstone [talcum] and *hu*-powder [carbonate of lead], several tens of catties each, and lute the mixture down with the six-one mud [a compound of seven minerals].[17] After this, heat it for thirty-six days and the medicine will then be ready. Take it during seven days and you will be an immortal. If one makes pills of this cinnabar, using *hsüan-kao* [an unidentified substance], and puts them on a strong fire, they will soon change into gold. Again if one mixes 240 *shu* [ten ounces] of it with 100 catties [784 ounces] of mercury and heats it, it will become gold too. If it has become gold, the medicine is ready too. If it has not become gold, then seal up the drugs again and heat them for the same number of days as before, and it will surely become gold.

[Descriptions of eight additional kinds of cinnabar follow.]

If one obtains only one of these nine kinds of cinnabar, one will become an immortal. One does not need to make all of them. Which one he is going to make, depends on his likings. If anyone, after having eaten of these nine kinds of cinnabar, wishes to ascend to heaven, he can depart. If he wishes to stay a while longer with men, he can follow his inclination. He is able in any way to enter or leave places where there is no opening at all. He is unable to suffer any harm. . . .

After having acquired the Tao, the superior men will rise up to be officials in heaven. The mediocre will congregate on the K'un-lun mountain, whilst the lowest class, after having obtained the Tao, will live on earth as immortals. The foolish people do not believe this but call it idle talk. From morning until evening they do nothing but what leads to death, not struggling for life at all. How can heaven thus force life upon them? The common crowd know only of delicious food, fine clothes, music

17. This "six-one mud" is commonly mentioned in the literature of popular Taoism; the substances of which it is composed vary according to different authorities.

and women, wealth and rank. They indulge in pleasure to their full satisfaction, being bound to perish within a short time. Be cautious and do not inform such people about the divine cinnabar, lest you should make them ridicule the Way and slander truth. . . .

The Way of longevity does not consist in worshipping *kuei* [demons] and *shen* [spirits] and doing service to them, nor does it consist in the practice of breathing and bending or stretching the body. The essential point in ascending to immortality lies in the *Shen-tan* (divine cinnabar). It is not so easy to know of it, but to prepare it is really difficult. If you are able to prepare it, you can live for ever. . . .

If one wishes to restore to life a man who has been dead for less than three days, mix a spoonful of the blue-coloured cinnabar with water and bathe the dead. Then open his mouth and pour another spoonful into it. The dead will immediately return to life. If one wants to prepare a meal, mix black-coloured cinnabar with water and smear it on the left hand. All wishes are fulfilled as soon as they are voiced. One can receive everything on earth. If you wish to disappear or to know the future or to stop age and remain a youth, take a spoonful of the yellow-coloured cinnabar and you will enjoy everlasting life in eternal youth. From your chair you will see to a distance of more than a thousand li; you will know all the auspicious and inauspicious omens, just as if everything were before your eyes. You will know man's destiny, his fortune and disasters, his span of life, whether he will be rich and honoured or poor and dejected. . . .

Pao-p'u tzu said: It was gold juice that T'ai-i took to become an immortal. Its efficiency is not inferior to that of the cinnabar nine times sublimated. When compounding it, use one catty [7.84 ounces] of yellow gold, weighed with the old scale. Aside from this use also *hsüan-ming* [purified sodium sulfate], *lung-kao* [gypsum], *t'ai-i hsün-shou-chung-shih* [arsenic sulfide], *ping-shih* [mountain salt], *tz'u-yu nü* [an unknown substance], a solution of *hsüan-shui*, *chin-hua-shih* [lead?] and cinnabar. Seal this up (for a hundred days). It will then change into a liquid.

When gold juice enters the mouth, the whole body will as-

sume a golden colour. Lao-tzu received this from [the immortal]
Yüan-chün said: This Way (recipe) is most impor-Yüan-chün.
tant, it comes to light only once in a hundred generations, so
keep it in a stone cave. All those who compound it, purify themselves and observe a diet during a hundred days. Any relation
with the common world should be avoided. On the slope of a
famous mountain, above a water flowing eastward build a separate, neat house. In a hundred days the elixir will be ready. If
one eats one ounce, immortality will be gained. He who does
not wish to leave this world but wishes rather to become a terrestrial immortal for the time being, needs only to purify himself and observe a diet for a hundred days. Those who wish to
ascend to heaven, must all abstain from grain food first for one
year and then the medicine is eaten. If he eats only half an
ounce, he will enjoy everlasting life and never die. No harm, no
poison whatsoever can injure him. He may nourish (keep) a
wife and children, become an official of rank, just as he likes,
and there is nothing that would be forbidden to him. Those who
desire to ascend to heaven, should undergo a purification and a
diet and then swallow one ounce. They will then fly up as
immortals. . . .

Buddhism

Introduction

The Buddhist religion in China acquired its first known adherents
in the first century A.D., more than half a millennium after the death
of its founder, Gautama.* Long established in India and parts of
Central and Southeast Asia at that time, it possessed a complex the-
ology and ritual far more sophisticated than any religious system

* For a discussion of Buddhist doctrines, see "Introduction to Buddhism" in
Volume IV of this series, *Classical India*.

hitherto known to the Chinese. Buddhism reached China in part via the sea lanes linking eastern India via the Straits of Malacca with the ports of Kwangtung, but the more important route led from northwest India around Tibet through the oases of Chinese Turkestan. Numerous Buddhists inhabited this oasis region: the great entrepot of Tun-huang, for example—site of extraordinary archaeological discoveries in the twentieth century—was a major Buddhist center. The introduction of Buddhism into China coincided with the extension of Chinese military power to the oases: Chinese officials and traders, as well as soldiers, came to reside there, and undoubtedly gained some acquaintance with the foreign religion. More importantly, the conquest linked the oases to China proper and facilitated the entry of Buddhist missionaries from Central Asia into China itself.

Most of the first Chinese Buddhists were originally associated with the Taoist church. To untutored Chinese eyes, Buddhism appeared to be little more than a variant of Taoism—an impression facilitated by certain genuine resemblances as well as others founded in misunderstanding. Both Buddhism and popular Taoism were religions of salvation. They agreed in revering an enormous pantheon of supernatural beings whose function was to help the believer toward liberation from earthly fetters. Neither doctrine included a supreme Deity who governed the world: the universe was thought to be largely self-regulating. Both codes of ethics rejected mundane ambitions and pleasures and cultivated intense sympathy for nature and for all living beings. Perhaps most importantly, Buddhism and Taoism were the only organized churches in China, providing their adherents with formalized outlets for religious emotion in worship services, public ceremonies, and festivals.

Other supposed similarities between the two doctrines were based upon ignorance. Not only were the concepts of Buddhism foreign to Chinese experience; confusion was compounded by a technique of translation which virtually ensured the interpretation of Indian Buddhist texts in accordance with Taoist preconceptions. The Chinese language lacked precise equivalents for Buddhist terminology; the closest available approximations belonged to the vocabulary of Taoism. Thus, for example, *dharma* in Chinese translation became "Tao"; *arhat* became "immortal"; Nirvana became "non-action or "immortality." Moreover, Chinese exponents of Buddhism practiced a type of exegesis known as "matching concepts" (*ko-i*), whereby Buddhist ideas were paired up with apparently similar Taoist ones.

Nirvana was almost universally equated with bodily immortality in early Chinese Buddhist literature, though the real analogy was with the classical Taoist concept of mystic unity. The ascetic practices of foreign Buddhist monks were compared to Taoist techniques, though they were in fact based upon quite different preconceptions. The respiratory exercises of Buddhist Yoga consisted of deep and regular breathing, the object of which was to produce concentration of mind as an initial step toward Nirvana. Taoist adepts, however, sought to "nourish the body" by holding their breath as long as possible; their usual goal was physical immortality, though the ultimate object in some cases was mystic union with Tao.

However, the prevailing mode of thought in Han China was Confucian; and between Buddhism and Confucianism the contrast was total. Buddhism was open to all mankind on nearly equal terms: its distinctions were based upon the believers' spiritual advancement. Confucianism, on the other hand, accepted a hierarchy of birth: the five relationships within the family and the state. The goal of Buddhist ethics was freedom from sin (*karma*) and its attendant consequences—future reincarnations upon earth; the Confucian ideal was an upright individual fulfilling his proper place in society. Buddhists had the characteristic Indian indifference to human history; they divided time into cosmic cycles of unfathomable length in which mythological beings played prominent roles. Confucians, on the contrary, cherished a deep respect for the achievements of humankind and assigned precise dates to past events. Buddhist doctrine and meditational techniques were based upon a complex analysis of individual human psychology; Confucianism was concerned rather with social forms and proper relations among people. The Buddhist Nirvana was a mystic state which detached the individual from his surroundings; its goal was the cessation of re-births in this world. Confucians, however, aspired to the respect of their fellow-citizens in life; after death they desired continuance of the ancestral line, with sons and grandsons to carry on the family sacrifices.

Given these fundamental differences, it is scarcely surprising that the great upsurge of Buddhism in China coincided with the decline of Confucianism in the Six Dynasties period (A.D. 222-589). Confucianism had been the officially sanctioned philosophy of the Chinese empire. But Confucian morality had not prevented the collapse of the Han dynasty; and its precepts were now largely irrelevant to the new political order. China in the Six Dynasties period was divided into a number of small states, none of which controlled more than a fraction of the former imperial territories. The new ruling houses were too ephemeral, and their legitimacy too doubtful, to inspire much respect. In north China most of them were also barbarian by origin and unable to comprehend traditional Chinese ways of behavior. Thereby the Confucian correlation between loyalty to the family and loyalty to the state was shattered; and Chinese of all social classes sought a philosophy of life unrelated to political and social achievements.

To be sure, several centuries of acclimatization were required before Buddhism in China was understood in anything like its Indian sense. Its basic ideas were too alien to the predominant Chinese modes of thought; and the difficulties of translation were overwhelming. No languages are farther apart linguistically than Sanskrit (or Pali) and Chinese. The early Buddhist missionaries knew Chinese only imperfectly, and their translations of Indian texts were woefully inadequate. But from the third century A.D. onward, an increasing number of Buddhist monks arrived in China from Central Asia and India. In collaboration with Chinese colleagues they translated a variety of both Hinayana and Mahayana texts; and they helped to correct many Chinese misconceptions about the faith. The greatest of these missionary translators was a monk of the Mahayana persuasion from Central Asia, Kumarajiva, who had learned to speak Chinese during a long period of captivity in western China. Arriving in Ch'ang-an in A.D. 401, he found a patron in the local ruler; and a group of Chinese monks was assembled to work with him. Kumarajiva undertook to explain orally the texts to be translated; his associates rendered them into good literary Chinese. In the short period until Kumarajiva's death in 409, this group produced an astounding number of high-quality translations, through which the ideas of Mahayana Buddhism appeared in the Chinese language with far greater clarity than ever before.

Introduction to the Treatise Removing Doubts

The *Treatise Removing Doubts* (*Li-huo Lun*) is the earliest extant original composition by a Chinese writer in defense of the Buddhist faith, and a work of high literary quality as well. Consisting of thirty-eight short colloquies between the author and his opponents, it eloquently illustrates the difficulties experienced by Chinese of traditional education in accepting the foreign religion. The author was himself a cultured gentleman of Confucian background who—like so many others of that period—came to Buddhism by way of Taoism. He understood the new religion largely in Taoist terms, and drew frequent parallels between Buddhist and Taoist conceptions. The objections to which he addresses himself, however, are mainly Confucian in nature. Wherever possible, he tries to demonstrate that Buddhism is perfectly consistent with good Chinese doctrine.

Nothing is known of Mou Tzu ("Master Mou"), the author of the *Treatise Removing Doubts*, except what he himself tells us in the preface to his work. As a man without official rank, he remains unmentioned in the Chinese dynastic histories, which did not usually concern themselves with religion unless it infringed upon the state's prerogatives. If the information in the preface is accurate, the *Treatise* was written shortly after A.D. 195, though some scholars have attempted to identify Mou Tzu with a certain Mou Jung, grand marshal under the emperor Chang Ti (A.D. 76-88). However, the work presupposes that Buddhism was already of sufficient importance to have aroused important opposition, which was scarcely the case before the final decades of the Han dynasty (ended A.D. 220); and the overwhelmingly Confucian frame of reference suggests a date when Confucianism was still the prevailing (and officially supported) philosophy of China. References in the text itself similarly support a date at the end of the second century A.D. The *Treatise Removing Doubts* is mentioned in Chinese bibliographic lists from various periods; but it seems to have been most popular in the fifth and sixth centuries A.D.

FROM THE TREATISE REMOVING DOUBTS
(LI-HUO LUN) BY MOU TZU

Mou Tzu had thoroughly studied the canonical books (Classics) and their commentaries, as well as the (writings of) the philosophers; and he loved all books, large or small. Though

From "Meou Tseu, ou les Doutes Levés," trans. from the Chinese by Paul Pelliot in *T'oung Pao*, XIX (1920), Leiden, The Netherlands, pp. 287-9, 293-9, 301-6, 309, 313-16. Translated from the French by J. Sedlar. Editorial additions from the original translation appear in parentheses; words in square brackets have been added by the present editors.

he had no liking for the military art, still he read (works) on the subject. Though he read books about gods and spirits and about immortality, assuredly he had no faith in them and considered them nothing but empty extravagances.

At that time, following the death of [the emperor] Ling Ti, the empire was in disorder.[1] Only Chiao province[2] was comparatively peaceful; the outstanding men from the lands of the North [of China] all went to live there. Many devoted themselves to the service of the gods and spirits, to abstinence from cereals, and to [the search for] immortality.[3] Numerous people of that time were addicted to such studies. Mou Tzu constantly suggested to them objections drawn from the Five Classics. None of the Taoists and magicians dared contend with him; he was like Mencius inveighing against Yang Chu and Mo Ti.[4]

Previously Mou Tzu had withdrawn with his mother to Chiao province. At the age of twenty-six he returned to Ts'ang-wu[5] and got married. The prefect (of Ts'ang-wu) heard that [Mou Tzu] devoted himself to study, and paid him a visit in order to appoint him to office. Now (Mou Tzu) had just reached the height of his powers; his whole will was turned toward learning. Moreover, he realized that the times were disturbed, and that he had no intention of assuming [official] functions. Therefore he did not accept.

At that time the governments [of provinces] and the commanderies all defied one another; no one crossed the boundaries from one into the other. The prefect, appealing to [Mou Tzu's] knowledge and experience, sent him to pay his respects to (the

1. Emperor Ling Ti died in A.D. 189 after a reign of twenty-one years. The disorders mentioned here occurred in consequence of the Yellow Turbans' revolt of 184.

2. Chiao province was in the far south, including present-day Kwangtung (China) and Tonkin (Viet Nam) and parts of Kwangsi and Annam. Until almost the end of the Han dynasty, it ranked as colonial territory rather than as a full-fledged province.

3. I.e., they were Taoists. Abstinence from cereals was supposed to promote longevity.

4. The followers of Yang Chu and Mo Ti (Mo Tzu) were Mencius' chief philosophical opponents. Ultimately Mencius' views, representing the main thrust of Confucian thought, largely prevailed over the others. For the ideas of Yang Chu see above, Introduction to the Lieh Tzu, pp. 194-5 and text on pp. 201-3; for Introduction to Mo Tzu see pp. 20-22.

5. Ts'ang-wu was a city on the West (Hsi) River in modern Kwangsi.

governor of) Ching province.[6] Mou Tzu reflected that it was easy to refuse an honor, but difficult to avoid a mission; and he made preparations for departure. At this same time the governor of (Chiao) province got a sample of [Mou Tzu's] erudition, and since [Mou Tzu] did not have any official function, offered him a position.[7] This time again (Mou Tzu) pretended to be ill and did not budge [from his house]. . . .

Then [Mou Tzu] meditated silently for a long time: "Because I debate well, I am entrusted with missions. Now the times are disturbed; this is not the moment to become illustrious." And sighing, he said, "Lao Tzu (said), 'Abandon righteousness and repudiate knowledge.'[8] No [external] object can affect the will of a man who takes care of his body and protects his true essence. The world cannot disturb his contentment. He is not the Son of Heaven's servant, nor the friend of lords. For this reason he may [truly] be considered noble." Thereupon [Mou Tzu] increased his inclination toward the Law of Buddha and examined closely the five thousand words of Lao Tzu.[9] He imbibed the Mysterious Perfection like wine and liquor,[10] and played the Five Classics like the lute or the organ.[11] Those people who held current opinions frequently thought him wicked, because he was believed to have abandoned the Five Classics and turned to heterodox doctrines. To discuss was (to be accused of) heresy; to remain silent was (to appear) incompetent. Thus in the leisure remaining from his notarial duties,[12] (Mou Tzu) drew up a

6. Ching province was in northeastern China (Shantung and Hopei).

7. The governor of Chiao province normally resided at Canton, through which Mou Tzu had to pass on his way north to Ching. However, the wording of the text suggests that this dignitary was in Ts'ang-wu at the time Mou Tzu refused his offer.

8. *Tao Te Ching*, ch. 19. See above, pp. 191-2.

9. I.e., the *Tao Te Ching*.

10. "Mysterious Perfection" is a symbol for the Way of the Taoists. The translator suggests that the comparison with wine and liquor is meant to indicate that Mou Tzu used the Taoist texts as ornaments rather than as essentials.

11. The word here translated as "organ" refers to an instrument called the *sheng*, which had metal keys that vibrated at the passage of air through pipes connected to a hollow gourd.

12. This phrase suggests that Mou Tzu may have acted as secretary to the prefect even though he refused official rank.

summary in which he cited the words of holy and wise men in order to justify and explain (his ideas). He entitled it *Treatise Removing Doubts, by Mou Tzu.*

V   People say: "Perfect truth is not embellished; perfect style is not ornamental. The more concise an utterance, the better it is understood; the rarer an object, the more splendid to acquire it. Pearls and jade are expensive because they are rare, while fragments of tile are worthless because they are plentiful. When the Sage[13] established the basic (text) of the Seven Classics,[14] he did not go beyond 30,000 words;[15] in them everything is found included. Today the chapters of the Buddhist books are counted in myriads, and their words by hundreds of millions; it is beyond the power of anyone to read to the end of them. I find this repugnant; I disapprove of it." Mou Tzu says: "What distinguishes the [Yangtze] River and the ocean from gutters of rain-water is their depth and breadth; what distinguishes the five mountains from knolls and hillocks is their height and massiveness. . . . The small cannot contain the large. The Buddhist books tell in advance of events for hundreds of millions of years and reveal the important matters of ten thousand generations. . . . Their great number renders them more complete; their great bulk makes them richer. Why object to this? Even though no one can finish them all, this is like someone's approaching a river in order to drink. Thirst quenched, he is content. Why inquire any further?"

VII   People say: "If the Way of Buddha is so venerable and noble, how is it that Yao, Shun, the Duke of Chou and Confucius did not practice it? Why are its doctrines not mentioned in the Seven Classics? You yourself are so fond of the (*Book of*) *Songs* and the (*Book of*) *History;* you delight in the (*Book of*) *Rites* and the (*Book of*) *Music;* how can you also appreciate the Way of the Buddha and take pleasure in heterodox practices? How can you

13. Confucius.
14. Mou Tzu's list of the Seven Classics probably included the present five plus the (now lost) *Book of Music* and the *Classic of Filial Piety.*
15. The origin of this figure (30,000 words) is mysterious. One Classic in itself (the *Book of Rites*) contains about 100,000 words.

rank them above the Classics and the commentaries and prefer them to the doctrine of the Sage? Really I can scarcely approve of this." Mou Tzu says: "A book is not necessarily composed of the sayings of Confucius; a medicine is not always (prepared from) a recipe of [the physician] P'ien-chüeh. If (a book) is in accord with righteousness, it should be followed; if (a medicine) heals, it is good. The superior man takes good [principles] from anywhere, just as he takes sustenance for his body. . . .

IX   People say: "The *Classic of Filial Piety*[16] says: 'We have received our body and our limbs, our hair and our skin from our parents; we may not injure or wound them.' When Tseng Tzu[17] was about to die, (he said): 'Uncover my hands, uncover my feet.'[18] Nowadays the monks shave their heads. Why do they violate the teachings of the Sage and depart from the conduct of filial sons? You always like to discuss the pro and the con and measure the straight and the crooked; contrarily (to all truth), can you approve of this?" Mou Tzu says: "To slander holy and perfect beings is not benevolent; to measure inaccurately is not to be wise. If a person is neither benevolent nor wise, how can he increase in virtue? If he fails to increase in virtue, he returns to [the ranks of] the wicked. Is the discussion so simple? In the old days some people from Ch'i[19] got into a boat to cross a river. The father fell into the water. The son bared his arms, seized his father by the head, and shook it up and down so that the water came out through the mouth. Thus the father returned to life. Now nothing is more contrary to filial piety than to seize one's father's head and shake it up and down. But as far as saving life is concerned, if [the son] had bowed with folded hands and performed the fixed (rites) of a respectful son, the father would have drowned. Confucius said: 'There are people who can rise to principle with (us), but who are incapable of acting with (us)

16. This is a short treatise which argues that filial piety is the basis of all virtue. Though attributed to Confucius or his disciple Tseng Tzu, it in fact dates from the third or second century B.C. and is little more than a reworking of some portions of the *Book of Rites*.
17. Confucius' disciple, known for his filial piety.
18. In order to show that he had not harmed his body.
19. Ch'i (in modern Shantung) was an important feudal state in Confucius' day.

according to circumstances.'[20] This is what is called 'bending to the necessities of the moment. . . .' "[21]

X   People say: "There is no greater happiness than off-spring; nothing is more unfilial than the failure to produce descendants.[22] The monks abandon their wives and children and give up their property, or never marry at all during their entire lives. Why do they violate the rules of happiness and filial piety in this way? They make a hard life for themselves; there is nothing wonderful about that. They retire from the world; nothing is remarkable about that [either]." Mou Tzu says: "What is more to the left is less to the right; what is larger in front is smaller in back. . . . Family and property are the superfluous things of the world; purification of the body, non-action (*wu-wei*), is the excellence of the Way. Lao Tzu said: 'Which touches us more closely, fame or the body? Which is more precious to us, the body or riches?'[23] . . . The monks cultivate the Way (Tao) and its power (*te*) in place of the pleasures of the world. They turn toward purity and wisdom and thus stand apart from the joys of the family. If this is not marvelous, then what is marvelous? If this is not remarkable, then what is remarkable?"

XII   People say: "The doctrine of Buddha teaches that man, after death, is reborn. I do not believe in the truth of this statement." Mou Tzu says: "When a man is about to die, his relatives climb up onto the roof to call him; (but) when he is already dead, whom do they call the second time? They call his vital spirits, you say.[24] Mou Tzu replies: If the spirit (*shen*) returns, the man lives; but if it does not return, where does it go? You tell me that it becomes demons (*kuei*) and benevolent spirits (*shen*). I answer you: the soul (*hun-shen*) surely does not die; only the

20. Citation from *Analects* IX, 29.
21. This alludes to a statement in the "Doctrine of the Mean," sec. II, 25; but Mou Tzu gives it a quite different meaning than it had in the original.
22. The second part of this phrase is a quotation from Mencius.
23. Quotation from the *Tao Te Ching*, ch. 44.
24. According to a common Chinese belief, each person had three heavenly souls (*hun*) and seven earthly souls (*p'o*). After death the *hun* became (benevolent) spirits; the *p'o* became demons. The Indian conception of *karma* was not understood in China before about the fourth century A.D.; Mou Tzu still thinks in terms of the soul's departure after death.

body decays. The body is like the roots and leaves of the five kinds of grain; the soul is like their seeds and kernels. The roots and leaves are born and will therefore die; but how can the seeds and kernels die? When the Way has been obtained, the body perishes. Lao Tzu said: 'The cause of my great suffering is that I have a body; if I had none, what evil could befall me?'[25] He also said: 'When one's merits are perfect, the body withdraws; this is the heavenly Way.' "[26] But, someone will say, "Those who follow the Way die; those who do not follow it die, too. What is the difference?" Mou Tzu says: "This is what is called never doing good for a single day but desiring praise for a lifetime. Those who have the Way die, but their spirits (*shen*) go to paradise. Wicked people die, but their spirits (*shen*) are the prey of evil. The stupid person scarcely understands an event which has happened; the sage foresees it before it begins. The Way in relation to what is not the Way is as gold to grass. Goodness is to happiness what white is to black. How can they be the same? And you ask what the difference is?"

XIII   People say: "Confucius said: 'When you don't know how to serve (living) men, how can you serve the spirits? When you don't understand life, how can you understand death?' This is how the Sage cut short (the questions of Tzu-lu).[27] Now the Buddhists speak thoughtlessly about matters of life and death and the affairs of spirits; certainly wise and virtuous men do not talk in that fashion. The follower of the Way should (attain) non-existence, maintain tranquillity, and bend his whole will toward simplicity. Why unsettle the mind by speaking of life and death and discussing idle questions about spirits?" Mou Tzu says: "Really, to speak as you do is known as seeing the external and not understanding the internal. Confucius was ill: Tzu-lu failed to ask for news of his illness. This is why (Confucius) responded harshly [to Tzu-lu's question about spirits]. The *Classic of Filial Piety* says: 'They prepare the ancestral temple

---

25. *Tao Te Ching*, ch. 13.
26. *Tao Te Ching*, ch. 9.
27. As reported in *Analects* XI, 11. Tzu-lu was one of Confucius' favorite disciples.

and make offerings to the spirits (*kuei*); in spring and autumn they sacrifice to them [the *kuei*] and think about them during the four seasons.' It also says: 'The living should be served with love and respect, the dead with grief and sorrow.'[28] Doesn't this teach people the worship of spirits and the knowledge of life and death? The Duke of Chou asked for (heavenly) instructions on behalf of King Wu, saying: 'I, Tan, have many abilities and skills and know how to serve the spirits.'[29] Now what does this mean? Isn't it the same sort of thing that the Buddhist books say about the succession of births and deaths? . . ."

XIV   People say: "Confucius said, 'The barbarian tribes of the East and North with their princes are still inferior to our great country even in these times of anarchy.'[30] Mencius laughted at Ch'en Hsiang because he changed (schools) in order to study the methods of [the foreign teacher] Hsü Hsing,[31] and said to him: 'I have heard of using Chinese (doctrines) to transform the barbarians, but I have never heard of using (the doctrines of) barbarians to transform the Chinese.'[32] You, who are of mature age,[33] have studied the teachings of Yao and Shun, the Duke of Chou and Confucius; and now you abandon them to study instead the methods of the eastern and northern barbarians.[34] Isn't this a mistake?" Mou Tzu says: ". . . The

28. This is the final verse of the *Classic of Filial Piety*; it refers to a person's parents and sums up the entire teaching of that work.
29. This incident is recounted in the chapter of the *Book of History* entitled "The Metal-Bound Coffer." When King Wu, the founder of the Chou dynasty, was ill and near death, his faithful brother, the Duke of Chou, implored the spirits to let him die in place of the king.
30. Reference to *Analects* III, 5. What Confucius actually said was: "The barbarians of the East and North have retained their princes. They are not in such a state of decay as we in China" (where in several states the ruling families had been ousted by usurpers). (Waley trans.)
31. Hsü Hsing opposed Mencius' theories about agricultural policy. The dispute between Mencius and Ch'en Hsiang about Hsü Hsing's doctrines occupies all of sec. 4, ch. 1, bk. III of the *Mencius* (Legge trans.).
32. *Mencius*, III, 1, 4, 12 (Legge trans.).
33. Literally, age twenty, or "the age of wearing the cap"—symbol that its wearer had passed from boyhood into manhood.
34. In Mou Tzu's day the barbarians who threatened China were located to the west and southwest. In Confucius' lifetime they were to the east and north; Mou Tzu has adopted Confucius' phrase.

words of Confucius were a means of combating the (disorders of his) times; and what Mencius said was in order to deplore the one-sidedness (of Ch'en Hsiang). In former times Confucius wished to reside among the nine barbarian tribes of the East, saying, 'If a superior man lives among them, what evil practice can withstand [his influence]?'[35] But Confucius was of no repute in (the states of) Lu and Wei;[36] Mencius was not given employment in (the states of) Ch'i and Liang.[37] How [much less] (could they) have held any position among the eastern and northern barbarians? Yü sprang from the western barbarians;[38] and he was both virtuous and wise. . . . The [Tso] Commentary[39] says: 'The polar star is at the center of Heaven but to the north of mankind.' From this point of view, it is not certain that the land of Han [China] is beneath the center of Heaven.[40] As for the Buddhist books, all living beings above, below, or all around depend on the Buddha. That is why I, too, respect and study (Buddhist doctrine). In what way does this mean abandoning the Way of Yao, Shun, (the Duke of) Chou, and Confucius? Gold and jade do not injure each other; red and green precious stones do not disturb one another. When you say that someone is mistaken, aren't you yourself in error here?"

XV   People say: "To take one's father's property and give it to a passer-by cannot be termed generosity; to sacrifice one's life

35. *Analects*, IX, 13.
36. Lu (in southern Shantung) was Confucius' native state; Wei was a small state directly west of Lu—the first place Confucius visited after setting out on his travels.
37. Mencius visited both these states in hopes of being offered a position. Ch'i was in Shantung; Liang (or Wei—not to be confused with the small state of Wei existing in Confucius' time) occupied the southeastern portion of the former state of Chin.
38. Yü (alleged founder of the Hsia dynasty) was one of the ancient kings revered by the Confucians. He came from a group of tribes living in Kansu and Szechuan, though his family is always said to be descended from the ancient Heavenly Kings.
39. The *Tso Commentary* is a historical account of the Spring and Autumn period. See above, pp. 120-31.
40. To Chinese Buddhists of that time, "Middle Kingdom" did not mean China, but rather the Ganges basin in India where Buddhism originated. However, the Chinese commonly regarded their country as the center of the world.

for others during the lifetime of one's parents cannot be termed humaneness. Now the Buddhist books say: 'The hereditary prince Hsü-ta-na took his father's goods and distributed them to strangers. He bestowed his country's precious elephant upon its enemies. His wife and children he gave to others.'[41] [But] to lack respect for parents while respecting others is an offense against propriety; not to love parents while loving others is contrary to virtue. Hsü-ta-na was neither pious nor humane. Still, the Buddhists honor him. Don't you find that strange?" Mou Tzu says: "The rule of the Five Classics is to designate the oldest son as heir; however, T'ai-wang,[42] after observing the good qualities of [his grandson] Ch'ang,[43] took his third son (Ch'ang's father) as heir. In this way the Chou [dynasty] became successful[44] and perfect peace was obtained. When a man marries the rule is to inform one's father and mother in advance; Shun did not inform them. . . .[45] People who see the broad picture don't get attached to details. How can a great man confine himself to ordinary rules? Hsü-ta-na realized that the world is impermanent and that riches are not one's own. That is why he carried out his idea of distributing (his wealth) in order to attain the great Way. His father's kingdom gained a greater good fortune thereby and its enemies were unable to invade it. When [Hsü-ta-na] became

41. This criticism refers to a famous Indian legend which was originally intended to illustrate the Buddhist virtue of charity. The prince Visvantara (Hsü-ta-na) gave away a magic white elephant which was the national treasure, for which his angry countrymen drove him into exile. As he was traveling various Brahmins approached, one asking for the gift of his horses, another for his carriage, another for his two small sons to be servants, and the last for his wife as a slave. Visvantara granted all requests. In the end the last of the Brahmins reveals himself as the god Indra in disguise; and Visvantara recovers his family and his property.

42. T'ai Wang (the name means "Great King") was the honored progenitor of the Chou dynasty.

43. Ch'ang was the personal name of the future King Wen, one of the founders of the Chou dynasty.

44. In conquering China (traditional date: 1122 B.C.).

45. The Book of Songs (Mao #101, Waley #71) says that a man must inform his parents before he marries. But the Mencius (bk. V, pt. 1, ch. 2, Legge trans.) reports that Shun's parents were so perverse that they would have prevented the marriage if they had known of it. Shun acted as he did because the relation of husband and wife (the purpose of which is to produce offspring) takes precedence over all other human relationships.

a Buddha, his father, his mother, and his brothers all were saved. If you don't regard that as filial piety and humaneness, then what is?"

XVI   People say: "The doctrine of Buddha is to revere non-action (*wu-wei*) and delight in almsgiving. A person who observes such precepts is as sensible as someone walking along the edge of a cliff.[46] Now the monks love wines and liquors; they even educate women and children; they buy [goods] cheaply and sell at a high price and practice nothing but deceit.[47] Such practices are the evils of the world. Does Buddhist doctrine call them non-action?" Mou Tzu says: "Kung-shu[48] could give men his axe and rope; he could not make them skillful [in using them]. The Sage could give people the doctrine, but not make them follow its precepts. Yao could punish thieves, but not make greedy people become like (Po) I and (Shou) Ch'i.[49] . . . Truly there is nothing to be learned from the wicked. In the same way, when a man well-versed in the Seven Classics is led astray by wealth and women, can you say that the six liberal arts are responsible for his vice and depravity? . . . Just because those who are addicted to evil cannot follow it, should we say that the doctrine of Buddha is bad?"

XIX   People say: "Of all the men who live under Heaven, there is not one who dislikes wealth and honors and loves poverty and misery. Everyone enjoys entertainment and leisure but fears exertion and fatigue. . . . At present the monks wear red cloth, take [only] one meal each day,[50] retract the six senses and

46. The expression is a quotation from the *Book of Songs* in *Analects* VIII, 3.
47. Criticisms of this type were frequently directed against Buddhists as the Buddhist church became more influential in the following centuries.
48. Kung-shu was a famous artisan of the state of Lu; he was the patron of wood-workers and masons.
49. According to legend, Po I and Shou Ch'i were princes of the Shang ruling house. Their father wished to leave the realm to his second son, who fled the country after the father's death in order not to stand in the way of his elder brother. The elder, out of respect for his father's wishes, refused to take the throne, which therefore passed to the third brother. After the fall of the Shang dynasty Po I and Shou Ch'i refused to serve the Chou overlords, and finally died of hunger.
50. This was the rule for monks all year; it applied to laymen only on fast days.

withdraw from the world. What is the good of that?" Mou Tzu says: "(Confucius said), 'Riches and honors are what everyone desires; if they can't be obtained by proper means, a person shouldn't get attached to them. Poverty and misery are what everyone detests; if they can't be avoided by proper means, one should accept them.'[51] Lao Tzu said: 'The five colors make a man blind; the five notes [of the scale] make him deaf; the five flavors pervert his palate; the gallop of the chariot and the hunt disturb his heart; objects which are difficult to obtain thrust him up against obstacles. Therefore the wise man acts for the sake of his stomach and not for his eyes.'[52] Are these words empty? . . ."

XXIV   People say: "You say that the Law of Buddha is highly deserving of respect, eminently pleasing, and that non-action (*wu-wei*) brings tranquility. Now there are numerous men of the present century, scholars, who laugh at it; they say that its words are endless and hard to apply in practice and that to believe in non-existence is difficult. What can be said to that?" Mou Tzu says: "The finest flavor does not please the palate of common people; the ideal sound fails to satisfy the people's ears. . . . The great Way, non-action, is not what ordinary folk see. What they fail to praise is noble; what they do not attack is worthless. . . ."

XXVI   People say: "You say that the books of Buddha are like the [Yangtze] River and the ocean [in breadth and depth], their style like brocade and embroidery. Why don't you reply to my questions with Buddhist texts instead of quoting the (*Book of*) *Songs* and the (*Book of*) *History?* Why do you bring diverse things together just to make them harmonize?" Mou Tzu says: "A thirsty person doesn't need to go to the Yangtze or to the ocean in order to drink; a hungry person needn't wait for the Ao granary[53] [to be opened] in order to fill his stomach. The Way is revealed to the wise; discussion is with those of pene-

51. *Analects* IV, 5.
52. *Tao Te Ching*, ch. 12.
53. The Ao granary was of enormous size; its purpose was to store food for years of dearth.

trating mind. Books are transmitted to the intelligent; things are
explained to the discerning. You already know the ideas [of the
Classics]; that is why I cite you the facts from them. If I borrowed statements from the books of Buddha in order to speak
of the principles of non-action, that would be like discussing the
five colors with a blind man or playing the five notes for a deaf
person. . . . That is why I reason with you by means of the
(*Book of*) *Songs* and the (*Book of*) *History*.

Introduction to the Correspondence
of Liu I-min and Seng Chao

Liu I-min (d. A.D. 410) was one of the many upper-class Chinese of
the Six Dynasties period who renounced government careers and
turned to religion as a way of life. A descendant of the Han imperial line, he was employed for a while in south China as a minor
official. When popular revolt threatened the existence of the dynasty
he served, Liu I-min abandoned his post and retired to the monastic
community on the Lu-shan mountain, in the central Yangtze region.
There he lived for many years, refusing to resume his official career
even after the re-establishment of peace. Buddhist legend subsequently told of his pure and simple life on the mountain and his
personal vision of the paradise of the Buddha Amida.

The Lu-shan community of which Liu I-min formed a part was
one of the principal centers of Chinese Buddhism. It was founded
in the late fourth century A.D. by the monk Hui-yüan as a reaction
against what he considered an over-emphasis on the doctrinal and
scriptural side of religion. Hui-yüan, though himself a learned man,
believed in salvation through faith in the saving powers of the
Buddha. A large contingent of both monks and laymen joined him
on the Lu-shan mountain, engaging in meditational practices addressed especially to the Buddha Amida (or Amitabha; in Chinese:
A-mi-to-fo). Amida was one of the best-loved saints of Mahayana
Buddhism. According to legend he was a former Bodhisattva who

had become a Buddha through the taking of forty-eight vows. Amida's attainment of Buddhahood in this way suggested that the vows themselves had an extraordinary efficacy. His worshippers believed that by meditating on him, repeating his vows, or even by merely mentioning his name they might be re-born in Amida's heaven, which was known as the Pure Land or the Western Paradise. From the Pure Land—a place supposed to be free of the evils and temptations of earth—they could easily and quickly attain Nirvana. The Pure Land sect soon became one of the major Buddhist groups in China; and Buddhists even of other schools commonly invoked the name of Amida in their prayers.

Seng Chao (A.D. 382-414) was perhaps the ablest Chinese Buddhist scholar of his day. Born to a poor family in the neighborhood of Ch'ang-an, he earned his living at an early age as a copyist of ancient texts. Evidently he was an eager learner; for he managed in this way to acquire a basic knowledge of Chinese literature as well as considerable facility in the classical style of composition. The mood of Taoism attracted him: he was particularly fond of the *Tao Te Ching* and the *Chuang Tzu*. But he was inspired to become a Buddhist by the *Vimalakirti Sutra*, a popular Mahayana text which recounts the efforts of an Indian nobleman (who is actually a Bodhisattva) to convert his fellow beings. Seng Chao joined the monastic community at Ch'ang-an, where he soon acquired a reputation for scholarship and proficiency in debate. Despite his youth, he was chosen as one of four principal Chinese assistants to the famous foreign monk Kumarajiva, who arrived at Ch'ang-an in A.D. 401. He took an active part in the translation project headed by Kumarajiva, where for the first time more than one hundred Mahayana Buddhist texts were made available in reasonably accurate Chinese versions. Apparently it was he who composed the Chinese texts after Kumarajiva—who could not write literary Chinese—had explained their meaning. Seng Chao was also a scholar in his own right. The collection of his essays known as the *Book of Chao* (*Chao Lun*) is one of the most important works of Chinese Buddhism from the Six Dynasties period. Marked by great piety as well as learning, it demonstrates the Taoist patterns of thought which still underlay the Chinese conception of the Indian faith.

In view of Seng Chao's scholarly eminence and his association with the famous Kumarajiva, it was only natural that Liu I-min should seek his guidance on matters of doctrine. In addition, the residents of the Lu-shan wished to maintain contact with their colleagues at Ch'ang-an, which was then the most important Buddhist center in China. The following letters, written in A.D. 409-10, breathe something of the atmosphere of that time, when Buddhism for the Chinese was still a new and wonderful revelation. Liu I-min and Seng Chao clearly regarded themselves as part of a mission, propagators of an ideal capable of replacing the old Confucian ethic and of a faith promising refuge from the uncertainties and suffering of life.

FROM THE CORRESPONDENCE OF LIU I-MIN AND SENG CHAO

The Questions of Liu I-min

I-min greets you.

The good news (that came from the Sangha[1] in Ch'ang-an) gave me great delight; my thoughts seek after you in the distance. The year is near the end; the frost is severe. How is your health? Because communication was interrupted[2] I had to store up my longing thoughts in my heart. Your disciple lies seriously ill in the wilderness, always plagued by a fever. As Brother Hui-ming is going to the North, there is now an opportunity to make my feelings known to you.

The men of old, though separated in body, kept their sentiments alive; if their thoughts harmonized, they were near each other. Though we are separated by streams and mountains, and up to now, there has been no possibility of our meeting, yet I have always longed to inhale the breeze (of your piety), to reflect the trace of your earthly existence (your scriptures) in

From *The Book of Chao*, trans. by Walter Liebenthal (Monograph XIII of *Monumenta Serica*), Peking, China: The Catholic University of Peking, 1948, pp. 86-9, 96-102. Reprinted by permission of *Monumenta Serica* Institute, University of California at Los Angeles.

1. The community of monks.
2. The hostilities which led to the temporary eclipse of the Eastern Chin dynasty occurred principally in the region north of the Lu-shan mountain.

the mirror of my heart. Yearning for this pleasure, I suffered torments. You were so far away that there was no hope of meeting you; I could only gaze at the sunset-coloured clouds and sigh deeply. Take care of yourself as the season requires. I hope that (for the future) there will be messengers, so that our correspondence may be lively.

Kneeling (before the image of the Buddha) I wish that the community (in Ch'ang-an) may continue in good harmony and that the foreign teacher (Kumarajiva) may be comfortable. You, my master, gifted with the power of understanding and explaining, participate in the discussions there concerning abstruse matters. I feel that your work of exegesis (translating and expounding the Scriptures) is equal to that done by the *T'uan Tz'u* of the *I Ching*.[3] Therefore, whenever I remember how far I am from you, I am deeply distressed.

The monks of the mountain (Lu-shan) lead a pure and regular life, the laws (*dharma*) and the rules are strictly observed. Outside the hours reserved for lonely meditation, they only study or lecture. They are so demure and well-ordered that it is a joy to see them. (Being allowed to belong to this circle) your disciple has achieved his desire, harboured from former incarnations. Watching this excellent course of conduct I feel that my gratitude will remain engraved on my heart (as durable as) the sun and moon.

The Dharma-teacher Hui-yüan[4] bears himself as well as ever. He progresses in insight and meditation; he resembles the gentleman in the *I Ching* who is "lordly in the daytime and cautious at night."[5] Only a man who is permeated by the Tao and whose mind is ruled by Reason could possibly, at an age of over sixty years, still keep his soul as pure as he does. Filled with confidence and consolation my gratitude knows no limits.

At the end of last summer I was introduced by the venerable

3. The explanations of each of the sixty-four hexagrams of the *I Ching* (*Book of Changes*) were called *t'uan*, "decisions," or *tzu*, "judgments." Tradition attributed them to King Wen of Chou (*ca.* 1150 B.C.).

4. Hui-yüan, the "Teacher of the Law (*Dharma*)" and founder of the Lu-shan community, died in A.D. 416 or 417, at the age of 83 or 84.

5. This is the explanation of the third line of the first (Ch'ien) hexagram of the *Book of Changes*.

Tao-sheng[6] to your book *"On Prajna[7] not Cognizant (of Objects)."* It is written in a dignified and elegant style and contains deep and convincing ideas. In expounding the *Scriptures* you lead the reader gradually to an understanding of their conceptions. (I found its thesis so interesting that) I was unable to put it down. Truly, you have bathed your heart in the ocean of the *Mahayana Scriptures* and obtained insight into their transcendental subjects. When the book is published, then Prajna will be understood all over the world without further explanation. What joy! What joy!

It is difficult to put the subtle subject (you are concerned with) into words. He who sings such strange songs has few accompanists.[8] The reader who cannot disentangle himself from words and symbols but sticks to them, will be lost. . . . Your criticism [of your opponent] is elaborate and conclusive, very ingenious and leaving no possibility of objection. But one as stupid as I cannot comprehend all at once. So I have still a few doubts which I shall now lay before you one by one. When time allows, I hope you will give me a brief explanation.

[In the remainder of the letter, Liu I-min raises specific questions concerning Seng Chao's views on the nature of Prajna.]

Chao's Answer to the Questions of Liu I-min

For a long time I have hoped to see you but my wish has always been frustrated. When Brother Hui-ming[9] arrived, I received the letter of the twelfth month of last year, containing your questions. I unrolled and perused it over and over again and

6. Tao-sheng was a monk of Lu-shan who went to Ch'ang-an after hearing of Kumarajiva's arrival there. He returned to the Lu-shan in A.D. 408. Himself the author of some important works (all of which have since disappeared), he opposed some of the key ideas of his fellow monks on the Lu-shan, e.g., Amida's paradise, rewards for good deeds, and illumination by degrees.

7. According to Mahayana Buddhism, *Prajna* (wisdom) reflects or illuminates the things of the world; it is the insight of the Bodhisattva who is ready to become a Buddha. Prajna is a kind of intuition into the essense of the world in which single objects are not distinguished.

8. Allusion to a popular story.

9. The monk who carried the letter.

was filled with joy as if you were with me in person. Autumn has brought cool winds. How is your health? An old disease often pesters this unworthy one. Since the messenger is leaving for the South, I must be short.

The 15th day of the 8th month (A.D. 410).

Reply of Seng-chao.

Though our garb is not the same[10] our religious aspirations are one. Though separated by mountains and rivers, we are neighbours in that we agree about (main) principles. Therefore, turning my mind in your direction, my thoughts meet you and my longings are soothed. By living of your own desire in proud retirement you manifest a more than common beauty of mind; leading a solitary life in seclusion, your heart is filled with joy. (The members of your community resemble Juan Ssu-tsung who) never gossiped but discussed only the philosophical principles underlying a case.[11] (Your songs remind me of) the noble poems (composed by the Seven Philosophers in the Bamboo-) grove.[12] (I admire) your high aspirations which reach forward to the supramundane sphere. I trust that your peace will not be disturbed and that you will take care of yourself. (I hope that) I shall receive a letter from you whenever there is a messenger available.

I wish the monks on your mountain good health and all happiness to the clergy and the laymen.[13] I was comforted to hear that the Dharma-teacher Hui-yüan is well as ever. Though I cannot yet join your pure life, my wish to submit to your high regulations becomes more ardent from day to day. (I admire) Hui-yüan who, though over sixty now, still leads a life of the

10. Liu I-min was a layman; Seng Chao was a monk.
11. Juan Ssu-tsung was a famous Neo-Taoist, one of the Seven Sages of the Bamboo Grove (see next note).
12. The Seven Sages (or Philosophers) of the Bamboo Grove were a group of Neo-Taoist philosophers and poets of the middle of the third century A.D. They frequently gathered in a certain bamboo grove to enjoy nature, wine, and conversation.
13. The laymen on the Lu-shan—some of them poets and painters—gave the community a cultural eminence not possessed by the much larger Buddhist colony at Ch'ang-an.

strictest austerity, watching his fold in the remoteness of the
mountain, "embracing unity in the emptiness of the valley."[14]
People from far and near revere and praise him. Can there be
anything more beautiful?

I stand on tiptoe and peer in your direction but the horizon
is covered with clouds. Being unable to express my veneration,
I am deeply grieved. You are fortunate to be in the presence of
this model of pure life all day long, and (growing in) understanding you rejoice.

The large community here (in Ch'ang-an) is as usual, the
Dharma-teacher Kumarajiva is well. Piety is the very nature
of the King of Ch'in.[15] His abilities are extraordinary. He is a
wall and moat to the Three Jewels,[16] he feels that propagating
the Law is his official duty. This induces eminent monks from
foreign countries to come here from afar. The spirit of the
Grdhrakuta Mountain[17] permeates this country.

Chih Fa-ling[18] went abroad (to get scriptures which will be)
fords and bridges for thousands of years to come, and brought
back from the West more than two hundred new *Mahayana
Sutras*. (The King) invited a teacher of Mahayana meditation,[19]
a teacher of the *Tripitaka*[20] and two teachers of the (Hinayana)
Vibhasha.[21] Kumarajiva is translating the Sutras which recently

14. Citation from the *Tao Te Ching*, ch. 10.
15. The Later Ch'in was a short-lived dynasty founded in A.D. 384 by a general of Tibetan origin; it ruled the area of western China which included
Ch'ang-an. This king was Kumarajiva's patron.
16. The Buddha, the Dharma (doctrine), the Vinaya (monastic order).
17. A place where many Buddhist sermons were preached.
18. Chih Fa-ling was a member of the Lu-shan community. In A.D. 393
Hui-yüan sent him on a journey to Khotan (in Central Asia) for the purpose of collecting Buddhist manuscripts. Fa-ling stopped at Ch'ang-an in
about 408 on his return trip.
19. Buddhabhadra, a monk renowned for his supernatural powers, arrived in
Ch'ang-an from Central Asia in A.D. 410 or slightly before.
20. The Tripitaka ("Three Baskets") is the Buddhist canon. The teacher was
Buddhayashas, the friend and former teacher of Kumarajiva from Kashgar.
21. The (Sanskrit) *Vibhasha* was the canon of the Sarvastivadin (also called
Vaibhashika) school—one of the two principal divisions of Hinayana Buddhism. The two teachers of the *Vibhasha* were Dharmayashas and Dharmagupta, both of whom reached Ch'ang-an in A.D. 407.

arrived in the Great Stone Monastery.[22] The store house of the Law is deep and wide, it daily shows unexpected features.

The teacher of meditation (Buddhabhadra) in the Palace Monastery (Hsiao-yao Park)[23] is teaching and practising meditation. He has several hundred disciples who work without rest day and night. They are reverent and harmonious. It is very gratifying.

The teacher of the *Tripitaka* (Buddhayashas) is translating the *Vinaya*[24] in the Central Monastery.[25] His recitation is as completely free from mistakes as if it came from the lips of the Tathagata[26] himself.[27]

The teachers of the *Vibhasha* (Dharmayashas and Dharmagupta) are translating the *Shariputra-abhidharma Shastra*[28] from a Sanskrit manuscript in the Stone-sheep Monastery.[29] Though the translation is not yet complete, whenever one asks about the content, one hears very interesting details.

My unworthy self has had the unique opportunity to share regularly in this noble endeavour, to join in these thriving cultural activities. Since I cannot see the disciples of Shakyamuni,[30] assembled in the Jetavana Garden, I have no other wish left except that you gentlemen, who prosper by standing aloof (from business and politics) could belong to our community.

The venerable Tao-sheng[31] was with us for several years.

22. The Great Stone Monastery was the largest monastery in Ch'ang-an and the residence of most of the monks. Its size was such that it was later divided into four separate monasteries.
23. This was the monastery in the park northwest of Ch'ang-an where the king had built a palace.
24. The *Vinaya Pitaka*, containing regulations for the monastic life; it is the third major division of the Buddhist Tripitaka.
25. Another monastery in Ch'ang-an.
26. Tathagatha is a title of the Buddha in his character as an eternal principle.
27. Buddhayashas, who had an extraordinary memory, knew this whole text (which ocupies 447 pages in one modern edition) by heart.
28. The two Hinayana teachers wrote out this text in Sanskrit in A.D. 407-8, but were obliged to improve their command of Chinese before attempting a translation. The work was finished in 414.
29. A third monastery at Ch'ang-an.
30. Gautama, the historical Buddha, is most often referred to in Chinese by his family name and title, Shakyamuni ("Sage of the Shakyas").
31. Tao-sheng was a monk formerly of Lu-shan. See above, n. 6.

Whenever there was time for conversation, we spoke of you with affection. Unexpectedly he went South and you have met him (as I learn from your letter). Apart from that news I have had no word of him and feel unspeakably uneasy.

Brother Wei[32] brought (from the Lu-shan) your *Song* called *Meditation upon the Buddha,* another with the same title by Hui-yüan and Hui-yüan's *Introduction* (to the whole collection).[33] Everybody with literary taste praises this work for its high intention and clear and beautiful wording. One might say, you have wandered to the dwelling of the Sage and knocked at his gate. There must be other papers composed by you and the teacher. Why don't you send them?

In the year *wu* (A.D. 406) Kumarajiva translated the *Vimalakirti Sutra.*[34] I then attended regularly and, between the sessions, took down what the Master said, in order to make a commentary of it. Though this cannot be considered as a literary composition it derives some value from being based upon authority.[35] So I use the occasion of this letter to send you a copy. You might, in your leisure, judge if it is worth reading.

Your questions are beautifully put and to the point. In answering them I feel like the man from Ying.[36] My thoughts do not reach very deep and I am not skilful in expressing them. Besides, final truth cannot be reached through a definition; any attempt to define it must result in a failure. Words, words only—, and what is finally achieved? But let us set to work and answer your objections as far as my inadequate powers allow.

[Seng Chao now replies to Liu L-min's questions.]

32. Otherwise unknown.
33. This collection of songs was written on the Lu-shan in A.D. 402, when about one hundred monks and laymen led by Hui-yüan took the vow to be reborn in Amida's paradise. This act marked the founding of the Pure Land sect.
34. I.e., he made a new translation of this work.
35. Apparently because Vimalakirti was supposed to have been a companion of the Buddha himself.
36. According to this story, a man from Ying (a place in Hupeh) had a piece of chalk the size of a fly on his nose, which a mason removed by swinging a hammer so cleverly that the man was not hurt.

V

Society

Introduction to Chinese Poetry

Much of the literature of ancient China is either didactic or historical—and often both at once. It concerns itself with the way in which persons and governments ought to behave, or with the great events of the past which affected entire states and nations. Chinese poetry, on the other hand, is personal in nature, dealing with the lives of individual men and women as they were in reality. As such it gives insights into ancient Chinese society which are lacking in the theoretical and historical works.

The best imaginative talent of China has always employed the lyric poem as a favorite medium of expression. The Chinese have no important epic or dramatic literature; and they have always regarded the novel as an inferior genre. Ancient Chinese poetry was reflective and analytical, rather than openly emotional. It touched on a great variety of subjects taken from daily life. In contrast to European poetry, for which the love of man and woman constitutes an all-important theme, in China love was a fairly minor subject. Far more attention was devoted to the joys of friendship, or to what might be called social commentary and criticism. Chinese poetry, like European, made use of metaphor, simile, and play on words: a favorite device was the juxtaposition of metaphors, by which an event in the world of nature was implicitly contrasted with a personal experience. Euphony was produced through length of line and through rhyme, which might occur at the beginning, middle, or end of a line. Translation can scarcely even suggest the complexity of language which gave classical Chinese poetry much of its effectiveness.

Social consciousness appeared at an early date in Chinese poetry. According to one tradition, in early Chou times the king's officials went out among the people collecting folk songs in order to learn the state of public opinion. Confucius placed a high value on poetry as one of the foundations of social order. Later Confucian literary theory held that poetry was the most appropriate vehicle for political and social criticism. The *Book of Songs*—one of the Five Classics—

was supposed to consist of allegories on political subjects; and other ancient poems were similarly interpreted as statements of moral principles.

No doubt some of these poems were actually intended as political or moral statements. In the symbolic and suggestive language of lyric verse, a poet could express thoughts which, if openly stated, would subject him to punishment by the state. But the interpretative tradition which discovered a hidden significance in the most innocent-sounding poems strikes modern critics as farfetched and absurd. It seems reasonable to assume that many classical Chinese poems are exactly what they appear to be—candid and eloquent expressions of purely personal feelings. For modern readers, they also provide valuable evidence about ancient Chinese society.

Introduction to the Book of Songs

The *Book of Songs* (*Shih Ching*)* is one of the Five Classics and a genuinely ancient work of Chinese literature. Consisting of 305 short poems, it was probably compiled about 600 B.C., though parts of it are certainly several centuries older. According to tradition, its contents were selected by Confucius himself out of an original collection of over three thousand poems, though historically this is doubtful. However, the book is a valuable source of information about Chinese society in the early Chou period. Except for a few verses found on archaeological objects, it contains the only known examples of Chinese poetry from pre-Confucian times.

Most of the poems seem to be folk songs by origin; most, and perhaps all, were designed to be sung rather than recited or read. Their musical settings, however, have long since disappeared, and nothing specific is now known of them. The language of the *Songs* is often archaic, the style lyric and impressionistic. The ends of the lines rhyme, as in English poetry; head-rhymes, internal rhymes, alliteration, and play on words appear as occasional ornaments. Occurrences in nature frequently symbolize or provide contrast to a human situation: however, the comparison is usually implied rather than openly stated.

In the traditional arrangement, the *Book of Songs* is divided into

*Also rendered in English as *Book* (or *Classic*) *of Poetry* or *Book of Odes*.

four sections, known respectively as "airs of the states," "lesser odes," "greater odes," and "hymns." "Airs of the states" is the largest category, containing 160 folk songs depicting various aspects of the lives of common people. The "airs" touch upon subjects common to folk poetry the world over—courtship and marriage, the harvest and the hunt, games and festivals. Allegedly the "airs" originated in fifteen different feudal states; but at an unknown date they were given some literary polish and rendered into a standard dialect. The "lesser odes," by contrast, deal with life at the Chou court. Unlike the "airs," they contain specific references to historical persons or events; presumably their authors were aristocrats or courtiers. The "greater odes" deal with the founders of the Chou dynasty—how they rose to power, their exemplary conduct and heroic deeds; these poems record some of the same legends found in the older portions of the *Book of History*. The "hymns," finally, are ceremonial pieces praising the achievements of the Chou dynasty and the peace and prosperity which is said to have characterized their rule.

The *Songs* have an unaffected simplicity and depth of feeling which is apparent even in translation. Some of them are considered masterpieces of lyric style. But their importance in Chinese history derives very largely from the assumption that they contain profounder meanings than appear at first sight. Tradition regards them as veiled statements of political and moral principles. The alleged association of the *Songs* with Confucius lent substance to this belief: it was difficult to imagine that the wisest man in history, as Confucius was reputed to be, would have considered simple folk ballads worthy of his attention. However, the tradition of allegorical interpretation of the *Songs* probably antedates Confucius. In the Spring and Autumn period (722-481 B.C.), quotations from them were part of every diplomat's arsenal—indispensable means for giving discreet expression to one's views. The *Tso Commentary*, for example—the most complete source for that period—records innumerable instances of this practice.

Eventually all of the poems acquired more or less standard allegorical meanings. The source for many of these was a scholar of the second century B.C. named Mao, whose edition of the *Book of Songs* is today the only one which survives complete. Taking phrases out of context, and identifying key words with others of similar sound but different meaning, Mao managed to associate each of the poems with specific historical events or personages. However arbitrary his conclusions appear to modern eyes, they received high praise in Han times; and subsequent commentators on the *Songs* imitated his methods. Indeed, his interpretations received official sanction as "correct" answers on the civil service examinations, and encountered no serious criticism until the famous scholar, Chu Hsi, challenged some of them in the twelfth century. For more than a thousand years, the much-quoted *Book of Songs* was viewed through Mao's eyes: his interpretations were the source of innumerable allusions both in formal literature and in popular speech. Mao's work, in fact, stands to the *Book of Songs* like the *Tso Commentary* to the *Spring and Autumn Annals* or the "Wings" to the *Book of Changes*. It fulfilled a felt need to enhance the importance of an ancient Classic by endowing it with political and ethical meaning, and to make its often obscure and archaic language understandable.

FROM THE BOOK OF SONGS (SHIH CHING)

Airs of the States

COURTSHIP*

3 (106)†

Hey-ho, he is splendid!
Magnificent in stature,
Noble his brow,
His lovely eyes so bright,
Nimble in running,
A bowman unsurpassed.

Hey-ho, he is glorious!
Lovely eyes so clear,
Perfect in courtesy,

From *The Book of Songs,* trans. by Arthur Waley, Boston and New York: Houghton Mifflin Company, 1937. Reprinted by permission of George Allen & Unwin, Ltd., London.
* These classifications were provided by the translator; they do not appear in the Chinese text.
† The first number is the translator's; the second (in parentheses) is that of the Mao text by which these poems are usually identified.

Can shoot all day at a target
And never miss the mark.
Truly a man of my clan.

Hey-ho, he is lovely!
His clear brow well-rounded,
When he dances, never losing his place,
When he shoots, always piercing.
Swift his arrows fly
To quell mischief on every side.

11 (75)

[In praising the man's coat, the lady is probably referring rather to his social status than to his taste.]

How well your black coat fits!
Where it is torn I will turn it for you.
Let us go to where you lodge,
And there I will hand your food to you.

How nice your black coat looks!
Where it is worn I will mend it for you.
Let us go to where you lodge,
And there I will hand your food to you.

How broad your black coat is!
Where it is worn I will alter it for you.
Let us go to where you lodge,
And there I will hand your food to you.

24 (76)

[The speaker of this poem is a lady waiting for the secret nocturnal visit of her lover. In China, as in parts of Europe, this custom was widespread and at least partially condoned.]

I beg of you, Chung Tzu,
Do not climb into our homestead,

Do not break the willows we have planted.
Not that I mind about the willows,
But I am afraid of my father and mother.
Chung Tzu I dearly love;
But of what my father and mother say
Indeed I am afraid.

I beg of you, Chung Tzu,
Do not climb over our wall,
Do not break the mulberry-trees we have planted.
Not that I mind about the mulberry-trees,
But I am afraid of my brothers.
Chung Tzu I dearly love;
But of what my brothers say
Indeed I am afraid.

I beg of you, Chung Tzu,
Do not climb into our garden,
Do not break the hard-wood we have planted.
Not that I mind about the hard-wood,
But I am afraid of what people will say.
Chung Tzu I dearly love;
But of all that people will say
Indeed I am afraid.

MARRIAGE

72 (158)

[This song appears to say that marriage is a simple matter to arrange; the services of a matchmaker (the traditional go-between)
are not necessary.]

How does one cut an axe-handle?
Without an axe it is impossible.
How does one take a wife?
Without a matchmaker she cannot be got.

Cut an axe-handle? Cut an axe-handle?
The pattern is not far to seek.
Here is a lady with whom I have had a love-meeting;
Here are my dishes all in a row.[1]

93 (14)

[Marriages traditionally were arranged between a man and the parents of his prospective bride. The girl usually saw her husband for the first time at the wedding ceremony.]

Anxiously chirps the cicada,
Restlessly skips the grasshopper.
Before I saw my lord
My heart was ill at ease.[2]
But now that I have seen him,
Now that I have met him,
My heart is at rest.

I climbed that southern hill
To pluck the fern-shoots.[3]
Before I saw my lord
My heart was sad.
But now that I have seen him,
Now that I have met him,
My heart is still.

I climbed that southern hill
To pluck the bracken-shoots.
Before I saw my lord
My heart was sore distressed.
But now that I have seen him,
Now that I have met him,
My heart is at peace.

1. To contain the ritual offerings for the marriage ceremony.
2. The bride was expected to weep before seeing her husband, then become calm upon catching sight of him.
3. To purify her in preparation for marriage.

WARRIORS AND BATTLES

124 (110)

I climb that wooded hill
And look towards where my father is.
My father is saying, "Alas, my son is on service;
Day and night he knows no rest.
Grant that he is being careful of himself,
So that he may come back and not be left behind!"

I climb that bare hill
And look towards where my mother is.
My mother is saying, "Alas, my young one is on
    service;
Day and night he gets no sleep.
Grant that he is being careful of himself,
So that he may come back, and not be cast away."

I climb that ridge
And look towards where my elder brother is.
My brother is saying, "Alas, my young brother
    is on service;
Day and night he toils.
Grant that he is being careful of himself,
So that he may come back and not die."

LAMENTATION

276 (113)

[The "rat" of this poem is presumably a rapacious lord or tax-collector.]

Big rat, big rat,
Do not gobble our millet!
Three years we have slaved for you,
Yet you take no notice of us.
At last we are going to leave you

And go to that happy land;
Happy land, happy land,
Where we shall have our place.

Big rat, big rat,
Do not gobble our corn!
Three years we have slaved for you,
Yet you give us no credit.
At last we are going to leave you
And go to that happy kingdom;
Happy kingdom, happy kingdom,
Where we shall get our due.

Big rat, big rat,
Do not eat our rice-shoots!
Three years we have slaved for you.
Yet you did nothing to reward us.
At last we are going to leave you
And go to those happy borders;
Happy borders, happy borders
Where no sad songs are sung.

MARRIAGE

Lesser Odes

105 (188)

I went into the country;
Deep the shade of the ailanto.[4]
It was as bride and wife
That I came to your house.
But you did not provide for me—
Sent me back to land and home.

I went into the country;
I plucked the dockleaf.[5]

4. A tree with small pointed leaves, fine-grained wood, and clusters of small, greenish leaves.
5. A coarse weed with small green flowers and large leaves.

It was as bride and wife
That I came to live with you.
But you did not provide for me—
Back to my home you sent me.

I went into the country;
I plucked the pokeweed.[6]
You thought nothing of the old marriage—
Found for yourself a new mate.
Not for her wealth, oh no!
But merely for a change.[7]

WARRIORS AND BATTLES

126 (181)

The wild geese are flying;
Suk, suk go their wings.
The soldiers are on the march;
Painfully they struggle through the wilds.
In dire extremity are the strong men;
Sad are their wives, left all alone.

The wild geese are flying;
They have lighted in the middle of the marsh.
The soldiers are walling a fort;
The hundred cubits have all risen.[8]
Though they struggle so painfully,
At last they are safely housed.

The wild geese are flying;
Dolefully they cry their discontent.
But these were wise men
Who urged us in our toil,

6. A weed used for staining.
7. The last two lines may very likely be corrupt. (Tr.)
8. Cubit-square frames held the earth in position when the walls were being
built. (Tr.)

And those were foolish men
Who urged us to make mischief and rebel.

127 (185)

Minister of War,
We are the king's claws and fangs.
Why should you roll us on from misery to misery,
Giving us no place to stop in or take rest?

Minister of War,
We are the king's claws and teeth.
Why should you roll us from misery to misery,
Giving us no place to come to and stay?

Minister of War,
Truly you are not wise.
Why should you roll us from misery to misery?
We have mothers who lack food.

135 (227)

[The final years of the Western Chou dynasty (1122-772 B.C.)
were marked by wars on its southern frontiers. This poem is about
the Lord of Shao, holder of a fief near the Chou capital, who went
south to fortify the stronghold called Hsieh.]

Lusty is the young millet;
Copious rains have fattened it.
Long, long was our march to the south;
But the Lord of Shao has rewarded it.

Oh, our loads, our barrows,
Our waggons, our oxen!
But now the marching is over
And at last we are going home.

Oh, our footmen, our chariot-drivers,
Our armies, our hosts!

But now our marching is over
And at last we are going back.

Noble is the palace at Hsieh;
The Lord of Shao planned it.
Glorious was the army on its march;
The Lord of Shao gave it victory.

The highlands and the lowlands were made safe;
The springs and streams cleared.
The Lord of Shao has vanquished,
And the king's[9] heart is at rest.

BLESSINGS

168 (170)

The fish caught in the trap
Were yellow-jaws and sand-eels.
Our lords have wine
Good and plentiful.

The fish caught in the trap
Were bream and tench.
Our lords have wine
Plentiful and good.

The fish caught in the trap
Were mud-fish and carp.
Our lords have wine
Good and to spare.

Things they have in plenty,
Only because their ways are blessed.
Things they have that are good,
Only because they are at peace with one another.

9. King Yu, the last ruler of the Western Chou dynasty (r. 781-772 B.C.).

Things they have enough and to spare,
Only because their ways are lovely.

THE CLAN FEAST

195 (165)

Ting, ting goes the woodman's axe;
Ying, ying cry the birds,
Leave the dark valley,
Mount to the high tree.
"Ying" they cry,
Each searching its mate's voice.

Seeing then that even a bird
Searches for its mate's voice,
How much the more must man
Needs search out friends and kin.
For the spirits are listening
Whether we are all friendly and at peace.

"Heave ho," cry the woodcutters.
I have strained my wine so clear,
I have got a fatted lamb
To which I invite all my fathers.[10]
Even if they choose not to come
They cannot say I have neglected them.

Spick and span I have sprinkled and swept,
I have set out the meats, the eight dishes of grain.
I have got a fatted ox,
To which I invite all my uncles,
And even if they choose not to come
They cannot hold me to blame.

They are cutting wood on the bank.
Of strained wine I have good store;

10. Paternal uncles. (Tr.)

The dishes and trays are all in rows.
Elder brothers and younger brothers, do not stay afar!
If people lose the virtue that is in them,
It is a dry throat that has led them astray.

When we have got wine we strain it, we!
When we have none, we buy it, we!
Bang, bang we drum, do we!
Nimbly step the dance, do we!
And take this opportunity
Of drinking clear wine.

Greater Odes

A MORAL PIECE

271 (256)

[The following advice, directed to a prince, is not concerned with
any abstract standard of morality but with the conduct appropriate
to a man in high position.]

Grave and dignified manners
Are the helpmates of power.
Men indeed have a saying,
"There is none so wise but has his follies."
But ordinary people's follies
Are but sicknesses of their own.
It is the wise man's follies
That are a rampant pest.

Nothing is so strong as goodness;
On all sides men will take their lesson from it.
Valid are the works of inward power;
In all lands men will conform to them.
He who takes counsel widely, is final in his commands,
Far-seeing in his plans, timely in the announcing of them,
Scrupulously attentive to decorum,
Will become a pattern to his people.

But those that rule to-day
Have brought confusion and disorder into the government;
Have upset their power
By wild orgies of drinking.
So engrossed are you in your dissipations
That you do not think of your heritage,
Do not faithfully imitate the former kings,
Or strive to carry out their holy ordinances.

Therefore mighty Heaven is displeased;
Beware lest headlong as spring waters
You should be swept to ruin.
Rise early, go to bed at night;
Sprinkle and sweep your courtyard
So that it may be a pattern to the people.
Put in good order your chariots and horses,
Bows, arrows, and weapons of offence,
That you may be ready, should war arise,
To keep at due distance barbaric tribes.

Ascertain the views of gentlemen and commoners,
Give due warning of your princely measures,
Take precautions against the unforeseen,
Be cautious in your utterances.
Scrupulously observe all rules of decorum,
Be always mild and good-tempered.
A scratch on a sceptre of white jade
Can be polished away;
A slip of the tongue
Cannot ever be repaired.

Do not be rash in your words,
Do not say: "Let it pass.
Don't catch hold of my tongue!
What I am saying will go no further."
There can be nothing said that has not its answer,
No deed of Power that has not its reward.
Be gracious to friends and companions

And to the common people, my child.
So shall your sons and grandsons continue for ever,
By the myriad peoples each accepted.

.   .   .   .

Hymns

AGRICULTURE

153 (275)

[Hou Chi, "The Lord of Millet," was a legendary figure reputed to be the inventor of agriculture and ancestor of the Chou people.]

Mighty are you, Hou Chi,
Full partner in heaven's power.
That we, the thronging peoples, were raised up
Is all your doing.
You gave us wheat and barley
In obedience to God's command.
Not to this limit only or to that frontier,
But near, far and for ever throughout these lands of Hsia.[11]

156 (279)

Abundant is the year, with much millet, much rice;
But we have tall granaries,
To hold myriads, many myriads and millions of grain.
We make wine, make sweet liquor,
We offer it to ancestor, to ancestress,
We use it to fulfil all the rites,
To bring down blessings upon each and all.

WELCOME

178 (284)

A guest, a guest,
And white his horse.

11. I.e., China. The Hsia dynasty was supposed to have preceded the Shang as rulers of China.

Rich in adornment, finely wrought
The carving and chiselling of his spearshafts.

A guest so venerable,
A guest of great dignity.
Come, give him a tether
To tether his team.

Here we follow him,
To left and right secure him.
Prodigal is he in his courtesies;
He will bring down blessings very joyful.

SACRIFICE

204 (302)

[This is a song of the Sung people, who counted themselves as descendants of the Shang (predecessors of Chou). The Sung people told much the same stories about their founder, T'ang the Victorious, as did the Chou about King Wen. T'ang is supposed to have come to the throne in 1766 B.C. (Tr.)]

Ah, the glorious ancestors—
Endless their blessings,
Boundless their gifts are extended;
To you, too, they needs must reach.
We have brought them clear wine;
They will give victory.
Here, too, is soup well seasoned,
Well prepared, well mixed.
Because we come in silence,
Setting all quarrels aside,
They make safe for us a ripe old age,
We shall reach the withered cheek, we shall go on and on.
With our leather-bound naves, our bronze-clad yokes,
With eight bells a-jangle
We come to make offering.
The charge put upon us is vast and mighty,

From heaven dropped our prosperity,
Good harvests, great abundance.
They come,[12] they accept,
They send down blessings numberless.
They regard the paddy-offerings, the offerings of
    first-fruits
That T'ang's descendant brings.

DYNASTIC SONG

217 (269)

Renowned and gracious are those rulers, those sovereigns
That bestow upon us happy blessings.
Their favour towards us is boundless;
May sons and grandsons never forfeit it!
There are no fiefs save in your land;
It is you, O kings, who set them up.
Never forgetting what your valour won
May we continue it in our sway!
None are strong save the men of Chou,
Every land obeys them.
Nothing so glorious as their power,
All princes imitate them.
Ah, no! The former kings do not forget us.

12. The ancestors.

MISCELLANEOUS LYRICS

Hymn to the Fallen

[Fourth Century B.C.?]

"We hold our flat shields, we wear our jerkins of hide;
The axles of our chariots touch, our short swords meet.
Standards darken the sun, the foe roll on like clouds;
Arrows fall thick, the warriors press forward.
They have overrun our ranks, they have crossed our line;
The trace-horse on the left is dead, the one on the right is
     wounded.
The fallen horses block our wheels, our chariot is held fast;
We grasp our jade drum-sticks, we beat the rolling drums."

Heaven decrees their fall, the dread Powers are angry;
The warriors are all dead, they lie in the open fields.
They set out, but shall not enter; they went but shall not
     come back.
The plains are empty and wide, the way home is long.
Their tall swords are at their waist, their bows are under
     their arm;
Though their heads were severed their spirit could not be
     subdued.
They that fought so well—in death are warriors still;
Stubborn and steadfast to the end, they could not be
     dishonoured.
Their bodies perished in the fight; but the magic of their
     souls is strong—
Captains among the ghosts, heroes among the Dead!

The poems "Hymn to the Fallen," "The Great Summons," "Woman," and
"The Scholar in the Narrow Street" appear in *Chinese Poems*, trans. by
Arthur Waley, London: George Allen & Unwin, 1946, pp. 35, 36-7, 84-5, 88.
Reprinted by permission of George Allen & Unwin, Ltd.
"Lament of Hsi-chün" and "The Ruins of Lo-yang" are from *A Hundred
and Seventy Chinese Poems*, trans. by Arthur Waley, New York, Alfred A.
Knopf, 1919, pp. 75, 86. Copyright 1919 by Alfred A. Knopf, Inc. Renewed by
Arthur Waley. Reprinted by permission of Alfred A. Knopf, Inc. and Con-
stable Publishers, London.

The Great Summons

(Invocation to the soul of a dead or sick man)

[Anonymous, Third or Second Century B.C.]

Green Spring receiveth
The vacant earth;
The white sun shineth;
Spring wind provoketh
To burst and burgeon
Each sprout and flower.
The dark ice melts and moves; hide not, my soul!
O Soul come back again! O do not stray!

O Soul, come back again and go not east or west, or
    north or south!
For to the East a mighty water drowneth
    Earth's other shore;
Tossed on its waves and heaving with its tides
    The hornless Dragon of the Ocean rideth;
Clouds gather low and fogs enfold the sea
    And gleaming ice drifts past.
O Soul go not to the East,
To the silent Valley of Sunrise!

O Soul go not to the South
Where mile on mile the earth is burnt away
And poisonous serpents slither through the flames,
Where on precipitous paths or in deep woods
Tigers and leopards prowl,
And water-scorpions wait;
Where the king-python rears his giant head.
O Soul go not to the South
Where the three-footed tortoise spits disease!

O Soul go not to the West
Where level wastes of sand stretch on and on;

And demons rage, swine-headed, hairy-skinned,
With bulging eyes;
Who in wild laughter gnash projecting fangs.
O Soul go not to the West
Where many perils wait!

O Soul go not to the North,
To the Lame Dragon's frozen peaks;
Where trees and grasses dare not grow;
Where the river runs too wide to cross
And too deep to plumb,
And the sky is white with snow
And the cold cuts and kills.
O Soul seek not to fill
The treacherous voids of the North!

O Soul come back to idleness and peace.
In quietude enjoy
The lands of Ching and Ch'u.
There work your will and follow your desire
Till sorrow is forgot,
And carelessness shall bring you length of days
O Soul come back to joys beyond all telling!

Where thirty cubits high at harvest-time
The corn is stacked;
Where pies are cooked of millet and water-grain,
Guests watch the steaming bowls
And sniff the pungency of peppered herbs.
The cunning cook adds slices of bird-flesh,
Pigeon and yellow-heron and black-crane.
They taste the badger-stew.
O Soul come back to feed on foods you love!

.   .   .   .

Lament of Hsi-chün

[About the year 110 B.C. a Chinese Princess named Hsi-chün was
sent, for political reasons, to be the wife of a central Asian nomad

king, K'un Mo, king of the Wu-sun. When she got there, she found her husband old and decrepit. He only saw her once or twice a year, when they drank a cup of wine together. They could not converse, as they had no language in common. (Tr.)]

My people have married me
In a far corner of Earth:
Sent me away to a strange land,
To the king of the Wu-sun.
A tent is my house,
Of felt are my walls;
Raw flesh my food
With mare's milk to drink.
Always thinking of my own country,
My heart sad within.
Would I were a yellow stork
And could fly to my old home!

The Ruins of Lo-yang

[By Ts'ao Chih (A.D. 192-233), third son of (the famous general) Ts'ao Ts'ao. He was a great favourite with his father till he made a mistake in a campaign. In this poem he returns to look at the ruins of Lo-yang, where he used to live. It had been sacked by Tung Cho. (Tr.)]

I climb to the ridge of Pei Mang Mountain
And look down on the city of Lo-yang.
In Lo-yang how still it is!
Palaces and houses all burnt to ashes.
Walls and fences all broken and gaping,
Thorns and brambles shooting up to the sky.
I do not see the old old-men:
I only see the new young men.
I turn aside, for the straight road is lost:
The fields are overgrown and will never be ploughed
        again.
I have been away such a long time

That I do not know which street is which.
How sad and ugly the empty moors are!
A thousand miles without the smoke of a chimney.
I think of the house I lived in all those years:
   I am heart-tied and cannot speak.

Woman

[by Fu Hsüan (A.D. 217-278)]

How sad it is to be framed in woman's form!
Nothing on earth is held so cheap.
A boy that comes to a home
Drops to earth like a god that chooses to be born.
His bold heart braves the Four Oceans,
The wind and dust of a thousand miles.
No one is glad when a girl is born;
By *her* the family sets no store.
When she grows up, she hides in her room
Afraid to look a man in the face.
No one cries when she leaves her home—
Sudden as clouds when the rain stops.
She bows her head and composes her face,
Her teeth are pressed on her red lips.
She bows and kneels countless times,
She must humble herself even to the servants.
While his love lasts he is distant as the stars;
She is a sun-flower, looking up to the sun.
Soon their love will be severed more than water from fire;
A hundred evils will be heaped upon her.
Her face will follow the year's changes;
Her lord will find new pleasures.
They that were once like substance and shadow
Are now as far as Hu and Ch'in.[1]
Yes, Hu and Ch'in shall sooner meet
Than they, whose parting is like Shen and Ch'en.[2]

1. The land of the barbarians and China. (Tr.)
2. The morning and the evening star.

The Scholar in the Narrow Street

[by Tso Ssu (died *ca.* A.D. 306)]

Flap, flap, the captive bird in the cage
Beating its wings against the four corners.
Sad and dreary, the scholar in the narrow street;
Clasping a shadow he dwells in an empty hut.
When he goes out, there is nowhere for him to go;
Thorns and brambles block his every path.
His plans are all discarded and come to nothing;
He is left stranded like a fish in a dry pond.
Without—he has not a single farthing of salary;
Within—there is not a peck of grain in his larder.
His relations all despise him for his lack of success;
Friends and companions grow daily more aloof.
Su Ch'in toured in triumph through the North,
Li Ssu rose to be Premier in the West;
With sudden splendour shone the flower of their fame,
With like swiftness it withered and decayed.
Though one drinks at a river, one cannot drink more than
    a belly-full;
Enough is good, but there is no use in satiety.
The bird in a forest can perch but on one bough,
And this should be the wise man's pattern.

A PEACOCK FLEW

[The respect of children for their parents' wishes, the submission
of the wife to her mother-in-law and of an unmarried woman to the
decisions of her male relatives, were traditional Confucian virtues.
The following poem shows the darker side of this morality.]

[Anonymous, Third to Fifth Century A.D.]

A peacock flew, far off to the south-east;
Flew for a mile, then always dallied in its flight.

From *Chinese Poems*, trans. by Arthur Waley, London: George Allen &
Unwin, 1946, pp. 89-100. Reprinted by permission of George Allen & Unwin, Ltd.

"At thirteen I knew how to weave silk,
At fourteen I learnt to make clothes.
At fifteen I could play the small lute,
At sixteen I knew the Songs and Book.
At seventeen I was made your wife;
From care and sorrow my heart was never free,
For you already were a clerk in the great town
Diligent in your duties and caring for nothing else.
I was left alone in an empty bridal-room;
It was not often that we two could meet.
At cock-crow I went to the loom to weave;
Night after night I toiled and got no rest.
In three days I would finish five bits,
And yet the Great One[1] chid me for being slow.
Husband, it is not because I weave too slowly
That I find it hard to be a wife in your house.
It is not in my power to do the tasks I am set;
There is no use in staying for the sake of staying.
Go then quickly, speak to the lady my mistress
And while there is time let me go back to my home."
The clerk her husband listened to her words;
Up to the Hall he went and "Mother," he said,
"The signs of my birth marked me for a humble course;
Yet luck was with me when I took this girl to wife.
Our hair was plaited, we shared pillow and mat,
Swore friendship until the Yellow Springs of Death.
We have served you together two years or three,
Since the beginning only so little a while.
In nothing has the girl offended or done amiss;
What has happened to bring trouble between you?"
Then spoke the clerk's mother:
"Come, my son, such love is foolish doting;
This wife neglects all rules of behaviour,
And in all her ways follows her own whim.
Myself I have long been discontented with her;
You must not think only of what pleases you.
Our neighbour to eastward has a steadfast daughter;

1. The mother-in-law. (Tr.)

She calls herself Lo-fu of the house of Ch'in.
The loveliest limbs that ever yet you saw!
Let mother get her for you to be your wife,
And as soon as may be send the other away;
Send her quickly, and do not let her bide."
Long her son knelt down before her and pleaded:
"Bowing before you, mother, I make my plea.
    If now you send her away
I will live single all the days of my life."
And when his mother heard him
She banged the bed, flying into a great rage,
And "Little son," she said, "are you not afraid?
Dare you answer me in such a wife's praise?
By this you have forfeited all my love and kindness;
Do not dream that I will let you work your will."
He did not speak, he made no cry.
Twice he bowed, and went back to his room;
He lifted up his voice to speak with his young bride,
But his breath caught and the words would not come.
    "It is not *I* that would send you away,
It is my mother that has scolded and harried me.
Do you live at your father's, just for a little while,
For I must be going to take my orders in town—
Not for long; I shall soon be coming home,
And when I am home, I will fetch you back again.
Let this put down the doubts that rise in your heart;
Turn it over in your thoughts and do not disobey me."
The young wife spoke to the government clerk:
"Give me no more of this foolish tangled talk.
Long ago, when the year was at its spring,
I left my father and came to your grand home.
I obeyed my mistress in every task I plied;
Day and night I hurried on with my tasks
In solitude, caught in endless toil.
Never in word or deed was I at fault;
In tender service I waited on Madam's needs,
Yet even so she sought to send me away.
It is no use to talk of coming back.

These things are mine: a broidered waist-jacket,
Lovely and rare, shining with a light of its own;
A canopy of red gauze
With scented bags hanging at the four corners,
And shuttered boxes, sixty, seventy,
With grey marbles strung on green threads—
So many boxes, and none is like the last;
And in the boxes, so many kinds of things!
If I am vile, my things must also be scorned.
They will not be worth keeping for the after-one;[2]
Yet I leave them here; they may come in handy as
     presents.
From now onward we shall not meet again.
Once in a while let me have your news,
And let us never, never forget one another."

A cock crowed; outside it was growing light.
The young wife rose and tidied herself.
She puts about her a broidered, lined gown,
Takes what she needs, four or five things,
And now on her feet she slips her silk shoes;
In her hair are shining combs of tortoise-shell.
Her waist is supple as the flow of rustling silk;
At her ear she dangles a bright crescent moon.
White her fingers as the slender onion stem;
She seems in her mouth to hold cinnabar and pearls.
Slender, slender she treads with small steps,
More fine, more lovely than any lady in the world.
She goes to the Hall, low she bows her head;
But the stubborn mother's anger did not cease.
"When I was a girl," the young wife said,
"I was brought up far from any town,
A wild thing, never schooled or taught,
And needs must shame a great man's house.
From you I have taken much money and silk,
Yet was not fit to do the tasks that you set.
To-day I am going back to my father's home;

2. Her successor. (Tr.)

I am sorry to leave you burdened by household cares."
From her little sister[3] it was worse work to part;
Her tears fell like a string of small pearls:
"When new-wed I first came to your home,
You had just learnt to lean on the bed and walk.
   To-day, when I am driven away,
Little sister, you have grown as tall as me.
Work for Madam, cherish her with all your heart,
Strive to serve and help her as best you may.
Those seventh-days and last days but one[4]
Do not forget what nice romps we had!"
She left the gate, mounted her coach and went;
Of tears she dropt many hundred rows.
The clerk with his horse was riding on before;
The young wife rode in her carriage behind.
A pattering of hoofs, a thundering of wheels—
And they met each other at the mouth of the great road.
He left his horse and sat beside her in the coach,
He bowed his head and into her ear he spoke:
"I swear an oath that I will not give you up
If for a little while you go back to your home.
I for a little must go back to the town;
It will not be long before I am here again.
I swear by Heaven that I will not abandon you."
"Dear husband," the young wife cried,
"Of your fond love I have not any doubt,
And since you have said you still accept me as your wife
It will not be long, I hope, before you are back.
You now must be like the great rock;
And I will be like the reed that grows by the stream.
The reed by the stream that bends but does not break;
The great rock, too mighty to move from its place.
I have a brother, my own father's son,
Whose nature and deeds are wild as a summer storm.
I fear he will not let me have my way,
And the thought of this fills my heart with dread."

3. [Sister]-in-law. (Tr.)
4. Holidays. (Tr.)

They raise their hands, bidding long farewell,
Her heart and his equally loath to part.

She enters the gate, she mounts her father's Hall,
Languidly moves with no greeting in her face.
"Child," cries her mother, and loud she claps her hands,
"We little thought to see you home so soon.
For at thirteen I taught you to weave silk,
At fourteen you could cut clothes.
At fifteen you played on the small lute,
At sixteen you knew the customs and rites.
At seventeen I sent you to be a bride
And fully thought that nothing had gone amiss.
What is your fault, what wrong have you done
That uninvited you now come back to your home?"
Then Lan-chih, ashamed before her mother,
"Oh nothing, nothing, mother, have I done amiss;"
And a deep pity tore the mother's heart.

She had been at home ten days or more
When the local magistrate sends a go-between.
Saying: "My master has a third son,
For grace and beauty none like him in the world;
He is eighteen or nineteen years old,
A lovely boy, gifted and of ready speech."
　　Then said the mother to her daughter,
"Daughter, this offer cannot be refused."
　　But the daughter weeping answered,
　　"When I left my husband's house,
He looked kindly upon me and an oath he swore
That come what might he would not abandon me.
And to-day, false and wicked should I be,
Were I untrue to this our great love.
It would surely be better to break off the parley;
There is no hurry; we can answer them later on."
Then said her mother to that go-between:
"In our humble house there is indeed a daughter,
Was once married, but came back to us again.

If she was not fit to be a clerk's wife
How can she suit a magistrate's noble son?
Pray go further and seek a better match;
At the present moment we cannot give our consent."
Not many days had the messenger been gone
When a deputy-prefect[5] came on like quest:
"They tell me that here is a lady called Lan-chih
Whose father's fathers long served the State.
My master would have you know that his fifth son
Is handsome, clever, and has not yet a wife.
His own deputy he sends as go-between
And his deputy-assistant to carry you his words."
The assistant told them: "In the Lord Prefect's house
Has grown up this fine young gentleman
Who now wishes to be bound with the Great Bond,
And therefore sends us with a message to your noble gate."
The girl's mother sent word to the messengers:
"This daughter of mine is already bound by a vow;
I cannot venture to speak of such a match."
When news of this reached the brother's ear
His heart within him was much angered and vexed.
He raised his voice and thus to his sister he said:
"The plan you follow is not well considered.
Your former husband was only a Prefect's clerk;
Now you have the chance to marry a young lord!
Wide as earth from sky is the space between;
Here is a splendour that shall brighten all your days.
But if you will not be married to this fine lord,
What refuge have you, whither else shall you turn?"
Then Lan-chih raised her hand and answered:
"Brother, there is good sense in what you say.
I left my home to serve another man,
But in mid-road[6] returned to my brother's house,
And in his hands must all my fortunes rest;
I must not ask to follow my own desire.

5. As messenger from the Prefect, who was much grander than a district magistrate. (Tr.)
6. In the mid-road of marriage. (Tr.)

Though to the clerk I am bound, yet now, I think,
To eternity we shall not meet again.
Let us now accept the offer of this match
And say that the wedding may take place at once."
The messengers left their couch, their faces beaming
With a bland "yes, yes" and "so, so."
They went to their quarters and to the Prefect they spoke:
"We, your servants, have fulfilled your high command;
The words we have uttered were not without effect."
When the Lord Prefect was told of all that had passed,
His heart was filled with great mirth and joy;
He read the Calendar, he opened the sacred book.
He found it written that in this very month
The Six Points were in fortunate harmony,
The Good Omen fell in the thirtieth day;
And now already the twenty-seventh was come.
"Go, my servants, and make this wedding for me."
With urgent message they speed the marriage gear;
Hither and thither they whirl like clouds in the sky.
A green-sparrow and white-swan boat;
At its four corners a dragon-child flag
Delicately curls in the wind; a golden coach
With jade-set wheels. And dappled coursers prance
With tasselled manes and saddles fretted with gold.
The wedding gift, three million cash
Pierced in the middle and strung with green thread.
Of coloured stuffs three hundred bits,
And rare fish from the markets of Chiao and Kuang.
The bridegroom's friends, four or five hundred
In great array go up to the Prefect's gate.

Then said the mother:
"Daughter dear, this moment a letter has come,
Saying to-morrow my Lord will fetch you away.
How comes it, girl, that you are not making your dress?
Don't leave it so late that the wedding cannot start!"
She did not answer, she did not make a sound;
With her handkerchief she covered her face and wept,

Her tears flowed like water poured from a jar.
She shifts her stool that is bright with crystal beads
And close to the front window she sets it down.
With her left hand she wields ruler and knife;
In her right hand she holds the silk gauze.
In the morning she finishes her lined, broidered gown;
By evening she has finished her thin gauze robe.
The day was over, and she in the gathering gloom
With sorrowful heart walked sobbing to the gate.

When the clerk her husband heard of what had passed
He asked for leave to return for a little while.
He had still to ride two leagues or three
When his horse neighed, raising a doleful moan.
The young wife knew the horse's neigh;
She slipped on her shoes and set out to meet him.
Woefully they looked on each other from afar,
When each saw it was his dear one that had come.
She raised her hand, she struck the horse's saddle,
Wailing and sobbing as though her heart would break.
"Since you left me—" she said,
"Things happen to one that cannot be foreseen—
It is true that I have not done as I wished to do;
But I do not think that you fully understand.
Remember that I have an own father and mother
Who with my brother forced me to do this,
Made me give myself over to another man.
How could I hope that you would ever come again?"
Then said her husband the clerk to his young wife:
"Well done!," he cried, "well done to have climbed so high!
The great rock that is so firm and square
Was strong enough to last a thousand years.
The river reed that once was thought so tough
Was a frail thing that broke between dawn and dusk.
From glory to glory will my fine lady stride,
While I go down to the Yellow Springs alone."
Then answered the young wife and to the clerk she said:
"What do you mean, why do you speak to me so?

It was the same with both; each of us was forced;
You were, and so was I too.
In the land of death you shall not be alone;
Do not fail me in what to-day you have said."
They held hands, they parted and went their ways,
He to his house and she back to hers.
That live men can make a death-parting
Is sorrowful more than words can tell;
To know they are leaving the world and all it holds,
Doing a thing that can never be undone!

When the young clerk had got back to his home
He went to the Hall and bowing to his mother he said:
"Mother, to-day the great wind is cold.
A cold wind shakes the bushes and trees.
A cruel frost has stiffened the orchids in the court.
Mother, mother, to-day I go to darkness
Leaving you to stay here alone.
For my mind is set on a very sad plan;
Let your grievance against me stop when I am dead.
May your life endure like a rock of the Southern Hills,
Your back be straight and your limbs ever strong!"
When the young clerk's mother heard this
Bitter tears at each word flowed.
"O woe, will you that are of good house,
Whose father's fathers were ministers at Court
Die for a woman? Little sense do you show
Of which things matter! Listen now to my plan.
Our eastern neighbour has good girl,
Dainty and pretty, the fairest in the town.
Let Mother get her to be your wife;
I'll be quick about it; you shall have her between dawn
    and dusk."
The clerk bowed twice, and turned to go;
Deep he sighed in the empty bridal room,
He was thinking of his plan and therefore sighing stood.
He turned his head, he moved towards the door,
Drawn by the grief that surged in his boiling breast.

That day, while horses whinnied and oxen lowed,[7]
The bride went in to her tabernacle green.
Swiftly the day closed and the dusk grew black;
There was not a sound; the second watch had begun.
"With the day that has ended my life also ends,
My soul shall go and only my body stay."
She lifts her skirt, she takes off her silk shoes,
She rises up and walks into the blue lake.
When the young clerk heard what had happened
And knew in his heart that they had parted for ever,
He hovered a while under the courtyard tree,
Then hanged himself from the south-east bough.

The two families buried them in the same grave,
Buried them together on the side of the Hua Shan.
To east and west they planted cypress and pine,
To left and right they sowed the *wu-t'ung*.
The trees prospered; they roofed the tomb with shade,
Bough with bough, leaf with leaf entwined;
And on the boughs are two flying birds
Who name themselves Birds of True Love.
They lift their heads and face to face they sing
Every night till the fifth watch is done.
The passing traveller stays his foot to hear,
The widowed wife rises and walks her room.

This tale is a warning for the men of the afterworld;
May they learn its moral and hold it safe in their hearts.

7. A bad omen. (Tr.)